THE SINKING OF THE PRINCESS SOPHIA

THE SINKING OF THE PRINCESS SOPHIA

TAKING THE NORTH DOWN WITH HER

KEN COATES &
BILL MORRISON

UNIVERSITY OF ALASKA PRESS

Library of Congress Cataloging-in-Publication Data

Coates, Kenneth, 1956-
The sinking of the Princess Sophia : taking the North down with her / Ken Coates & Bill Morrison.
p. cm.
Includes bibliographical references and index.
ISBN 0-912006-50-1
1. Princess Sophia (Steamboat) 2. Shipwrecks–Pacific Coast (Alaska) 3. Yukon Territory–Social conditions. 4. Alaska–Social conditions. I. Morrison, William R. (William Robert), 1942- .
II. Title.
G885.C63 1991 90-26927
910'.916434--dc20 CIP

 First printing of U.S. edition.
International Standard Book Number: 0-912006-50-1
Library of Congress Catalogue Number: 90-26927

Printed in the United States

This publication was printed on acid-free paper which meets the minimum requirements of American National Standard for Information Science—Permanence of Paper for Printed Library Material, ANSI Z39.48-1984.

Design by Marie Bartholomew
Cartography by C. Stuart Daniel

Published in the United States by:

University of Alaska Press
University of Alaska Fairbanks
Fairbanks, Alaska 99775-1580

Published in Canada by:

Oxford University Press
70 Wynford Drive
Don Mills, Ontario M3C 1J9

CONTENTS

ACKNOWLEDGEMENTS

We are indebted to a great number of people, both in Canada and in the United States, for their help in writing this book. The Social Sciences and Humanities Research Council's generous grant of a Research Time Stipend (to Ken Coates) and a sabbatical from Brandon University (to Bill Morrison) made much of the research possible. Both Brandon University and the University of Victoria gave welcome and essential financial support for our research. Additional support was provided by Peter Baskerville of the University of Victoria's Public History Group. Invaluable research work was done by Joy Dornian, Diane Fowler, Bruce Stadfeld, Rob McGarva, and Cory Neville in Brandon, and by Christina Nyers in Victoria. Archivists in Canada and the United States gave friendly and efficient help beyond any call of duty.

Particular thanks are due to Joyce Justice of the Seattle Branch of the United States Archives, and Kathleen O'Connor of the San Francisco Branch, to the staff of the Alaska State Archives at

Juneau, and the Yukon Territorial Archives. Our agent, Denise Bukowski of The Bukowski Agency, saved us from some of our more grotesque conceits. Our editor, Sally Livingston, did an excellent job with the text. Thanks also to Stuart Daniel, a first-rate cartographer, and to Allison Hastings of Intra Blaney Travel in Victoria, the country's most able travel agent. We also received valuable assistance and advice from Claus-M. Naske of the University of Alaska, Fairbanks, from Leonard McCann of the Vancouver Maritime Museum, and from anonymous reviewers who read early drafts of the manuscript. Special thanks are due to Juneau historian R.N. DeArmond, who provided valuable local information that saved us from several geographic and maritime howlers.

Particular thanks are also due to the people in the Pacific Northwest who helped us with their personal and family memories about the *Princess Sophia*: Mrs Carl Holsonbake, Wellon, AK; Meta R. Buttnick, Seattle; J.S. Merrill, US Coast Guard, Seventeenth Coast Guard District; Mrs P. DeMuth, Juneau; Ethel G. Michelsen, Seattle; Mrs Robert Kirchner, Seattle; W.A. Miller, Mukilteo, WA; Thelma R. Lower, Vancouver; Miss Joan E. Harding, Vancouver; Sheila Nickerson, Juneau; Mrs M.D. Brook, Atlin, BC; Mrs K.E. Pearsall, Victoria; Mr Craig, Richmond, BC; Alan F. Gosse, Victoria; Linda MacDonald, Mayo, Yukon; Mr Chuck Keen, Juneau; the Hon. Judge R.B. McD. Hutchinson, Victoria; Bruce Hutchinson, Shawnigan Lake, BC; Eileen Burke, Vancouver; Shirley Cuyler, Hastings, MN; Robert W. Very, Vancouver; L. McGrath, Snohomish, WA; Mrs W.E. Robinson, Delta, BC; India M. Spartz, Juneau; Mary Lou Spartz, Juneau; Rev. J.T. Horricks, Chilliwack, BC; Mrs B.M. Thompson, New Westminster, BC; R.F. Kennett, Port Moody, BC; Edward P. Madsen, Juneau; Mrs M. McCall, Victoria; Roy E. Macey, Fanny Bay, BC; J.R. Woosnam, Vancouver; Samuel Vint, Vancouver; Philip A. Hole, Victoria; Joan E. Vanstone, Vancouver; W. Jack Dalby, West Vancouver; H. Lake, Sidney, BC; Mrs D.C. Gough, Vancouver; Mrs K.L. Reid, West Vancouver; Esther Paulson, New Westminster; Mrs Jean Clarke, Granthams Landing, BC; Mrs G. Miller, Qualicum Beach, BC; Vern H. Ingram, Burnaby, BC; P.F.

Wolanski, Nanaimo, BC; Eric W.M. James, White Rock, BC; Tom Zacarelli Jr, Cobble Hill, BC; Mrs Audrey Hunt, Trail, BC; Doris M. Armstrong, Langley, BC; W.D. Campbell, Lantzville, BC; Ernie L. Plant, Langley, BC; Stan Wellburn, Vancouver; Mrs Grace Blackstock, Victoria; Mrs B.M. Thompson, New Westminster, BC; David W. Blackaller, White Rock, BC; W.J. Thorburn, Burnaby, BC; Dan Main, Parksville, BC; Vernon E.W. Finch, Vancouver; Miss R.M. Dallas, Vancouver; Richard F. Kennett, Port Moody, BC; Mrs D. Smith, Surrey, BC; James A. Haws, West Vancouver; Lloyd Bailey, Victoria; Steve Hites, Skagway; P.J. Buckway, Whitehorse, Yukon.

The successful completion of this book is in large measure due to the unending support and encouragement of our families. Bradley, Mark, and Laura Coates have now visited the 'Land of the Midnight Sun' and know much more about the land and people that preoccupy their father. Ruth, Claire, John, and Catherine Morrison have yet to venture northward, but they remain enthusiastic about their father's northern work. We wish in particular to acknowledge, with love and many thanks, the remarkable encouragement provided by our wives, Cathy Coates and Linda Morrison. Their support, enthusiasm, and patience are a constant source of inspiration to us.

Kenneth S. Coates
Department of History
University of Victoria

William R. Morrison
Centre for Northern Studies
Lakehead University

BEAUFORT SEA
Bering Strait
BERING SEA
NOME
ST. MICHAEL
ALASKA
YUKON RIVER
RUBY
Porcupine R.
Kuskokwim R.
IDITAROD
FAIRBANKS
Tanana R.
YUKON
Mackenzie River
Pee
YUKON
DAWSON
Stewart River
Bristol Bay
ANCHORAGE
VALDEZ
RIVER
Pelly River
U.S.A.
CANADA
Gulf of Alaska
KODIAK ISLAND
WHITEHORSE
SKAGWAY
JUNEAU
ADMIRALTY ISLAND
SITKA
PACIFIC
PETERSBURG
WRANGELL
BRITISH
KETCHIKAN
PRINCE RUPERT
OCEAN
QUEEN CHARLOTTE ISLANDS
COLUMBIA
ALERT BAY
VANCOUVER ISLAND
VANCOUVER
VICTORIA
Juan de Fuca Strait
SEATTLE
PACIFIC NORTHWEST
0 100 200 300 400 500 miles
0 200 400 600 km
© K.S. Coates & W.R. Morrison, 1989
DANIEL CARTOGRAPHY
170° 160° 150° 140°W
75° 70° 65° 60° 55° 50° 45° N
140° 130°W

INTRODUCTION

At first light on the morning of 26 October 1918, a small fleet of rescue vessels left the sheltered habours where they had spent the night and made their way to Vanderbilt Reef. The sight that awaited the men on board filled them with horror. A twenty-foot mast jutting forlornly out of the icy winter waters of Lynn Canal was all that could be seen of the Canadian Pacific steamship *Princess Sophia.* Grounded on the reef, for more than a day and half the *Sophia* had clung tenaciously to it as a bitter early winter storm swirled about her. Then the storm grew in intensity, and despite attempts at rescue, the *Sophia* was swept across the rock. Her bottom was torn open, and the ship and her passengers slipped into a frigid grave.

The sinking of the *Princess Sophia* killed 353 people and wrought havoc on the far northwest of North America. The story contains all the melodramatic elements that make up a classic adventure tale: hardship, heroism, the immense forces of nature, greed, love, wealth, pathos, and sudden death. In a sense it is a far more important story than that of the *Titanic*–the great 'unsinkable' ship that preceded it to the ocean depths by six years. The *Titanic* claimed many more victims–approximately 1,500–but its story was essentially no more than the sum of many personal tragedies. The *Princess Sophia*, on the other hand, not only struck down hundreds of lives but also dealt an almost lethal blow to the far northwest–a huge area of this continent. Hundreds of residents of the region died on the ship, including a significant percentage of the white population of the Yukon Territory. In that respect, the magnitude of the disaster far eclipses any result of the sinking of the *Titanic*.

The *Sophia*'s is also an international story, involving both the Alaska and Yukon Territories. The ship, though Canadian, sailed from an American port and sank in American waters; many of the would-be rescuers were American; the bodies of the victims were initially taken to an American town, and then transported to burial sites across Canada and the United States. At the same time, the sinking of the *Sophia* shows that in that era the far northwest was a distinct region, with common interests and a developing northern identity.

The mining districts of the far northwest made up a small world of their own, isolated by distance and climate from the rest of North America. These small communities were tied to the 'outside' by a single transportation route running from central Alaska up the Yukon River past Dawson City to Whitehorse, then to Skagway by railway. There, on the edge of the north, goods and travellers transferred to ships owned by the Canadian Pacific Railway's steamship service, or one of its competitors, for the voyage down the Inside Passage–the beautiful trip down the coast of the Alaska panhandle and British Columbia to the ports of Vancouver and Seattle.

Seventy years ago, the Canadian Pacific steamers played the same role in northern transportation that jet airliners play today; in a sense, they were even more important, since there was no road to the northwest then, and the ships were not only the quickest (and supposedly the safest), but the only really practical means of getting to and from the region. When a ship like the *Princess*

Sophia sank, it was bound to take with it not tourists, the people who fill today's cruise ships, but a cross-section of northern society–miners, businessmen, civil servants, steamboat men, their wives and children. When these people sailed on the *Sophia* in late October 1918 they were following an ordinary routine, much as people do today when flying from Whitehorse to Vancouver, or Winnipeg to Toronto, or Fairbanks to Seattle. Like today's travellers, they were leaving to find work, to visit relatives, to follow the sun in retirement, to seek medical attention–for all the reasons that people travel. But, like the victims of airplane crashes, they were in the wrong place at the wrong time. These are the people, ordinary and extraordinary, who fill the pages of this book.

It is hard to understand why the story of the *Princess Sophia* is not better known in North America, particularly in the Pacific coastal regions and the far northwest. Apart from maritime history buffs, readers of books on ocean shipping,[1] and a dwindling group of friends and relatives of the victims, few members of the general public are even aware of the episode. Most surprisingly, the *Princess Sophia* is virtually unknown in the Yukon and the interior of Alaska, the very part of the continent that was so cruelly affected by her sinking.

The *Titanic*, on the other hand, is remembered in stone as well as in folk memory. In Southampton, the English town from which many of the *Titanic*'s crew came, there are no fewer than five memorials to the men who died on her. Some of the victims of the *Princess Sophia* are buried under grave markers that mention the ship. But there is no public memorial–not in Dawson City, where scores of the victims came from, nor in Juneau, where the bodies were taken after the tragedy and where many lie buried, nor in Vancouver, Victoria, Seattle, Whitehorse, Atlin, Eagle, Iditarod, Ruby, or Fairbanks, the communities where so many of those men, women, and children had been well-known as business partners and lodge brothers, as fellow members of the IODE and the Yukon Order of Pioneers, as schoolmates. Why? This book is in part a search for answers to that question, a search that has cast new light not only on the disaster itself, but on the history and development of the far northwest of North America.

It is also a series of intensely human stories: of Frank Burke, the teenager from Vancouver who signed on the *Princess Sophia* for a few weeks' work; of Captain James Alexander, the veteran mining entrepreneur who had finally found his fortune; of Lulu Mae Eads, the former dance-hall queen; of John Zaccarelli, the Italian Klondiker turned grocer; of Chinese cooks and porters with names like Set Yip that the newspapers could not be bothered to spell correctly; of men so obscure they were buried in unmarked graves; and of over three hundred more.

The authors came to this story from different beginnings. Ken Coates was brought up in the Yukon, attending elementary and secondary school in Whitehorse and forming the kind of attachment to the territory and its history that comes from growing up there. Like all northern Canadians he had to go south for his university education, but decided to train himself to speak for his region to the rest of the country, and to write its history from a northern point of view. Bill Morrison is a native of Hamilton, Ontario, trained in Ontario universities, who came to the study of the north through a southern route–an interest in federal-government policy regarding the north, and the means by which Ottawa extended its sovereignty over the lands north of the 60th parallel.

Yet neither of the authors, whether as children, as schoolboys, or as undergraduates, had ever heard of the *Princess Sophia*. The story was not included in the curriculum of the Whitehorse schools, and it was certainly not mentioned in the schools of Ontario. They were, however, both familiar with the story of the *Titanic* from childhood, and at an early age Morrison, whose father was a keen sailor, could sing all the verses of the popular song about that disaster, an ironic ditty whose chorus includes the lines 'It was sad, mighty sad, it was sad when that great ship went down.' No one sang about the *Princess Sophia*, however,[2] and it was not until they began to read more deeply into Yukon history, in such books as Laura Berton's *I Married the Klondike* and the memoirs of Martha Black, that they found mention of the episode and the effect it had on the region.

Why are some disasters remembered and others largely forgotten? Part of the reason must lie in the images associated with them in the public mind. The *Hindenburg* disaster, for instance, was made famous by the horrifying picture of the great dirigible crashing in flames–one of the most famous photographs of this century–and the panic-stricken commentary of the radio announcer on the scene. But the *Hindenburg* killed far fewer people than did the *Princess Sophia*. The same is true of the *Challenger* space-shuttle disaster of January 1986, whose image has been etched into the minds of hundreds of millions of television viewers. The most telling comparison, however, is with the *Titanic*, a name that must be familiar to nearly every educated speaker of English. There are several reasons why the *Titanic*'s story is so much better known than the *Princess Sophia*'s, of which the least important is the fact that the first episode killed four times as many people as the second. More significantly, the sinking of the *Titanic* carried a dreadful irony that caught the interest of the world: people believed (apparently without foundation)[3] that the ship's builders had boasted it was unsinkable: men had challenged Fate, and Fate had crushed them.

There are several explanations for the obscurity of the *Princess Sophia* disaster. The *Titanic* sank in 1912, at the end of the Edwardian era, in a time of peace, after a century of relative calm and prosperity, when the wonders of technology fascinated the world and violent death seemed shocking and somehow unnatural. The 1915 torpedoing of the passenger ship *Lusitania* killed over 1200 people. For a supposedly unarmed passenger ship to be sunk by a submarine without warning seemed particularly appalling because it was unprecedented. By October 1918, when the *Princess Sophia* sank, the world had become all too accustomed to the horror of mass death. Indeed, the timing of the sinking could hardly have been worse from the point of view of public interest; not only was the world jaded from four years of carnage, but the ship sank just before the Armistice, and the grief of friends and survivors was eclipsed by the general rejoicing that greeted the end of the war. Finally, and perhaps most important, several of the people who went down with the *Lusitania* and the *Titanic* were famous–men like Colonel J.J. Astor, who bequeathed $100 million to his children, or Benjamin Guggenheim and Isidor Straus, both millionaires. The *Sophia*'s victims were not millionaires, though some were prosperous, and at least one, Captain Alexander of the Engineer Mine, was on his way 'outside' to sell his property for a reputed million dollars. Nor were they well-known outside the circle of their family and friends. Moreover, they came from the Yukon River valley, an area that had attracted the world's attention during the Klondike gold rush but had been largely forgotten for nearly two decades. In short, the passengers and crew of the *Princess Sophia* were simply ordinary people from the periphery of civilization; they were not famous, wealthy, glamorous people from its very centre. The story of the *Titanic* echoes this truth:

> In all disasters, it is the fate of the rich and famous that attracts the most fascinated attention; and of this squalid but universal truth the *Titanic* is a glaring example. Like the poor on land, drowned steerage passengers have no history. Common humanity has little interest in knowing what happened to other common people like themselves; shocked by the sudden intervention of chance and chaos in human affairs, they draw reassurance from the knowledge that even the privileged can come to an untimely end.[4]

The *Princess Sophia* story is a vital part of the history of the far northwest, and particularly of the Yukon River basin. It should be as important to that region as the great Halifax explosion of 1917 is to Nova Scotia, the fire of 1887 to Vancouver, the flood of 1950 to Winnipeg, the Galveston hurricane of 1900 (which killed 6,000) to that city, the San Francisco earthquake to California, the great hurricane of 1938 to the New England states, 1954's Hurricane Hazel to the Toronto area, or any number of other disasters to the regions where they occurred–part of the fabric of local history, part of what every child growing up there learns, not only in school but in everyday conversation. These events are not only history, but folklore. The *Princess Sophia* story should be all these things; one of the goals of this book is to make it so.

More than folklore, however, are the wider aspects of the disaster. The sinking of the *Princess Sophia* can serve as a kind of historical searchlight, illuminating little-known aspects of the history of the continent's northwestern regions. The disaster was made up of many individual stories–about fear, grief, bravery, stupidity, luck, and the importance of last-minute decisions. It was also an important episode in the history of a North American region–its economy, its growth, and its decline; a story of a northern society built on a 'boom and bust' philosophy.

The importance of the *Sophia* story hinges on a central aspect of northern life: the transiency of the non-Native people. It is a well-known fact that many northern residents lived in the region only during the summer, going north in the spring and returning to a southern home each fall. What is less well-known is how widespread the practice was in the early days. There were people on the *Princess Sophia* who had worked in the north for many years but had never sunk roots in the region; men and women who spent the summer months in the Yukon River valley and the winter in Vancouver, Seattle, or California; merchants who came north in the spring with their goods and departed in October with their profits. In particular there were those who had seasonal jobs in the north–steamboat captains like John Charles Green, master of the *Yukon*. He had worked on the river steamers since the gold rush; each spring he and his wife went north when the ice went out on the river, and each fall they returned to Seattle.

The *Princess Sophia* was an important part of this pattern; she and her sister ships were the arteries of commerce and transportation, carrying the lifeblood of goods and people north and south. Thus–to carry the metaphor a bit further–when an accident happened to this artery, the entire system was bound to suffer. In 1918 the health of the northern economy was far from good. And it is here that the tale begins.

This is the story of a maritime disaster that had its roots in the economic and social decay of the far northwest. As such, it must begin with an account of the Yukon and the Alaskan interior in the years after the Klondike gold rush, a period when the vital forces were draining out of the region. The passengers who died on the *Princess Sophia* were an integral part of this society in decline, and so the history of this period is drawn from their experiences. The story of their lives and their reasons for leaving the region in the fall of 1918 make painfully evident the fatalism that engulfed the northwest during the First World War. The collective trauma of regional decay casts into sharp relief the tragedy of the *Princess Sophia*.

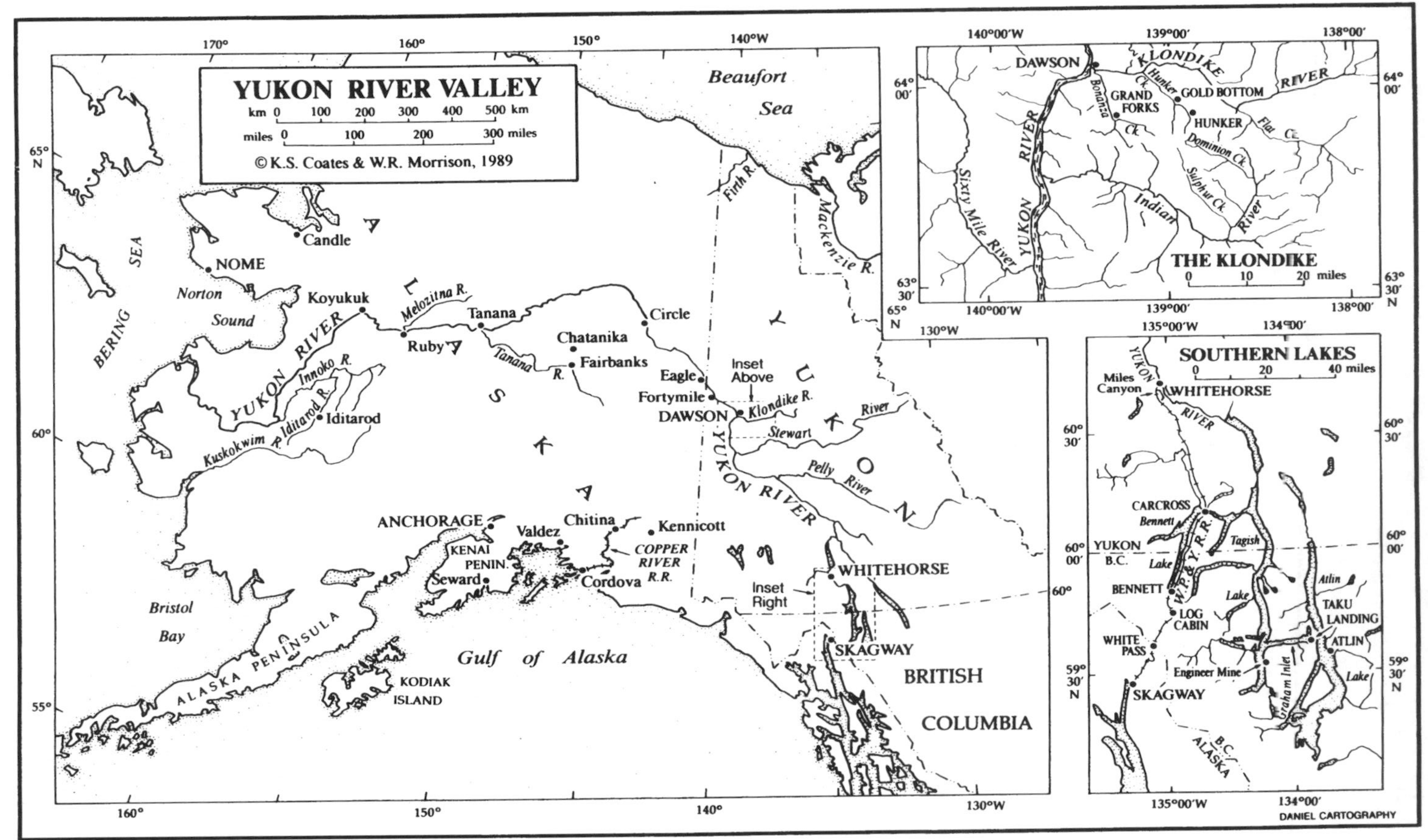

YUKON RIVER VALLEY
km 0 100 200 300 400 500 km
miles 0 100 200 300 miles
© K.S. Coates & W.R. Morrison, 1989
Beaufort Sea
BERING SEA
Norton Sound
ALASKA
YUKON
Candle
NOME
Koyukuk
Melozitna R.
Tanana
Ruby
Circle
Chatanika
Fairbanks
Tanana R.
YUKON RIVER
Innoko R.
Iditarod R.
Iditarod
Kuskokwim R.
Eagle
Fortymile
DAWSON
Inset Above
Klondike R.
Stewart River
Pelly River
YUKON RIVER
Firth R.
Mackenzie R.
ANCHORAGE
Valdez
Chitina
Kennicott
COPPER RIVER R.R.
KENAI PENIN.
Seward
Cordova
WHITEHORSE
Inset Right
SKAGWAY
Bristol Bay
ALASKA PENINSULA
Gulf of Alaska
KODIAK ISLAND
BRITISH COLUMBIA
THE KLONDIKE
0 10 20 miles
DAWSON
KLONDIKE RIVER
Bonanza Ck
Hunker Ck
GRAND FORKS
GOLD BOTTOM
HUNKER
Flat Ck
Dominion Ck
Sulphur Ck
Indian River
Sixty Mile River
YUKON RIVER
SOUTHERN LAKES
0 20 40 miles
YUKON
Miles Canyon
WHITEHORSE
RIVER
CARCROSS
Bennett Lake
Tagish Lake
W.P.&Y.R.R.
YUKON
B.C.
BENNETT
LOG CABIN
Atlin Lake
TAKU LANDING
ATLIN
WHITE PASS
Engineer Mine
Graham Inlet
SKAGWAY
B.C.
ALASKA
DANIEL CARTOGRAPHY

1. THE NORTH IN DECLINE

Once known round the world, by 1918 the Yukon River valley had been all but forgotten. The Klondike had achieved world-wide fame for a few years after the discovery of gold on Bonanza Creek in August 1896. Driven by dreams of Eldorado, thousands swarmed north in 1897 and 1898 in the world's last great gold rush. Dawson City exploded out of nothing in 1896; by the summer of 1898 the city and the surrounding creeks had at least 30,000 residents–no one knew for sure–and was the largest city in Canada west of Winnipeg. A number of lesser communities flourished on the creeks: Hunker, Gold Bottom, Sulphur, Dominion, Grand Forks. But the rush had ended in 1899. Though there was (and is) still plenty of gold to be found in the Yukon's tributaries, a new century brought new mining techniques to the gold fields. For gravel deposits where each cubic yard contained only a few cents' worth of gold, large machines were needed. By 1900 modern industrial techniques were replacing the small placer operations on the creeks; gold mining around Dawson was becoming capital- rather than labour-intensive. Naturally, fewer men were required to operate the huge dredges that now chewed up the creeks than had been needed to work them by hand. The miners moved on, pushed out by the mammoth dredges that replaced independent prospectors with wage labourers in the gold fields.

Very few of the people who came to Dawson during the rush and afterwards actually made much money from mining gold, and many of them left in disappointment to follow the 'echo-booms' spawned by the Klondike strike. In September 1898 'three lucky Swedes'[1] found gold on Anvil Creek, a few miles from Nome, and other prospectors made a strike in the upper reaches of the Yukon watershed at Atlin, BC. In July 1899 John Hummell discovered gold on the sandy beach of Nome, and another rush to that town began. In 1902 several important strikes were made in the Tanana River region, which led to the establishment of Fairbanks as an important rival to Dawson City. More strikes a decade or so later, near Ruby and Iditarod, accelerated the decline of Dawson. These 'echo-booms' were all important strikes, and they drew considerable attention, though their fame never equalled the Klondike's. There were heroics and privations in the Alaska fields as there had been in the Klondike, but not the same dramatic images–the men bent over as they toiled up the Chilkoot Pass, the suffering of Dead Horse Gulch, the armada of jerry-built boats floating down the Yukon River.

It was at Nome that the most famous of the Alaska rushes took place. There, on the sandy beaches facing the Bering Sea, gold was discovered at the end of 1898. The ensuing rush marked the beginning of the end of Dawson City's glory, and switched the attention of Americans from the Yukon to their own northern territory. In 1902 interest shifted from Nome to the Tanana Valley, deep in the interior. Here gold was discovered literally by chance: a trader-prospector named E.T. Barnette cached his supplies on a tributary of the Tanana River; an Italian miner named Felix Pedro was then able to purchase a grubstake from Barnette, and subsequently struck gold. The Tanana stampede, in the winter of 1902-3, led to the founding of the town of Fairbanks. Named after Indiana Senator Charles W. Fairbanks, the town became politically important when Judge James Wickersham, the federal judge for the region (and later Alaska's congressional representative) moved government offices there.[2] Within a year of the stampede Fairbanks had a population of 1,200, and by 1905 it was the largest community in Alaska.

The last great rush in the interior of Alaska in 1909 was launched by the discovery of rich deposits of gold on tributaries of the lower Yukon River. In the watersheds of the Kuskokwim and Innoko rivers a number of towns grew up around mining camps, the most important of which was Iditarod, founded in 1910. With the Fairbanks fields faltering, Iditarod boomed, and soon it was producing two or three million dollars' worth of gold per year (the region was still producing $1 million as late as 1940). Becoming the supply and commercial centre of a prosperous placer mining district, by 1911 it had a population of nearly 700. But by 1918 its best days were over, and in 1920 its residents numbered only 20.[3]

The rush moved on to Ruby, on the left bank of the Yukon River, south of the junction of the Melozitna River. Though gold was discovered in the district in 1907, the town was not founded until 1911, after a stampede to new discoveries on Long Creek. For several years the population of Ruby was over 1,000, but by 1920 it had fallen to only 128. Though the town is still in existence, its population has never again grown above 200.[4] In their heyday, both Ruby and Iditarod were typical Yukon River valley boom-towns, with plenty of saloons, gamblers, prostitutes, and others who went north on the Canadian Pacific passenger ships to mine the miners.

The *Princess Sophia* and her sister ships carried these people as well as businessmen, a few tourists, civil servants, soldiers, Mounted Policemen, wives, and children north and south. In late 1918 scores of people from all over the northland were making plans to travel 'outside' aboard her. One of them was John F. Kelly, known in the north as 'Broken Jaw' Kelly. Born in 1885, he had worked all over the Yukon valley, at Dawson, Ruby, and Fairbanks. Though a good worker, he never held a steady job for long. What he liked to do was 'to go to some new creek and sink a hole, he liked that better than anything else . . . in that country wherever you would happen to go [where] there was something new you would find Kelly.'[5] There were hundreds of rolling stones like him in the valley.

Clarence Porter also worked on both sides of the border. He had gone north in 1899 with his wife and worked as a blacksmith in Dawson. In 1904 he moved to Fairbanks, where he continued to work as a blacksmith, investing his earnings in mining properties in the Ruby district. Like many small businessmen and tradespeople, he made a fair amount from staking prospectors–at one time he took $30,000 from a claim, but lost most of it in properties that failed to pan out.[6]

But not all the people who went to Ruby and Iditarod were veteran northerners. Even the last echoes of the Yukon valley gold rushes were capable of drawing men from the south. Charles M. Castleman, a farmer's son born in Falls County, Texas, in 1879, was 29 at the time of the Ruby strike.[7] Tired of farming and working in a flour mill in Vernon, Texas, he went to Alaska in 1910 to try his luck. He worked in mines and did some prospecting on the side, and though he didn't strike it rich, he made enough money to send $100 south to his father each year. Eight years, however, had more than satisfied his appetite for northern adventure. He had seen his hopes for wealth disappointed, and since he had no real ties to the north, there was nothing to keep him there when better opportunities beckoned elsewhere. Towards the end of 1918 he decided to return south, and booked passage on the *Princess Sophia*.[8]

The mining industry had also attracted merchants, hotelkeepers, and other businessmen, and there was a small civil service on both sides of the border. One of its most prominent members in the Yukon was Edmund S. Ironside, born in 1879 on Manitoulin Island in Ontario, the son and grandson of senior officials in the Department of Indian Affairs. After working in his teens with the surveyors on the Crowsnest Pass railway route, he had gone to the far northwest in 1898. He then worked in the Canadian customs office at Skagway, tried his hand at mining, worked for a time with the contractors who built the White Pass & Yukon Railway, and eventually joined the Canadian Customs Service in the Yukon. He rose to the position of Collector of Customs in Dawson, 'one of the best qualified and most respected Government officials in the Dominion'.[9] By 1918 Ironside was one of the few federal civil servants left in the territory after the cutbacks of that year, and as such, one of Dawson's most prominent citizens. Unmarried (his mother had kept house for him since 1913), during the war he had been one of the organizers of the Yukon Patriotic Fund, responsible for getting the larger Yukon businesses to persuade their employees to donate one day's pay per month to the fund.[10] He also wrote poetry 'in the Service tradition';[11] one poem, entitled 'A Message', was published posthumously in the *Dawson Daily News*:

> I pray the prayer all Yukoners do,
> May the Golden Paystreak abide with you;
> Wherever you are, wherever you be,
> Old pal, your memory still lives with me;
> Though you may forget old times at last,
> Forget your friend of a day that's past;
> I'll always remember, most Yukoners do,
> May Life's Golden Paystreak abide with you.[12]

With the security of a civil-service job, Ironside was prepared to stay in Dawson City. But he preferred to take his holidays outside.

Oscar E. Tackstrom, his wife, and their two children, like most northerners, passed easily back and forth across the international border. Born in the United States in 1878, Tackstrom arrived in the Yukon as a young man during the gold rush, failed to make his fortune in the Klondike, and in 1906 went to Fairbanks, going on a few years later to the small mining community of Ruby to try his luck there. The ease with which Tackstrom and men like him moved between the Canadian and American mining frontiers underlines the fact that the two frontiers were part of a larger Yukon River community. Both Fairbanks and Ruby were linked to the outside through the Dawson-Whitehorse-Skagway route, so going from one community to another was as easy as moving from one stop to another on a long railroad line. In Ruby, Tackstrom went into business, becoming the manager of a lumber company and was soon recognized as one of the town's leading citizens.

In 1908 Oscar Tackstrom travelled to Dawson City to marry Christina McDonald. A member of a well-known family in Nanaimo, BC, she had gone to Dawson to visit her sister, who was married to a Yukon River steamboat captain. While on a side trip to Fairbanks she had met Oscar, who fell in love with her. It was easy to do; he was ready for marriage, and Crissie was not only 'lovable in disposition',[13] but strikingly beautiful–a 'perfect Titian type' with a 'tall and willowy figure'.[14] The Tackstroms soon had two children: George, who was just 10 in 1918, and Margaret, a few years younger. They were a close, warm family, popular in the community–the kind of people who gave the non-Native north what human stability it could claim.

George F. Mayhood's career similarly straddled the Alaska-Yukon boundary. Born near Napanee, Ontario, around 1858, he went to California in 1875 to seek his fortune, then joined the rush to the Klondike in 1898. That same year he was caught in the terrible Easter avalanche at Sheep Camp on the Chilkoot trail in which over sixty men were killed, and was lucky to escape with only a broken leg. Having gone into business in Dawson as part of the provisioning firm of Mayhood and Jackson, when the rush collapsed he opened a general store at Chatanika, on Cleary Creek near Fairbanks. Later he went to Iditarod, and became one of the first businessmen to join the rush to Ruby, where he set up a cigar store and pool room. Mayhood was another of the region's energetic optimists, seeking opportunities where they could be found. Though he seemed to have a commitment to the region, his family did not; when his sons grew up, they moved to California.[15]

Ulysses Grant Myers started his northern career in the Yukon but found prosperity in Alaska. He was born in New York City in 1864, in the next-to-last year of the Civil War; judging by his name, his parents must have been staunch Unionists. Unlike most men who went north in 1898, he had a university degree, from William and Mary College in Virginia. After trying his luck in the Klondike gold fields for two years, he moved downriver to Eagle, Alaska, where he got a job with the United States weather bureau. In 1904 he was appointed US Commissioner and Recorder at Eagle, and in 1905 he began practising law. Myers eventually became the mayor and coroner of the community, and in the summer acted as Customs House broker, meeting all the steamers coming downriver from Dawson City. He spent the rest of his life at Eagle, and became one of the town's leading citizens. His wife, however, preferred to winter at Poughkeepsie, New York.

Although he made a good living from his various government jobs–as Commissioner he received $3,000 a year in fees, and as Customs House broker about $2,500 each summer–Myers was always short of cash. He was a common type in the Yukon River valley, a man with faith in the region's future who was willing to back it with money. Over and over again he listened to the stories of prospectors, and over and over again he grub-staked them. His wife described the result:

> He laid aside no salary or accumulations . . . he outfitted many prospectors, sending them out to prospect and do the assessment work on located claims, paying all expenses in return for a share interest in the claim. I personally know of over fifty of such claims, every one of which cost him from $100 to $500 and several cost him in excess of $500. . . . all but his one-half interest in one group [were] worthless . . . this is the net result of his savings except for a half interest in farm land at Sunnyside, Washington, which never has produced any income . . .[16]

Arnoux Pellison had crossed even more borders during his life. French by birth, a native of the Basses Pyrénées, he prospected on Dominion Creek during and after the rush, and in 1910 sold his claim to the Treadgold Concession. After that he went to Alaska and tried his luck in a number of mining camps–Koyukuk, Nome, Candle, Fairbanks, Chatanika, and Kuskokwim, among others. When the war broke out in Europe Pellison followed it intently–his brother Jean was serving in the French army. When the United States entered the conflict, he was 36 years old, and could probably have escaped the draft. But he decided to serve his adopted country, and prepared to go south to San Francisco at the end of the 1918 mining season to enlist.

Thomas Turner had also ranged far afield during his life, not as a working miner but as a manager for large mining corporations. His presence in the far northwest was symbolic of the change from individual mining to the era of the large concessions. A graduate of Stanford University in geology and mining, he had first worked as superintendent and assistant manager of the Orsk Gold Dredging Company at Nikloaiersk, on the Amur River in Eastern Siberia. He then went to Dawson as assistant dredging superintendent for the Yukon Gold Company, to Ruby as engineer and accountant for the company, and then to its Iditarod operations. Like Pellison, Turner was headed for military service in 1918; at the age of 30, he had just received his draft notice.[17]

These people, and thousands more like them, moved up and down the Yukon River valley following the 'echo-booms'. By 1915 gold production at Iditarod had surpassed that at Fairbanks. But many of the older districts were still producing; even at that late date, there was considerable mining activity in the oldest gold-mining area in Alaska, around Circle, which predated the Klondike rush. As late as 1916 there were more than seventy mines in the Eagle-Circle region employing 265 men and producing $375,000 worth of gold.[18]

At Atlin, one of the best-known figures in the region had finally found success. Captain James Alexander, owner of the Engineer Mine on Tagish Lake, had worked for many years to develop his property. Each winter he spent at least a few weeks in the south trying to promote it. By 1918 he had twenty-five men working on the mine, and had finally aroused the interest of southern buyers; a purchase price of over $1 million was mentioned in the press.[19]

Though Alaska was more prosperous than the Yukon in the years leading up to the First World War, one part of the Yukon economy succeeded not only in maintaining its prosperity but in defeating its American rivals. This was river transportation. Although there were a number of routes to the Yukon River valley, each loudly touted by people who hoped to make money from exploiting it, the shortest and quickest–and therefore the best–was from Skagway to Whitehorse via the White Pass & Yukon Railway, then down the Yukon River by steamer. The British-owned White Pass & Yukon Railway Company also owned a subsidiary, the British Yukon Navigation Company, which operated sternwheelers on the river between Dawson and Whitehorse. Its control over the vital White Pass route to the sea gave the company the financial strength to expand its operations west of the 141st meridian. In 1914 it bought into another subsidiary, the American Yukon Navigation Company, operating along the lower part of the river in Alaska. Although this company continued to run boats between St Michael and Dawson, the route upstream from Dawson to Whitehorse was more popular, partly because the trip along the Inside Passage was more pleasant than the open sea voyage via the Bering Strait, especially for those with weak stomachs.[20]

As a result, the majority of people who entered or left the Yukon River valley did so by way of Dawson, Whitehorse, and Skagway, and the commercial traffic followed the same route. Alaskans living in Ruby and Iditarod were in fact much closer to the mouth of the Yukon River than to its source, and could have reached salt water more quickly by going down the river to the Bering Sea rather than up it into Canada. They could also reach salt water at Seward or Valdez by means of overland trails, but these were hard going. The success of the White Pass & Yukon Route and its subsidiaries, combined with people's reluctance to face a sea voyage, meant that traffic via the St Michael-Bering Sea route declined, and most Alaskans, like Yukoners, travelled 'outside' through Whitehorse.

The supremacy of this Yukon route, which lasted until the Alaska Railroad was completed in the 1920s, maintained the unity of the Yukon River valley community that had begun in the early days of the fur trade. It was only natural that such a community should exist, for before the Klondike gold rush the main field at Fortymile straddled the international boundary, and many of the men and women who moved to the Alaskan fields after 1900 had begun their careers in the Yukon. People like George Mayhood, Ulysses Grant Myers, Arnoux Pellison, Thomas Turner, and the Tackstroms–all passengers on the *Princess Sophia*–were members of a large, dispersed community with an economy based on the search for gold and other minerals. This community had its transportation hub at Dawson City, where boats coming up from the lower Yukon transferred passengers and freight to others leaving for the upper part of the river and the railway at Whitehorse. If the boats were making the entire journey from Fairbanks to Whitehorse, as some did, there would be a stop in Dawson for fuel, provisions, and passengers. The transfer at Dawson provided an opportunity for old friends to meet and exchange reminiscences for a few hours or perhaps a day.[21] Finally, everyone travelled the narrow-gauge railway from Whitehorse to the port of Skagway, where ships like the *Princess Sophia* waited to take them south. For hundreds of people this journey was an annual ritual that, like the medieval fairs, renewed personal ties and marked the passing of the years. For a people so joined by a common history and a single transportation route to the outside world, national boundaries were of secondary importance. The *Dawson Daily News* regularly spoke in terms of the entire Yukon valley, referring to it as 'the Northland'.

The lives of the valley's residents, bound up with the resource industry and the industries that served it, were also tied to its seasonal rhythms. Most of the passenger and virtually all of the commercial traffic in the region took place between the break-up of ice on the river in May and freeze-up in late October or early November. If this activity was notable in the early spring, it was even more so in the autumn. Most of the men who worked on the dredges were always laid off when increasing cold in the fall forced the dredges to stop operating, and would not be hired again until the spring. The same was true of those who worked on the steamboats, and in many other jobs in the region. Since there were few alternative jobs in the winter, many of these men left for the south each fall. Those who had their wives and children with them in the north took them along; the rest looked forward to rejoining their families.

Many of these seasonal workers were on the *Princess Sophia* in October 1918. Arthur D. Lewis, a Londoner born in 1866, had emigrated to British Columbia in his early twenties, where he worked for six years in the naval dockyard at Esquimalt. In 1898 he went to the Yukon to join the Bennett Lake Navigation Company, and later worked as a purser on the White Pass & Yukon steamers. His wife and children lived in Victoria, and when navigation on the Yukon stopped in the fall, he would return there; during the war years he had spent the winters selling real estate in Victoria. In the spring of 1918 he went north as purser on the *Casca*.[22] William McWaters of New Westminster also worked both north and south: in the summers he was a fireman on the steamer *Dawson*, and in the winter he went home to fish and find work wherever he could.[23] One of the most famous Yukoners, William Scouse, followed the same annual routine. He was a Scottish coal miner, born in 1862, who had come to America in 1880 to work in the Pennsylvania coal mines. He worked his way across the continent, spending time in Kansas, Washington, Nanaimo, and the Queen Charlotte Islands. In the spring of 1896 he and three partners had arrived in the Yukon River valley, and he was in the central Yukon when he heard of the great strike on Bonanza Creek. The man who took the first bucket of pay dirt from the richest creek in the world–Eldorado, where he owned claim number 15–Scouse held on to most of his money, and in 1918 was still making $10,000 a year from his properties. After his marriage in 1902, he went south every year at the end of October to spend the winter with his wife in Seattle, returning north in the spring.[24]

It is impossible to determine how many people followed a similar pattern, but the available evidence indicates that there must have been hundreds of them. This seasonal mobility affected the development of the north in a number of ways. Most damaging to the Yukon because of its small population–around 7,000 in 1914, and falling–was the lack of economic commitment to the north on the part of many of its residents. Hundreds of those who worked in the Yukon were only sojourners; by 1918 some had lived in the territory for twenty years, yet seldom spent a winter there. Because of the employment patterns of the Yukon, this seasonal migration was not always voluntary, but whether choice or necessity drove them south every autumn, the result for the north was the same: there was no long-term commitment to the region. Like boom-and-bust communities everywhere, it was a place people went to in order to make a living, not to live; to extract resources and wages, not to put down roots; a place for getting, not giving. William Scouse, for example, invested most of his earnings in the south; though he owned mining properties in the far northwest worth $25,000, his real-estate holdings in Seattle amounted to $100,000.[25] The Alaskan mines followed patterns similar to those of the Yukon, but the fact that the American territory had a population roughly ten times larger tended to give it greater stability.

Nevertheless, some Yukoners who had gone to the Territory during the gold rush had never left. Murray and Lulu Mae Eads had both arrived at the height of the rush, he originally from Kentucky and she from Alabama. Murray didn't have much money–he had been working in a Seattle drug store in 1897, when the first boat loaded with gold came south from the Klondike–but he came from a prominent family. (His uncle was a famous engineer who in the 1870s had built the Eads bridge at St Louis, the first railway bridge over the Mississippi River–a remarkable feat of engineering that still stands.) In Dawson City Murray Eads worked for a local transportation company, but he realized early on that the permanent wealth in Dawson was to be made by mining the miners, and as soon as he had amassed some capital he invested in hotel properties. As the owner of the Monte Carlo and then the Floradora, both prominent watering spots, he presented the most famous of the Klondike entertainers–Babe Wallace, Diamond Tooth Gertie, the Oregon Mare, and one of the town's most famous dance-hall queens, the seductive Lulu Mae. Even after Lulu Mae married her boss and settled down to a 'respectable' life, she was never accepted by polite Dawson society: as late as 1907 she was charged with allowing on her premises 'women of loose, idle or suspicious character and having no honourable occupation or calling, for the purpose of drinking and keeping company with men'.[26] Eventually the Eads changed the hotel's name from Floradora to the more sober Royal Alexandra, but even in the early 1910s it retained some of the flavour of the old days:

> There was always some of the aura of the golden era about it. In the lobby hung three giant oil pictures of nudes, seven feet high, in tremendous gilt frames. Eads had had them packed in on men's backs over the trail in the early days. That hotel lobby, with its enamel spittoons, its painted nudes, its black-leather Edwardian chairs and its endless poker games glimpsed through the doors in the rear, never changed in any single detail . . .[27]

By the First World War Murray Eads had diversified his interests. He was now part-owner and secretary-treasurer of the O'Brien Brewing and Malting Company, a passionate supporter of baseball in the town, and an active member of the Yukon Territorial Liberal Association. His career illustrates the taming of the Canadian gold mining frontier, the transition from the turbulent days of the gold rush to the more conservative period that followed. Although by 1918 the couple had achieved sufficient prosperity to invest in a Seattle bank, they had never once left the Yukon–a phenomenon unusual enough to be remarked upon in the press.

By the end of the war it was becoming obvious to Yukoners that their economy and society were disintegrating about them. The population was falling rapidly, Dawson City had lost much of its vitality, and steamer and other commercial traffic on the upper Yukon had declined significantly. The final blow occurred in 1918, the year of the *Princess Sophia* disaster. The war was in its fourth year, the national debt was rising, political bitterness across the country was the worst in a generation. The federal government, burdened by the costs of the war, was eager to save money in places that didn't seem to matter. It had no time to think about the Yukon, and no desire to throw more money away on governing or developing what looked like a lost cause. Without any consultation with local authorities, Ottawa abruptly decided that the Yukon had too much government. The position of Commissioner was abolished and replaced by a Comptroller, who was to serve a sort of chief clerk for the territory. The Territorial Council was swept away, and when anguished protests from Dawson led to its reinstatement a few months later, it had been reduced from ten members to three. The federal budget for the territory was cut by nearly half and a number of government offices closed. The most that local politicians and the Yukon's MP, Dr Alfred Thompson, could do now was to prevent Ottawa from abolishing the Council (and thus the last vestiges of representative government) altogether.

One of the *Sophia*'s passengers who was heading to war in 1918 was a man whose roots went back into the period of the region's history long before the gold rush, before the international border existed even on paper. Walter Harper was the son of one of the first men to explore the mining possibilities of the Yukon River valley. Arthur Harper, a native of northern Ireland, had come to North America as a boy in the 1830s, and had followed gold rushes in the United States for twenty years. Convinced that since there was gold in the southern Rockies, there should be more of it in the north, in 1872 he went to the far northwest with two partners, Jack McQuesten and Alfred Mayo. The three men engaged in prospecting and trading in several places throughout the valley–Harper and Joe Ladue laid out the streets of Dawson City in 1896–and though he never became rich, he lived to be called the 'Father of the Yukon'. The title was more than symbolic: during his years there he fathered eight children. Walter, whose mother was Native, was born around 1891, when Arthur Harper was nearly 70.

Walter Harper grew up in Alaska, educated by Episcopalian missionaries who saw in him a means of building bridges to the Native population. At Fort Yukon, Archdeacon Hudson Stuck took a particular interest in the young man, making him his private secretary and taking him along on his pioneering expedition to the top of Mount McKinley. Stuck later said of his protégé: 'In all the arts of travel, in all the wilderness arts, he was past master. With a rifle, an ax, a dog-team, a boat of any kind from a birch-bark canoe to a power launch he had few superiors in Alaska. I had rather he were by my side in time of stress or danger than any other I ever knew.'[28] In September 1918 Harper married Frances Wells, a nurse from Philadelphia who was serving at the Archdeacon's mission. He then fulfilled Stuck's fondest hopes by announcing that he wished to go south to train as a medical missionary, and eventually return to Alaska to serve among his mother's people. He was also liable for military service, however, and as he and his bride prepared to leave Alaska, he was hoping to serve as a military doctor.

The entry of the United States into the First World War in 1917 dealt a blow to the economy of Alaska's interior too. In addition to draining many miners off into the military, the war raised the cost of materials and supplies. A series of dry summers curtailed dredging and hydraulic mining just as the 'bonanza deposits' were giving out, leaving dredging and open-cut mining as the most viable methods. More than half the placer operations in the region closed down between 1917 and 1921; with the annual cost of a small miner's provisions amounting to over $400 and the average annual return to the individual miner only $398,[29] it is easy to see why. The youngest and most active men in the region were leaving for military service or better jobs, most of them never to return. Finally, in the summer of 1918 the German army began to crumble, and residents of the far northwest could rejoice that peace and victory were close at hand. But for Alaska and the Yukon, fate had reserved a cruel blow almost for the moment of triumph.

2. ESCAPING FREEZE-UP

Seventy years ago, even more than now, life in the Yukon River valley was governed by the rhythms of the seasons. Each fall the north went into hibernation. For six or seven months the thick ice of the Yukon River and its tributaries brought an end to river transportation, with the result that economic activity slowed almost to a standstill. It was possible to travel from Dawson to the railhead at Whitehorse in the winter via the Overland Stage–a large coach on runners, drawn by six horses, that carried passengers and mail over a 360-mile trail from Whitehorse to Dawson one week and back the next–but by 1918 the service had deteriorated. Originally there were roadhouses every 22 miles where passengers could rest, but now many of them were closed; travellers had to carry their own lunches, and the trip sometimes took ten days each way.[1] Compared with steamboat travel, the overland route was slow, expensive, and uncomfortable, and no one took it except for the most compelling reasons.

For most northerners, the gradual onset of winter required careful preparations. Wood had to be cut and piled before the snows came to stay; the river steamers had to be laid up for the season; supplies had to be gathered and stored, for there would be few opportunities to replenish stocks once the steamers stopped running. Fish from the Yukon River were split, cleaned, and hung up to smoke over a fire–a traditional method used by the Yukon Natives, and a source of cash income for them. Some work continued, particularly in the few hardrock mines operating in the region, but the hectic pace of the intense summer season could not be sustained through the short, dark days of winter.

Each fall, some residents of the Yukon valley admitted to themselves that they could not bear to face another six-month bout of cabin-fever. The thrill of seeing the ice set on the rivers in the fall and then trying to guess when it would break up in the spring had long since worn thin, and they had had their fill of cold, darkness, and ice-fog.

Nor were the miners and other summer workers the only part-time northerners. There was not nearly enough year-round work for Dawson's lawyers, and a number of them regularly wintered in the south. The *Yukon Sun* noted in October 1902 that H.E. Ridley of the firm of Pattullo and Ridley had left with his wife for a vacation in America and Europe: 'Last year Mr Pattullo had the winter's vacation and it is Mr Ridley's turn this winter.'[2] Even the territory's two judges were not permanent residents; they took turns spending the months from September to March outside the Yukon.[3]

Every year, then, some northerners made their preparations for winter while others got ready to leave. But as the war years progressed there were more ominous signs associated with the annual fall departures. With the northern mining economy shrinking each year, the number of people leaving for good increased steadily. In earlier days the annual migration had been part of a cycle of regeneration, as each year the population of the Yukon River valley shrank for the winter only to burgeon again as old friends and new adventurers arrived with the spring. But by the end of the First World War, the ritual had taken on an almost funereal tone. Now everybody knew that many of those who left were not coming back, and the familiar promises to 'see you next year!' at the docks in Tanana, Dawson, and Whitehorse had a hollow ring. Town after town, already suffering from the effects of prolonged depression, took each new departure as a body-blow. From the mines around Iditarod at least twelve people were preparing to leave in the late fall of 1918, draining the spirit and vitality from a once-prosperous region.

Laura Berton, one of the region's best chroniclers, witnessed the depressing annual ritual that signalled the gradual decline of the northland. To her, the year's last boat–the final opportunity to leave before ice captured the river–symbolized the painful disintegration of Dawson City:

> The last boat's departure was a considerable rite in Dawson City, for it effectively marked the beginning of winter. It was invariably a sad and sentimental occasion. The dock was jammed with people, for the entire town turned out for the ceremony of leave-taking. The last boat was always packed with the wealthy going out for the winter, the fortunate going out forever, and the sick going out to die. The atmosphere was electric with brave untruths. Every last soul on the boat pretended to be returning the following spring, but in point of fact, few ever did so. The last boat had a curious and depressing finality about it. For some reason those people who were quitting the country for good, always waited for the last boat, and the last moment, before they did so. Thus it became more than just another boat leaving town; it became a symbol of the town's decay.[4]

This sad ceremony involved the entire Yukon River valley, although its effects were perhaps most evident in the old boom town at the junction of the Klondike and Yukon Rivers. Some of the steamers that picked up Laura Berton's friends in Dawson had already collected the last travellers of the year in Alaska, bringing all of them together for the final journey up the Yukon to Whitehorse and then along the White Pass & Yukon line to Skagway, where they could board the coastal steamers for the south. It was the White Pass & Yukon Route's schedule that determined the timing of the departure ritual for the entire northern interior. From Iditarod and Ruby in western Alaska to Atlin in Northern British Columbia, the boats' last run of the year would carry scores of northerners on the first stage of their trip outside. At its longest the process took almost two weeks, from the time passengers boarded a WP&YR steamer in Iditarod until they disembarked to catch the train at Whitehorse. The 111-mile trip to Skagway, the American port where the large steamers like the *Princess Sophia* waited to take the travellers south, took the better part of a day.

In early October 1918 four boats, the *Washburn*, *Alaska*, *Yukon*, and *Seattle No.3*, made their last call of the season for passengers and freight along the lower Yukon. The *Washburn*, having already picked up passengers in Iditarod,[5] pulled into Tanana in the chilly early-morning hours of 5 October. At about the same time, the *Alaska*, *Yukon*, and *Seattle No.3* pulled out of Fairbanks for their final run of the year to Dawson.[6] The journey ahead–to Dawson and then, for all but the *Seattle No.3*, to Whitehorse–carried few dangers. The boats stopped frequently at wood camps along the river, taking on fuel to feed the hungry boilers. The upriver journey was slow, often tedious, even at this late time in the season. The *Washburn*, for example, took ten days to cover the roughly 500 miles from Tanana and Dawson City on its last run on 1918.[7] Though the river was easily navigable below Whitehorse, the shallow waters and frequently shifting channel called for constant attention and careful manoeuvering by the captain and pilot.

Most of the captains operating the river boats in the fall of 1918 could claim many years of experience. The master of the *Yukon*, Captain John Green, 43 years old in 1918, had worked on steamers since 1890, following in the footsteps of his father, a well-known Seattle steamboat man. At times he operated his own steamer, but for the most part he worked as a river pilot, starting in 1897. He went to work on the WP&YR boats in 1912, and although a winter resident of Seattle, he remained a fervent believer in the future of the north. He owned several mining properties in Alaska, which his wife, Harriet, operated on his behalf. She went north each summer, staying until the last run of the year when she would accompany her husband south. As the *Yukon* steamed up the river towards Dawson City, Harriet and John Green talked of the friends they had left, of the impending trip south on the *Princess Sophia*, and of the winter to come in Seattle.[8]

Many of the people these steamboats carried up the Yukon River from the Alaskan mining communities to the *Princess Sophia* could ill be spared. Iditarod, for instance, lost one of its civic leaders in the 1918 migration. Florence Beaton, reputed to be the first white woman to live in the district, had gone with her husband John, the co-discoverer of the Iditarod field, to the new mining camp in 1909. Beaton, by all accounts a wealthy man, owned a number of placer claims and had also invested in dredging equipment. Florence, 28 in 1918, had been outside several times–such luxuries were available to the families of those who struck it rich. Her children, 6-year-old Loretta and 4-year-old Neil, had been born in Alaska and had never before taken the long journey up the river.[9] But any sadness Florence and her children may have felt at leaving husband, father, and community was tempered by the belief that they would return in the spring.

The same could not be said for Ilene Winchell. As she took leave of her husband Al, a miner employed by the Yukon Gold Company, she could think only of her illness. Although she was just 31, the northern winters had already proven too great a strain on her frail constitution, and she was going to California to recover her health. Their parting was filled with distress, for in addition to her illness, Ilene Winchell had premonitions of impending death. Her husband later recalled that she had left him with a request: 'Al, I can't tell you how I know it, but you will outlive me. If you do, Al, tell me that you will see that I am buried with my mother.' He was reluctant to encourage her morbid fancies, and after all there was nothing to fear; the river and train journey were perfectly safe, and she had booked passage on the *Princess Sophia*, one of the newest ships on the west-coast run. Still, anxious to put her mind at ease, he agreed to her request.[10]

Ellen Lenez was also leaving the north for reasons of health. A native of Antigonish, Nova Scotia, she had gone north early in the gold-rush days with her husband, Peter, who worked on mining claims and on the steamboat docks in Dawson. By 1918 she was 52 and crippled with rheumatoid arthritis–'the rheumatics', as the contemporary phrase went. She had been in an invalid chair for several years, and the couple finally decided that she should seek a cure at the famous Mayo Clinic in Rochester, Minnesota.[11]

In Ruby, George Mayhood, the cigar-store and pool-hall owner, was leaving for California via the *Princess Sophia* to visit his two sons. Like others, he was aware of the decline of the mining camps, which he attributed to the chronic labour shortage associated with the war and the high prices endemic to the north. More than a dozen of Ruby's hundred citizens were departing in the 1918 exodus, most of them for good.[12] Despite wartime problems, of which the fall migration was the most obvious symbol, Mayhood and some others remained confident that Alaska and the Yukon would eventually reward their patience with sustained prosperity. Mayhood backed up his sanguine outlook with the declaration that he, like all true northerners, would be back in the spring.

Not everyone shared his optimism. Many of those leaving in the fall of 1918 were glad to go and had no intention of returning. The golden images of instant wealth that had at first sustained them had become tarnished through years of economic depression, high costs, and disappointments. Charles Castleman, the Texan who went north in 1910, had had enough. Like so many others, he had not struck it rich, although he kept looking, and he grubstaked his mining operations by working as a wage miner for the Otter Dredging Company. But the years had chipped away at his enthusiasm, and when in the summer of 1918, his brother wrote of the great new opportunities in the oil fields around Breckenridge, Texas, Castleman finally succumbed.[13] Though by all accounts a likeable sort, he would probably not have been greatly missed. Young men like him came and went through the Yukon mining camps like the migrating birds–up in the spring, gone in the fall, and hard to tell one from another. Few of those who stayed paid much attention.

The same could not be said for the Tackstroms. Oscar had been in the north since the early days of the Klondike rush and was one of the first businessmen in Dawson, but the fact that he was generally acclaimed as one of the small community's leading citizens was due in large measure to the activities of his wife. Unlike some northerners' wives, Crissie had stayed with her husband in the north. Their happy marriage–so described by several observers–and their family gave a sense of permanence sadly lacking in the mining community. Crissie's interests extended far beyond the borders of the isolated camp. She was an active supporter of the local church, and raised money in the community for the support of war orphans in France.

But for the Tackstroms 1918 was the year to leave. Their son George was 10 that year, and in need of better education than was available in the gold fields. Crissie worried, too, about the prospects for her young daughter in such an isolated setting. Sadly, for they loved the region, they decided to leave. It was agreed that Oscar should return the next summer to attend to his lumber business; Crissie and the children, however, were not coming back.[14]

Leaving her home in Ruby was painful both for Crissie and for the community of which she had been such an important member. But the departure could not be postponed any longer, for the steamers were ready for their final run of the season. Just before leaving, Crissie Tackstrom sent $73 on behalf of the Ruby Sunday school to the Alaska Committee for the Fatherless Children of France, for the support of two French orphans for a year. 'I hope', she wrote the committee, 'to be able to do my share toward the support of the French orphans and the Red Cross when we get established [in the south], and will write you where we will be located.'[15]

In mid-October the Tackstroms bought tickets for the *Princess Sophia*, boarded the *Alaska*, and headed for Dawson City. As the steamer fought the current up the flat, bleak reaches of the lower Yukon, the family had plenty of time to anticipate the journey ahead and their arrival in California at the home of Crissie's sister.

Peter W. Peterson was also looking forward to the trip outside that would take him to a new career and a reunion with his wife and daughter. He was Norwegian, born in 1885, and had gone with his family as a boy to Oconomowoc, Wisconsin. In 1904 he went to the Yukon and got a job with the Yukon Gold Company in its thawing plant, stoking the boilers that produced live steam to free the gold from the permafrost, until he was badly burned in an accident. Peterson then went into the wood business, where he prospered–by 1918 he employed four men on two saws, and supplied all of Dawson City's wood for heating and cooking[16]–although he suffered another severe accident here as well, losing an arm to one of his machines. By the time war broke out, however, his business, like everything else in Dawson, was declining, and he finally decided to sell out and seek a new career in Wisconsin, either in the fishing or the shipping business. In 1917 he sent his wife and daughter south to live with his relatives for a year, and in the fall of 1918 he prepared to follow them.[17]

Thomas A. LePage was another who had no regrets in leaving the Yukon valley. He was a native of Switzerland, born in 1882 near the Italian frontier. After emigrating to Canada he found work in Victoria as a gardener on the grounds of the Empress Hotel. In 1917 he married, and in the spring of 1918 he signed on with the White Pass & Yukon Route as a steward on the steamboat *Dawson*. The job paid $170 a month and keep, and LePage hoped to be able to save enough over the summer for a down payment on a house in Victoria; before leaving for the north he had talked to a real-estate agent about properties. In October 1918 his work was done for the season, he had money in his pocket, and he was preparing to go south to be reunited with his wife and to plan for their new home.[18]

Dave Williams, 'one of the most enterprising and popular of Dawson's business men', 'one of the most capable colored men ever in the North', with 'an endless number of friends', was also leaving the town for good that fall. Born in Lisbon, Ohio, in 1873, he had worked for a number of years as a porter on Pullman sleeping cars before heading north during the rush. He tried mining, then opened a barber shop on Dawson's Queen Street. He lived in several mining towns in the Yukon and Alaska, then opened a bath house in Dawson. He also operated a successful florist shop with a collection of tropical plants kept warm by a large hot-water heating system. But by 1918 his flower business was declining and in October of that year he got a telegram from Frank and William Nolan, old-time Yukoners, urging him to move to Tampa, Florida, and join them in the orange-growing business. In short order he sold his shop and booked his passage south.[19]

Why Robert Hager was leaving the Yukon is not known, but he

was an interesting example of a way of life chosen by a handful of Yukon pioneers. He was born in 1873 and went north during the rush, working as a miner and fur trader. In 1905 and 1906 he served as a Special Constable for the Mounted Police at McQuesten Post. About this time he took the fairly unusual step of formally marrying a Native woman, a resident of Mayo named Liza Jimmy, and during the war he worked for a time as a carpenter in the Mayo district. His wife died, leaving him with a young son who was cared for by her parents. In the summer of 1918 he was panning the bars of the Stewart River, making between six and nine dollars a day.[20]

Dawson City was a hive of activity in October 1918, its seasonal bustle belying the decade-long depression that was slowly sapping the life from the Yukon. Ships coming downriver from Whitehorse pulled into the docks on the Dawson waterfront, discharged their cargoes, took on passengers and their effects and, as soon as they could, headed back upstream to Whitehorse. The crews worked quickly, knowing they were on the last trip of the year, and that at the end of it they could return south to their families and friends. For both the people leaving Dawson and those passing through from further down the Yukon River, the hectic activity on the docks only heightened their sense of change and loss.

At 5.00 p.m. on Saturday, 12 October 1918, the White Pass & Yukon Route steamer *Washburn* pulled into Dawson, and by nine the next morning the boat was ready for its last trip to Whitehorse. On Monday the *Alaska* and *Seattle No.3* arrived. For the latter's crew there was extra work. Their ship was to go into dry-dock at Dawson, and they had to work quickly to prepare her for the winter. If they wished to make it out of the territory in time, the job had to be completed in a day or two, before the last boat left for Whitehorse.

Richard Harding Davis, 25 years old, was one of the *Seattle No.3*'s crewmen who were impatient to go. Born in Pittsburg, after working for several years on the dredges of the Yukon Gold Company, one of the north's largest mining concessionaires, he had signed on with the White Pass & Yukon Route as a deckhand for the fall of 1918. This pattern of work–several months on the dredges, then a final trip or two on the Yukon River as part of a steamboat crew–was not unusual; the steamship company hired many like him to help with the end-of-season rush. Davis's interest in finishing work on the *Seattle No.3* was increased by his desire to join his wife, Louise, who worked for the Cascade Laundry in Dawson to supplement the meagre salary–$4.50 per day plus board–he earned from the Yukon Gold Company.[21] The couple's aspirations went far beyond their jobs as dredgehand, deckhand, and laundress; they shared dreams of northern wealth. In the short term, though, all they wanted was to leave the Yukon before the ice came. The buzz of activity around the *Seattle No.3* carried extra excitement for Richard and Louise Davis,[22] for they were heading for Skagway and the *Princess Sophia.*

While the Tackstroms and other pioneers from the lower Yukon spent their stopover in Dawson visiting old friends, the Davises were not the only ones anxious to be on their way. One of the steamers from Alaska, either the *Seattle No.3* or *Alaska,* carried two such men from Eagle. One was Ulysses Grant Myers, the town's mayor, coroner, and Customs House broker. The other, James Dubois, was cut from the classic American frontier mould: his career had taken him across North America in search of the elusive bonanza, but his lack of any noticeable success had not discouraged him. Unlike his travelling companion, Dubois had no wife to disapprove of his northern enthusiasm. Born in Oregon in 1861, he had worked as a cowboy for Theodore Roosevelt, later President of the United States. Then, infected with the Klondike fever, he had joined the rush to the Yukon in 1898 and went on mining until 1910, when he sold most of his holdings and purchased the Riverside Hotel in Eagle. There, with Myers, he joined a local fraternal organization, the Eagle Lodge of the Red Men. Like his friend, Dubois continued his investments in local mining operations, maintaining his optimism in the eventual prosperity of the district.[23]

For both Dubois and Myers, the trip outside in 1918 seemed like a long-delayed holiday. Owing his wife a visit, Myers was going to New York via the *Princess Sophia* and the transcontinental railway. He left word in the north that he intended to make the journey a short one, and would be back sometime in the winter. Dubois, on the other hand, had few personal ties to the south, though he may have been headed to his sister's in Portland, Oregon. More probably, like other miners and townsfolk 'bushed' after several years in an isolated mining camp, he was simply looking for the bright lights and fast action of a southern city. Certainly neither man would have seen the stopover in Dawson City as any more than an interruption in this journey, particularly since their memories of the wide-open boom town of the gold rush bore little resemblance to the sedate, decaying government centre that was Dawson City in October 1918.

It came as a shock to Dawsonites when Murray and Lulu Mae Eads announced that they too were taking one of the last boats out of town. They had not been south for twenty years–a fact that caused some comment, since they were well off, and almost everyone else went outside as often as they could afford to. But one or both of the Eads had a secret terror of travelling by sea; indeed, in the fall of 1918 one of them had a premonition of 'death in the icy waters of the North'.[24] They had a Dawson lawyer draw up a will, stipulating that if they died at the same time, their estate should be shared equally between Lulu Mae's two sisters.[25] They were scheduled to go south on the *Princess Sophia*, then change to another ship, sail through the Panama Canal, and finally, using a small portion of the money they had stockpiled through their investments, travel around the United States visiting family and friends. Lulu Mae made elaborate preparations for her journey, carefully selecting $5,000 worth of the fine jewellry–mostly diamonds and gold–that had become her trademark.[26]

John R. Maskell was particularly anxious to leave Dawson that fall. Born in England, he had gone to the Yukon to find work, first at Stewart and then on a dredging crew near Dawson. During the winter he, like Louise Davis, had worked in the Cascade Laundry. Maskell was well known in the town as a singer and elocutionist, often singing and giving readings at public and patriotic entertainments–his specialty was recitations of Robert Service's poems. He was also a champion swimmer, reputed to have once swum the English Channel.[27] When he boarded the steamboat in Dawson, Maskell was on his way to a more distant destination than anyone else on the boat, for at the age of 32 he was headed for Manchester, England, to marry Miss Dorothy Burgess.

For others planning to catch one of the last steamers the final days before departure required considerable work. Dawson City Council, struggling with declining revenues, a dwindling tax base, and hints that municipal administration was about to be taken over by the federal government,[28] faced the loss of two members–and thus its quorum–to southern travel. Two councillors, J. Austin Fraser and W.J. O'Brien, were planning to go; Max Salter had already left. A meeting was hastily called for 10 October to deal with outstanding business, and then the Council was adjourned until the spring, when some of its members were scheduled to return. In the Dawson City of that era there was little business that would not keep another six months.[29]

In O'Brien Dawson City had one of its leading and favourite citizens. He was both a Territorial and a Dawson City councillor, a member of the Loyal Order of the Moose (Lodge No. 1393) and a prominent Liberal. Born in Toronto in 1878, Bill O'Brien had moved with his parents to Detroit, Michigan. In 1901 he went north to work with his uncle Thomas O'Brien on the construction of the Klondike Mines Railway and on the O'Brien and Moran fleet of steamers, which operated on the Yukon River during the boom years. O'Brien found a friendly home in the territorial Liberal Party, and was employed for a time as the secretary to Commissioner Alexander Henderson. But he eventually struck out on his own, opening an insurance company and continuing his political activity.

On a return visit to Detroit in 1902, Bill O'Brien had met and married Sarah Kane, who followed him back to Dawson shortly after the birth of their first child, Grace. Bill and Sarah, known to all as Sadie, soon rose to the top of Dawson society. He was well-known throughout town for his excellent baritone and sang at numerous community gatherings, while she, although an American, joined the George M. Dawson chapter of the Imperial Order Daughters of the Empire. Her participation in this most patriotic of anglo-Canadian organizations was not untypical. The founding member of this particular chapter happened to be Martha Black, another recently transplanted American, who would later become the second woman ever elected to the Canadian parliament. Black's interest in the club–like Sadie's, no doubt–rested on the knowledge that participation in such groups was important to her husband's career and a mark of distinction within the extremely status-conscious community of Dawson.[30] Sadie participated in many of the town's other societies and clubs, and was particularly active in St Paul's Anglican church. Many of her commitments, particularly within the church, involved one or other of her five children, who in 1918 ranged in age from 14 to just over 2.

A family of two young and attractive parents and five healthy children was an ornament to Dawson, a community that still had more men than women, quite a number of them lonely, ageing bachelors. All children were popular in the town, and particularly the O'Briens. A contributor to the Dawson newspaper described Grace, the eldest, as 'thoughtful and considerate of the rest of the children, and greatly devoted to her parents'. She was 'exceptionally bright in school, and did especially clever work in connection with the school newspaper, both as writer and illustrator. Her drawings were remarkably good. She was a good pianist, patrol corporal in the Dawson Girl Guides, and also a member of St Paul's Junior Auxiliary.' Her younger sister, Pearl, aged 10 in 1918, led her class in school, played the piano and sang, and was also a member of the Girl Guides and the church auxiliary. Together, the two sisters had knitted 'many socks for the boys at the front'.

The three other children were also highly regarded in Dawson:

> Robbie, age 8 years, was a very bright and intelligent lad, full of life and fun, always a leader amongst his chums, and was well known to all Dawsonites as a little lad of ceaseless boyish activities. Billie, age 6 years, was a dear little chap, full of life and fun; very good with his studies, and, like his sister, Pearl, was the top student in his class the last month in school here, of which fact he was very proud. Ruth May, the baby, was 2½ years old, a lovely, bright, nice, toddler.[31]

Although, like almost everyone else, the O'Briens spoke cheerfully of returning to Dawson City the following spring, they were seriously considering the possibility of remaining permanently in the south. They planned to see Sadie's father, a prominent building contractor in Detroit, about a job in that industry. As an alternative, they were also considering settling in Vancouver and using their contacts in the Liberal party to line up a new career. One way or the other, they felt they had gone as far as they could in Dawson, and that a move outside was necessary to support their large and active family. Before they left, therefore, Bill gave up his post as secretary for the Loyal Order of the Moose and the family cut many of the ties that bound them to the north.[32]

William Scouse, the dapper Scots coal miner turned Klondike entrepreneur, was also preparing to leave the north in October 1918. His wealth–estimated at more than $125,000–afforded him the luxury of going south every year on the *Princess Sophia* or one of her sister ships. His wife lived in Seattle year round, while he returned to Dawson each summer to work his properties. For Scouse the fall departure was a familiar ritual, a voyage that took him from the land that had given him prosperity to the place he actually considered home.[33]

Men like William Scouse who had made a good enough living to travel outside regularly were of course a minority in the mining community. Much more typical were Sven Anton Nelson and Oscar Poppert, two miners who worked in partnership in the Ruby district. Nelson, born in Sweden in 1865, had come to America to work in the grocery business in Chicago. He went north after the Klondike rush, and was one of the first miners to prospect in the Ruby camp. A friend who lived in Dawson City described him as 'straightforward, a sterling friend . . . a typical prospector, and one who followed his calling in the silent places from the upper reaches of the Novikaket to the north fork of the Innoko'.[34] Much of time he worked in partnership on Midnight and Poorman Creeks where he earned $1,000 to $3,000 a year, depending on his luck–not much, considering the cost of living in the north–though in one good year he took $15,000 out of his property.[35] His main partners were Oscar and Walter Poppert, 40-year-old twin brothers from Milwaukee, Wisconsin. Oscar Poppert had tried his hand at a number of things since leaving home for the north. For a time he worked on whaling ships, and when that industry was killed by the development of substitutes for whale oil and whalebone, he 'drifted into mining'[36] with his brother at Ruby. There the Popperts met Nelson, and the three of them tried prospecting on their claims. They had spotty success, but remained hopeful of getting a good return on at least one of their properties.

In the fall of 1918 the three men decided that since they had the price of the passage, they might as well go down to Seattle and look for winter work in the shipyards. A number of other men from Poorman Creek, near Ruby–Billy Furhman, William Lesky, Charles Cook, and Andy Johnson–decided to go along, but when they tried to book passage on the steamer *Alaska* and travel as a group, there was not enough space. So Walter Poppert got a ticket on the *Alaska*, while the rest waited a day or two longer.

If the men from Poorman Creek were 'typical' miners, others leaving that fall were not typical of anything except, perhaps, the eccentricities that life in the north seemed to stimulate in some people over the years. John A. Hellwinkle was one such. He was a native of Germany, born in the port of Bremen in 1858, and as a young man had sailed all over the world in the merchant marine. At one time he had found himself in a South American port during an epidemic of yellow fever, a disease for which at that time there was no cure, and had distinguished himself by volunteering to nurse the sick. He was one of the oldest residents of the Yukon mining district, having gone to Fortymile in 1895, a year before the great Bonanza strike.[37] He moved to Dawson City with the original stampeders but, finding no gold, decided that the road to wealth lay through real estate. When the boom started to fade he began to buy up property in the town until by 1918 he owned fifty-five properties, including a grocery store, and was one of the largest private landowners in town. This did not make him a rich man, however, for by that time there were few buyers left in Dawson–only sellers. He was in fact considered somewhat of a local oddity:

> In Dawson he had failed to find gold, so he became instead a real-estate crank. With an optimism that was so typical of the town, he began to buy up real estate in the firm belief that the Klondike would boom again and he would make a killing. He devoted all his energies to it . . . His cabins are still in Dawson crumbling away.[38]

Hellwinkle had never married, and had no ties to the north except his hoard of real estate. In the fall of 1918 he decided to go south on the *Princess Sophia* to spend the winter with his brother in California.

Sam Henry was another old Yukoner heading south that October. A native of Lincoln, Nebraska, the nephew of 'prominent hotel people', he was one of thousands of people in Canada and the United States working in humdrum jobs–he was a streetcar conductor in Lincoln–when they decided to try their fortune in the north. He arrived in the Yukon in 1896 at the age of 36 and prospected with Chris Sonnickson, another well-known pioneer; his wife Josephine followed in 1899, bringing their two young daughters with her, and a third daughter was born in Dawson.

Henry made no fortune in gold, but he held on and diversified his operations. He had a grocery store in Dawson City, worked as a teamster, and started a ranch at Mazie May on the Stewart River where he experimented with farming and stock-raising. The Henrys were pillars of a number of community organizations; Sam served on several committees and belonged to both the Shrine and the Masonic Lodge, while Josephine, an active member of the IODE, 'did much patriotic work, and was a tireless knitter' of socks for the boys in France.[39] By 1918 their two older daughters were married and living in the south, and the youngest was attending school in New Westminster, BC. Neither Sam nor Josephine Henry had been south since before the turn of the century, and they were more than ready for a trip outside.

An anecdote in connection with the Henrys' preparations for leaving lingered on for years after in the territory. They could not decide whether they would come back in the spring: having at first announced that they were going south only for the winter, they then decided to leave forever, and sold all their household furniture. But this seemed too final, so they proceeded to buy all their possessions back again. It was the kind of ambivalence that marked many departures from the north. As Laura Berton commented, the Henrys had 'missed too many boats'.[40]

Some of the people leaving the far northwest in the autumn of

1918 were ordinary, almost obscure men and women with few real links to the region. This was particularly true of the river steamboat crews. Most of them had a northern address–Dawson, Whitehorse, Tanana, Fairbanks–but since they spent little time in one place, and often lived seven months of the year in the south, they made little impact on their communities. Charles Guy, a 45-year-old chef on the *Seattle No.3*, picked up his mail in Whitehorse, but the most that anyone remembered about him was that he was a good baker.[41] Not even that much was known about W.K. Murphy, a deckhand on the same boat: only that his northern address was Tanana and he wintered in Seattle.

Charles Tetsujiro Kagawa was another whose departure few Yukoners would have noticed. At the age of 37 he had travelled a long way from his birthplace at Odawara, Japan, about 25 miles from Yokohama. He and his brother Hirozo had come to Canada as young men, braving the hostility of white British Columbians in their search for a better life. Hirozo got a job in a mine at Britannia Beach, BC, while Charles came to the Yukon some time after the gold rush and took what work he could get. He tried prospecting on a number of different creeks around Dawson, worked for other mine owners, and served as a cook in the kitchens of a couple of the larger dredging companies. He probably had to put up with a certain amount of racial hostility; he was described in the Dawson newspaper as being 'well liked by his countrymen', meaning, presumably, the local Japanese community–a qualification that says a good deal about the racial attitudes of Yukoners.[42] By 1918, with $800 saved in a Vancouver bank and another $200 in gold dust, Kagawa came to the conclusion that he was never going to get much more than that out of the Yukon. Hearing that there were promising gold prospects in Russian Siberia, he decided to re-cross the Pacific. He wound up his affairs in Dawson and bought a through ticket to Vancouver via Skagway and the *Princess Sophia.*

T. Laughlin McNeil, by contrast, was not on the periphery of northern society; when he left, the news made the local paper. 'Lockie To Hit Trail,' said the *Dawson Daily News:*[43] 'a man with a happy word for everyone, and Yukon will miss him.' Lockie

McNeil, born in Inverness County, Nova Scotia, in 1866, came from a large and prominent Maritime clan–his uncle was the Archbishop of Toronto–and as a young man worked as a hoisting engineer and a whaler. He went to Dawson in 1900, in the closing days of the gold rush, and after working in saloons and hotels eventually becoming part-owner of a number of them. By 1918, however, business had declined to the extent that he could hardly make a living; he wrote his brother in Black Hawk, Colorado, that things were falling off and he was coming outside to stay. All the same, the Dawson newspaper said he was 'not sure but what the call of the [south] would wear off before many moons, and he likely will follow the ducks back to Dawson in the spring.'[44]

Leaving to join the US Army was Albert D. Pinska, though since he was 45 years old[45] and married, he might well have been rejected; his second option was winter work in the Seattle shipyards. Pinska was a native of St Paul who had gone to Dawson City in 1906 to manage a store owned by his brother Martin. In Dawson he met and fell in love with Olive Geer, daughter of a pioneer Yukon River steamboat captain. Like almost all of the local business and professional class, the Pinskas were active in clubs and community service organizations. A member of the Dawson Women's Ambulance Corps, Olive was also the secretary of the Klondike Knitting Klub, which merged during the war with the Dawson branch of the Canadian Red Cross; interestingly, her husband too was a tireless knitter, 'and both turned in a great many socks which were forwarded to the Yukon Boys at the front'.[46] (Indeed, knitting socks appears to have been one of the major leisure occupations of Yukoners during the war. Although it might seem that the job could have been done much more efficiently by machine, those hand-knitted socks served a psychological as well as a practical purpose. A symbol to the men in the trenches that the people on the home front cared about them, they also served to concentrate the minds of the knitters on the war and the war effort–they gave the civilian population a feeling of participation, of 'doing their bit' for Canada and the Empire.)

The Pinskas engaged in a variety of other activities as well. They had a summer cottage at Sunnydale, across the river from Dawson, where they held parties for their friends. Albert Pinska was a keen duck hunter and bowler–he had played with the St Paul Minnesota Capitals, a championship team that won prizes all over the middle west. Both husband and wife were also expert curlers; Olive Pinska skipped a ladies' team that won a prize in the Dawson patriotic bonspiel of 1917.

They did not announce why they were leaving the Yukon the fall of 1918. Most likely, the store's winter business had declined to the point where Albert was simply not needed; his brother could manage it easily by himself. The Pinskas turned over their cottage and motorboat to the Dawson Returned Soldiers' Club and joined in the general pandemonium of departure.

The river steamers continued to come and go, forcing hasty good-byes at dock-side and busy work in the warehouses along the river. In the midst of it all a US government vessel, *General Jeff. C. Davis*, arrived from Fort Gibbon, Alaska, with eighty American recruits drawn from the lower reaches of the Yukon River valley and destined for the battlefields of Europe. They were draftees, 'fine, husky young lads ... from the Tanana valley and other points from Eagle to St Michael. They are the last contingent Uncle Sam is sending out of the Yukon this year.'[47] The upstream journey had been tedious, and when they arrived in Dawson the soldiers were in the mood to let off some steam.

Auris W. McQueen was among the Alaskan doughboys headed eventually for France.[48] Not a miner but a telegrapher and wireless operator by trade, he was born in 1883 and educated in Kansas, then moved to the west coast where he worked as a telegrapher for newspapers in San Jose, Stockton, and Fresno. On joining the United States Army Signal Corps he was posted to Fort Gibbon, Alaska, and every month he sent a small sum of money to his widowed mother in Long Beach, California. He wrote to her describing the boat trip from Fort Gibbon to Dawson:

> The man who wrote 'On a Slow Train Through Arkansas' could write a true story of a 'Slow Trip Through Alaska' if he had been with a party of a few soldiers. We were sure making a slow trip. We were on a government steamer from Fort Gibbon to Whitehorse and had no pilot who knew the river, so had to tie up nights, and at that got stuck on six sandbars. We were 19 days on that 11-day trip up the Yukon.[49]

Still, there were diversions along the way. As the *General Jeff. C. Davis* neared the international boundary at the 141st meridian, the steamer encountered a huge herd of caribou crossing the river. The herd stretched from horizon to horizon, and 5,000 animals could be seen from the deck:

> We had great difficulty in navigating among the swimming animals. For three hours at least we were steaming upstream among them. The barge in front of the steamer plowed down some of them, but they seemed to bob up from beneath afterward. The crew got ropes and lassooed a dozen, and dragged them aboard and slew them, and we had the finest of fresh caribou cutlets and roasts. The captain would not allow anyone to kill any more, as he deemed it would be wanton destruction to take more than could be used.[50]

Dawsonites, glad at last to have the United States in the war, welcomed McQueen and his comrades with open arms. The soldiers were chauffeured about the town by local car-owners, and were greeted enthusiastically by the Royal Northwest Mounted Police:

> The boys had not had a foot on shore for days, so they enjoyed themselves hugely during the two hours here, accepting the hospitality of Dawson automobile owners and others. The town throbbed with them, and they had a great time, shouting incessantly as the boat pulled out. . . . The greatest of good feeling existed between the boys representing the Union Jack and the Stars and Stripes, and cheers were exchanged incessantly as the boat pulled out at midnight.[51]

When, after a few hours, the *General Jeff. C. Davis* left the docks, hundreds of townsfolk gathered along the river to cheer on the young men as they took the first step of their long journey to the front.[52] It was Tuesday, 15 October.

Also leaving that evening were the last two river steamers of the 1918 season, the *Yukon* and the *Casca*. The *Yukon*, piloted by Captain Green, arrived in Dawson at 9.30 p.m. Passengers and baggage were hastily loaded, and by midnight both vessels were ready to leave for Whitehorse. Haste was important, for winter was just over the horizon, and already there were touches of morning frost in the quiet eddies along the edge of the river. The two boats were filled to capacity. Huge crowds formed along the docks in the early dark of that October night, the air filled with the false frivolity of parting friends and well-intentioned promises to keep in touch. Shouts of 'I'll be back' and 'See you soon' hung over the throng, although few could have really believed the brave words.[53]

Travelling on one of these boats was a 'well known old Yukon character' named Edine Neil. Discreetly referred to in the *Dawson Daily News* as 'Oregon M., a noted artist here in the days the ceiling was the limit',[54] under her full stage name, the 'Oregon Mare', she had been one of the most famous dancehall girls in Dawson's gold-rush era. The reason for her departure is not known; no longer young, perhaps she was retiring to the south; or maybe she was simply going outside for the winter. Fortunately, she had not booked her passage on the *Princess Sophia*.

For those on the docks the scene was by now all too familiar. Good friends, community leaders, work-aways, and others clambered on board, most never to return. Two years earlier, in October 1916, Laura Berton had been a passenger on that year's 'last boat':

> There was always a forced joviality among those on the dock who called 'see you next spring' to those on the deck, but when the final whistle sounded everybody on dock and deck began quite openly to weep. Then the boat pulled out into the river and turned its prow towards the south, leaving a little crowd of people standing on an empty wharf, looking cold and miserable and quite forlorn.[55]

No other event brought home the collapse of northern society quite so directly. The 'last boat' cast a pall that lingered over the river communities for days.

For those on board, however, the departure was probably a relief. Even those who were sorry to be leaving must have been glad to have the painful goodbyes over with, and the gentler climates of British Columbia or California undoubtedly offered some compensation. The rest–the ones whose time in the north had brought nothing but hardship and shattered dreams–could hardly wait to see the last of the Yukon River valley.

In the early hours of Wednesday 16 October the *Yukon* and *Casca* turned upstream and rounded the sweeping bend that soon obscured the view of Dawson City. When Laura Berton left Dawson in 1916, 'the ice was already forming along the shore and great lumps were floating sluggishly down the river. The hills around us were brown and dead and there was a smell of snow in the air.'[56] The first leg of the trip–from Dawson to Whitehorse–took about four days. Although the journey upriver along the middle Yukon is one of lonely beauty, of vast distances, low mountains, and a wide, pulsing river, most travellers found it tedious. Their attention was focussed further south.

Some had guaranteed reservations on the *Princess Sophia* or one of the other ships plying between Skagway and southern ports, but others had left that leg of their trip up to chance, and were hoping to find space on a ship once they got to tidewater. The demand for passage south was so great that season that steamship companies were making special trips to Skagway; the Grand Trunk Pacific Steamship Company's *Prince Rupert* and the Alaska Steamship Company's *Alaska* both made unscheduled runs there in the third week of October 1918.[57]

As the *Yukon* steamed towards Whitehorse, a committee of passengers from Alaska staged an impromptu campaign to sell bonds for the Fourth Liberty Loan. They canvassed everyone on board, most of them 'hard working men and women . . . the argonauts to Alaska [who had] been developing her resources'. By the time the boat reached the dock, the committee had sold $14,500 worth of bonds, and an extra $300 in donations for the Red Cross branch at Fairbanks. On the steamer *Alaska* Captain J.T. Gray held a raffle: he turned the profit of $57 over to the Skagway Red Cross.[58]

Now the river steamers docked at Whitehorse, completing their last runs of the season. When the *Washburn* pulled into town on Thursday 17 October, the crew helped the passengers to disembark, unloaded the cargo, and then took the boat back downstream to Lake Laberge. While the WP&YR wintered some of its steamers in the company shipyards in Whitehorse, others, like the *Washburn*, spent the winter by the shores (in memory of Robert Service, one is tempted to say 'on the marge') of Lake Laberge. There the boilers were drained, the machinery oiled, the cabins tidied and the decks cleared. The vessels were then pulled from the water and left for the season. Because the ice on the river below the lake went out several weeks earlier than at Whitehorse, this practice added precious days to the short Yukon River navigation season (although the benefits were soon eaten up by the added costs of transporting supplies from Whitehorse to the lake). Having readied the ship for winter, the crew of the *Washburn* returned to Whitehorse, where most caught the train for Skagway. When the *Casca* and *Yukon* reached Whitehorse on Saturday 19 October, their crews followed the same procedure.[59]

The travellers passed through Whitehorse as quickly as they could, though some had to stay overnight. The town had been built in 1900 at the lower end of the Whitehorse Rapids and Miles Canyon, a notorious obstacle to navigation that had drowned several men during the early stages of the gold rush, and now served as the connecting link between the White Pass & Yukon Route railway and the river steamboats. On the eve of the First World War its population numbered about 800, although, like Dawson's, it fell considerably in the winter months. Nevertheless, buoyed by its strategic location and vital function, Whitehorse appeared to have a solid and reasonably secure future, in stark contrast to the decay of Dawson.

The White Pass & Yukon Route,[60] which was the reason for the town's existence, dominated every aspect of Whitehorse.[61] The community was built around the railway and the sternwheeler docks; the company's Main Street station was the focal point for all commercial activity. Although the signs of permanence were growing–more stores, more solidly built homes, more WP&YR warehouses, and increasing activity in the wide copper belt that surrounded the town–Whitehorse was still primarily a way-station. And as the passengers filed off the sternwheelers and sought passage on the next train to Skagway, its function was only too evident.

They faced a journey of 111 miles over a narrow-gauge track. The trip was not dangerous–only later in the winter did snow slides pose a threat–but it was cold, and with short stops at Carcross, Bennett, Log Cabin, and White Pass, it took about seven hours. Trains ran every day except Sunday in the navigation season, but only twice a week in winter. The cars had little insulation and were heated by a small stove at one end, around which fall and winter travellers commonly huddled to keep warm.

The train stopped at Carcross just long enough for the passengers to stretch their legs inside the station, and to pick up a few people from the Atlin district. The town of Atlin was and is one of the most beautiful, yet least known parts of British Columbia. It was founded in late 1898 as the result of a short-lived gold rush that year, and had survived into the twentieth century as a service centre for a number of mines that continued to operate in the region. Because of its natural beauty, it became a mecca for tourists travelling in the far northwest. A gas-powered lake boat, the MV *Tarahne*, built in the winter of 1916-17, carried cargo, regular passengers, and tourists on Atlin Lake. Tucked into the extreme northwestern corner of the province, the town was accessible from the outside by a route that went across Atlin Lake to Taku Landing. There a narrow-gauge railway, built in 1899 and known locally as the 'world's shortest railway', carried passengers the two and a quarter miles to Graham Inlet on Tagish Lake. From there the WP&YR's *Tutshi*, built in 1917, took the travellers to the railway station at Carcross.[62] It was a complicated route, with a slightly longer navigation season than the lower Yukon. But the trip between Atlin and Skagway could be made in less than a day, and the country was so beautiful that the Atlin run was maintained until 1936, when waning tourist interest led to its cancellation.

Among those following this route to Carcross in October 1918 was Captain James Alexander, affectionately known as 'Cap', his wife Louise, and two business associates, C.E. Watson, manager of the Mining Corporation of Canada, and Toronto mining expert George Randolph. Alexander rarely travelled this early in the year; he and his wife usually headed for their southern haunts–Vancouver, New York, and other eastern cities–later in the season.

Cap Alexander, a 50-year-old veteran of the Boer war, had been active in mining in British Columbia and the Yukon from 1903. While travelling with an engineering party along the southern shore of Tagish Lake, he and his wife had discovered a promising gold property. Alexander named it Engineer Mine and operated it on and off for more than ten years. Now he was entertaining purchase offers from one of the largest mining concerns in the country. Watson, Randolph, and C.S. Verrill, a mining engineer from Vancouver, visited the Engineer Mine in October 1918 and wired a favourable report back to their corporate superiors. The Alexanders happily changed their annual routine in favour of accompanying the men back to the south so that negotiations could continue. The future looked prosperous for the region and for Captain Alexander; the newspapers reported that the selling price of his property was more than a million dollars.

This rosy prospect was due in large measure to Louise Alexander's grit and determination. While her husband had considered selling the property on occasion over the years, she had argued against it. That Cap Alexander listened to her was indicative of the strength of their relationship. They had met in 1914, when he lay near death in a Chicago hospital and Louise was assigned as his nurse. They fell in love and were married while he was recovering–or so the story went. There was a considerable difference in their ages, but Louise and James were by all accounts incurable romantics, seldom separated and much in love. The news that the Mining Corporation of Canada was about to buy their mine must have seemed the fulfilment of their dreams, for they now had almost within their grasp the wealth to satisfy their material needs forever and to allow them to continue their travels across North America. It was with great anticipation, therefore, that the Alexanders boarded the steamer *Tutshi* on 19 October for the first stage of their journey.[63]

Clarence S. Verrill, the Alexanders' travelling companion, had also had an interesting career. Born in New Haven, Connecticut, in 1877, he was the son of a professor of natural science at Yale University. As an undergraduate at Yale, studying mining and metallurgy, he went with his father on a scientific expedition to Bermuda, collecting specimens for the university's Peabody Museum; 'his exploits in diving for devil-fish were so extraordinary as to furnish material for magazine writers.'[64] He had taken the 'Grand Tour', travelling though most of the European countries, and was also enough of a poet to have his verses published in *Scribner's* and the *Atlantic Monthly*. Having worked for mining concerns in Colorado, California, Washington, and the West Indies, he moved to Vancouver in 1908 to work as a consulting geologist. He was a personal friend of Captain Alexander and had twice visited the Engineer Mine, so it was only natural that he would be asked to take the party of eastern buyers north to Atlin to examine the property.

The last stage of the journey lay ahead. The travellers from all over the Yukon watershed went south from Whitehorse on different trains, spaced over several days, but in a short time all would be gathered in Skagway, awaiting the steamer that would carry them south at last. The train that left Whitehorse on 21 October was made up of four baggage cars, six passenger cars, three observation cars, and the general manager's private car, and carried 392 passengers, picking up 34 more at Carcross for a total of 426–at least 70 more than the previous record number.[65] Those, like the Tackstroms, whose trip had started two weeks and many hundreds of miles earlier, must have faced the final leg with a combination of weariness and anticipation. Carcross lay only a few hours by train from Skagway and the Pacific Ocean. The worst of the trip was almost over.

The remaining train journey, even in the grey, unfriendly days of late October, was spectacular. The narrow-gauge line clutched the hillside as it curved around the shore of Lake Bennett. After a brief stop for lunch at Bennett, a way-station at the end of the lake, the train headed off across the top of the hill, a bleak tundra that in this season was usually covered with a light dusting of snow. Suddenly, almost without warning, the train descended, moving more slowly now as it inched down the steep grade of the White Pass; in one place it hung out over space, with only a frail-looking bridge between it and the rocky floor of the canyons below. Snaking through short tunnels, across spidery trestles, and around a series of hairpin curves, the train gradually descended into the Skagway River valley. Just before the final drop to the valley floor, the passengers got a panoramic view of Skagway below and, beyond the small community, the waters of Lynn Canal, the whole scene framed by the snow-capped coastal mountains.

Most of those disembarking at Skagway had been there before. Some remembered it from the days of the Klondike gold rush, when the notorious crook 'Soapy' Smith ruled the boom town before he met his just end at the hands of vigilante Frank Reid. There were few signs now of those raffish glory days. Skagway had a population of 500 in 1918, less than a sixth what it had been in 1900, and its sole reason for existence was its role as a transshipment port for the White Pass & Yukon Route. A scattering of old buildings along the main streets harkened back to better times, but few remained open to serve the hundreds of travellers–an unusually large crowd–leaving the north in October 1918.

The exodus had snowballed as it approached Carcross, and when the crowds from the last boats out of Dawson reached Skagway, the town was almost overwhelmed. Travellers jostled one another for tables at local restaurants, and though hotel managers juggled their rooms judiciously, some travellers had to camp out in abandoned cabins–there were plenty of them in town–or improvise some other temporary shelter.

The end-of-season migration had long been celebrated with a 'Sourdough dance', and the tradition seemed especially appropriate in 1918. As the local newspaper reported it:

> The Sourdough dance on Saturday night was one of the most enjoyable affairs ever given in Skagway. In fact, it reminded one of old days, when everyone knew everyone else, and all strived to make the others happy. The music was good and almost everyone who dances in Skagway as well as all the strangers within our gates were there and until a late hour dance followed dance in rapid succession and at last when 'Home Sweet Home,' was played it was with great reluctance the happy throng left the hall.'[66]

On Monday night the revelry continued with a dance at the White Pass Athletic Club 'in honour of the many people who are enroute to the south'[67] and the next evening a fund-raiser was held at the Skagway Popular Picture Palace to refurnish the rectory of St Mark's church. Movies were shown, then Mrs Theodore Armstrong of New York, a 'writer of Grand Opera', was heard in some songs of her own composition. William O'Brien, passing through from Dawson City, was presented as a man who 'hardly needs an introduction', and sang some songs in his 'rich baritone voice'; Miss Lois Butt, the elocutionist, provided 'something better than usual'; and there were 'songs and dances by the kiddies'. The house was packed.[68]

Getting out of Skagway proved to be more difficult than most had anticipated. The onslaught of travellers, many of whom did not have reservations for any of the steamships serving the coast, swamped the booking agents in Skagway: there were simply not enough spaces to go round. Auris McQueen and the other soldiers who had taken the *General Jeff. C. Davis* upstream from Fort Gibbon to Whitehorse found themselves caught in the crush. Auris wrote to his mother: 'at Skagway the stampede of people out of the interior had got ahead of us and we had to miss three boats and only got this one [the *Sophia*] by good luck.'[69] For those eager to continue their journey, the delay must have been a painful anticlimax. Days of tedious river travel, topped off with the discomfort of the train trip from Whitehorse to Skagway, had tried their patience, and tempers understandably frayed as people jockeyed for passage on the next available steamer.[70] Ed P. Bemis, purser on the steamboat *Tanana*, later reported that even among those who had wired ahead to Skagway for reservations on the *Princess Sophia*, dozens found when they got there that the ship was full. Instead, the company found space for them aboard the *Prince Rupert*, which was leaving a day earlier. 'We had a great time guying those who had gotten in their applications for reservations on the Sophia early and therefore had to wait for her, while those who were late were placed on an earlier boat . . . "We'll see you in Seattle," was the general remark as we left.'[71]

On Wednesday 23 October, the Canadian Pacific vessel *Princess Sophia* pulled into the dock at Skagway. For some 280 passengers, the long-awaited moment had come. They were the lucky ones; others had arrived too late and would have to wait a few days for the next ship. They were scheduled to leave late that evening, and the certainty that in three and a half days they would reach Vancouver, Victoria, and Seattle added to the relief of boarding the *Sophia*. For them, the journey was almost complete.

3. THE *PRINCESS SOPHIA*

The town of Skagway lies at the head of Lynn Canal, a fiord about ninety miles long that runs from the town in a southerly direction, forming the northernmost part of the Inside Passage. The flat estuary of the Skagway River, on which the town lies, contrasts with the dramatic meeting of land and sea elsewhere along Lynn Canal, where mountains hundreds of feet high drop precipitously into the frigid water.

In 1918 Skagway's role was immediately apparent to anyone who looked at the town. The railway ran up to dockside, facilitating the tasks of loading and unloading the goods that fed, clothed, and supplied the interior communities of Alaska and the Yukon. The docks were on the east side of the harbour, south of town, protected from the strong winds that frequently blew up and down Lynn Canal. The tracks ran from the docks down the middle of the main street, and by the time they crossed the edge of town, the grade was already beginning to rise. At the top of the climb lay the spectacularly beautiful White Pass through the mountains that loom a few miles behind the town.

Skagway has not changed a great deal in appearance over the past seventy years. One difference, though, is that it is now not just a way station but a tourist mecca in itself, the terminus of an important west-coast cruise-ship route that brings many thousands of visitors to the town each summer. Knowing a good thing when they see it, the merchants of Skagway regularly give their wooden buildings a fresh coat of paint, and most of the seedier bars and stores have been replaced by boutiques offering a variety of craft work and souvenirs. The other difference is that the train tracks no longer run down the middle of the main street. In the old days, when the trains stopped at the passenger station (now a tourist information centre run by the National Parks Service), they completely blocked the main business district, hampering commerce and polluting shops and shoppers with ash and cinders. After the Second World War, the tracks were rerouted; they now run from the docks along the east side of town. The railway was always a world-famous tourist attraction, but by the 1960s it was dependent for most of its freight traffic and profits on the output of a single mine in the Yukon. In the early 1980s falling world mineral prices led to a shutdown of the mine, and in 1982 the White Pass & Yukon Railway, by then one of the last of North America's narrow-gauge lines, closed. It was partially reopened in the summer of 1988 to take tourists on excursions from Skagway to the international boundary at Log Cabin, but its role as freight carrier now appears to be finished for good.

Skagway once had a sister town. Lynn Canal is like an arm terminating in two fingers; looking north, Skagway is the finger on the right. Around a point of land is the left finger, which used to terminate in the town of Dyea. During the rush of 1897-8, before the completion of the railway, many goldseekers had gone from Skagway around this point of land to Dyea. The town, which in 1898 had a transient population of as many as 10,000, marked the beginning of the trail leading over the Chilkoot Pass–a route made famous by the photographs of men bent like beasts as they toiled in an endless chain up the snowy slope. By 1918 Dyea had long been abandoned, and there is hardly a trace of it now: only a cemetery and a few rotting shacks. Skagway, on the other hand, though quieter than it had been in the days of the notorious Soapy Smith, was still fairly prosperous as the trans-shipment point for a huge hinterland. Like Whitehorse, it had come into being because of its strategic location. It lay at the transfer point of the main route linking the south with the far northwest, so that the great majority of people and goods coming in and out of the Yukon valley went across its docks. Into the harbour of this town the *Princess Sophia* steamed on Wednesday 23 October and tied up to the dock beside the WP&YR tracks.

The *Sophia* was one of the newest ships of a proud fleet–the British Columbia Coast Steamship Service of the Canadian Pacific Railway Company. The CPR was the most famous private corporation in Canada. In 1885 it had completed the country's first transcontinental railway–the 'National Dream' of Pierre Berton's book[1]–but the company had been in the business of water transport almost as long as it had been in railways. Incorporated in February 1881, it had ordered its first ships just two years later, before the railway was even finished.[2] In fact, ships were as important to the CPR as were trains, since the basic plan behind the company was not only to span Canada but to build a great transportation route 'stretching from Liverpool to Hong Kong', as George Stephen, its first president, put it.[3] In 1889 the CPR ordered the first of the famous 'Empress' line–the *Empress of India*, *Empress of Japan*, and *Empress of China*–for service on the route between Vancouver and the Orient.

It was not until the early years of this century, however, that the CPR got into coastal shipping on a permanent basis. In 1901 it spent $531,000 for control of the Canadian Pacific Navigation Company, a firm that had been providing passenger and freight service between Victoria, Vancouver, and Washington State, around the coast of Vancouver Island, and north to Skagway. With controlling interest in this company came a fleet of nine propeller-driven steamers and five paddle steamers. One of these, the *Princess Louise*, was the first of a line of thirty-two 'Pacific Princesses' that the company was to operate in BC coastal waters and north to Prince Rupert, Juneau, and Skagway.

The CPR immediately reorganized and expanded its Pacific

coastal service. Placed in charge of the new operations was Captain James W. Troup, then running the company's steamship service on BC's lakes and rivers. Troup was a man with long experience in the field. Born in Portland, Oregon, in 1855, he was the son and grandson of Columbia River steamboat captains, and had been a riverboat captain himself while still in his teens. One student of the Canadian Pacific steamships described him as an

> excellent choice for the position of manager. He was experienced, having operated river steamers on the Columbia River, both in Oregon and in British Columbia. He was an imaginative, capable administrator and a man of vision [who] left his mark on both the design of the new ships and the standards established for the service.[4]

Others judged Troup not by his administrative efficiency but by his personality. He seems to have been a hard master. A man still living in 1988 who worked on the CPR steamers for over forty years and served on the *Princess Sophia* in 1915 considered him a 'son of a bitch', very much a company man, who would sacrifice the welfare of his men for the sake of the CPR.[5] Another called him a 'real stinker'.[6] But this was a hard, competitive era. Troup was responsible for running an efficient, profitable operation in the face of stiff competition, and courting popularity with his subordinates was not high on his agenda. He held his job as general superintendent of the Pacific coastal service until his retirement in 1928, and was thus directly in charge of all the 'Princess' ships when the *Princess Sophia* sailed into Skagway in October 1918.

The CPR company always put great emphasis on the safety of its ships, and regularly issued instructions to its captains to take no chances in bad weather. An early order from Troup's office, dated 28 July 1904, emphasized this policy in the running of the 'Princesses'; some of its details would later prove ironic in light of what happened to the *Sophia*:

> Do not neglect Article 16 of these regulations which requires that 'every vessel shall in a fog, or in a heavy snow or wind storm go at a moderate speed, having careful regard to existing circumstances and conditions'. While we have a published schedule, bear in mind that the Company do not wish any risk whatever run in order to maintain this schedule, take no chances in foggy or stormy weather.[7]

The route from Vancouver to Skagway ran up the Inside Passage, winding through the coastal islands of British Columbia and Alaska. The CPR used this route in preference to the open ocean because it facilitated stops at the intermediate points of Prince Rupert, Sitka, Wrangell, Ketchikan, and Juneau; it was also protected to some extent from ocean storms. Moreover, ships like the *Princess Sophia* were licensed to operate only within 50 miles of shore. Within a year of the CPR's acquisition of the Canadian Pacific Navigation Company, however, an event took place that showed the dangers of the Vancouver-Alaska run.

The steamship *Islander*, a 240-foot twin-screw steamer built in 1888, left Skagway on 14 August 1901 under the command of Captain Hamilton Foote, bound for points south. Ice was sighted in the Lynn Canal, yet the ship maintained full speed of 14 knots. At 2.15 the next morning, in clear weather, the ship hit an iceberg off Douglas Island, near Juneau.[8] There was some confusion at first as to how severe the damage was, and more confusion as the ship rapidly began to fill with water. Passengers and crew scrambled for the lifeboats. The watertight doors were closed, trapping eleven stowaways who had been put in the coal bunker. The ship sank in a little over fifteen minutes, amidst scenes of panic and horror:

> Struggling from their stateroom up the steeply inclined decks, Dr W.S. Phillips of Seattle, his wife and daughter finally reached the upper deck. However, the suction caused by the rapid inrush of water was so great that all three were sucked into one of the ventilators and Mrs Phillips and her daughter were carried to their deaths. Fortunately, the doctor's chin caught on the rim of the ventilator and he was able to extricate himself. Then the *Islander* took her final plunge, carrying the doctor with her. When he surfaced, he was pulled onto a life raft and later taken to shore. There, to his horror, he found the body of his little girl washed onto the beach.[9]

In all, the captain, sixteen crew members and twenty-three passengers drowned or died of exposure.[10]

At the inquiry into the sinking of the *Islander*, allegations were made that the captain and crew had been drinking at the time of the accident, but no evidence was found to support such charges, which seem to arise whenever there is a maritime disaster. Instead, the inquiry commended the crew on its efforts to save as many passengers as possible, though the pilot, Captain LeBlanc, was censured for not slackening speed as soon as ice was spotted, and it was suggested that if the ship's captain had realized sooner the seriousness of the situation, more lives could have been saved.[11]

The *Islander* was replaced in the company's fleet by a fine new ship, the *Princess Victoria*, in 1903. In the same year she was joined by the *Princess Beatrice*, the first of the line built in British Columbia. The *Beatrice* was put on the Victoria-Seattle run after a 1904 disaster which showed that no amount of engineering skill or luxury could protect a ship against bad luck, bad weather, or bad judgement. In January of that year the *Clallam*, a ship owned by the the Puget Sound Navigation Company of Seattle, was headed for Victoria when she ran into rough weather in the Strait of Juan de Fuca, took on water in the engine room, and lost power. When the ship seemed about to founder, the captain ordered the women and children into the lifeboats. But the *Clallam* stayed afloat long enough for a rescue vessel to arrive and take off the crew and the rest of the passengers. Meanwhile, all the lifeboats were lost in the heavy seas; 54 people, mostly women and children, were drowned. It was sobering proof that lifeboats were not necessarily a safe refuge, and that sending passengers into them was not always the best course to take in an emergency.

Between 1907 and the outbreak of war in 1914 no fewer than nine 'Princesses' were built for the CPR's passenger service (others, such as the *Princess Ena*, handled mostly freight)–the *Princess Royal* (1907), *Princess Charlotte* (1908), *Princess Adelaide*[12] and *Princess Mary* (1910), *Princess Alice* and *Princess Sophia* (1911), *Princess Maquinna* (1912), *Princess Irene* and *Princess Margaret* (1914)[13]–while a tenth ship, the *Princess Patricia*, was bought from another company in 1912. Of these, the *Maquinna*, *Mary*, and *Sophia* were specifically designed for west-coast and northern service, as opposed to inter-city and local service between ports in the Straits of Georgia and Juan de Fuca, and Puget Sound.

The *Princess Sophia* had been ordered early in 1911, when J.W. Troup, on behalf of the CPR, asked several large British shipbuilders to submit bids on a contract for another 'Princess'. The new ship was intended to fill a gap in the Company's operations:

> She would be suitable for the Skaguay [sic] business and for Prince Rupert, and other northern British Columbia traffic. We have been greatly handicapped by not having suitable freight steamers to do our work. . . . we have in this case planned a vessel that would make a fairly good freighter as well as passenger boat. She would operate cheaply, and would be able to do a large amount of business when it is offered.
>
> My idea is that this boat would be used in the Skaguay trade in the busy season-spring and fall, and in the British Columbia local business at other times. She is a little large at the present time for the British Columbia business, but with the growth of Prince Rupert, I do not think we will miss it in the building of such a boat.
>
> The idea is not to make this one at all elaborate-a plain, workable vessel. The specifications show pretty well what we want.[14]

The specifications called for a ship 245 feet long, with a breadth of 44 feet and a gross tonnage of 2320. The contract was won by Bow, McLaughlan and Company of Paisley, Scotland, at a price of £51,000, or about $250,000. In design, the *Sophia* was a typical passenger and freight steamer, with a prominent superstructure and a single funnel. Cargo holds were located forward and aft of the centrally located passenger acoommodations. A triple-expansion engine powered the vessel's single screw. When completed she was licensed to carry 250 passengers (though in a pinch, and with special permission, she could carry more-her passenger capacity was 500), and a crew of about 70.

Leaving Scotland for British Columbia in February 1912, the *Sophia* was a substantial vessel, with nearly all the passenger accommodations arranged on the four top decks. The lower decks were devoted to cargo space, bunkers, and machinery. On the top or Boat Deck were the wheelhouse and, immediately behind it, officers' quarters and the wireless room. Next were 16 two-berth staterooms. These were typical of the era; each contained a built-in upper and lower berth, a sink with running water, electric lights, a mirror and other conveniences, and a stool or small chair. Each outside cabin had a single window. Below this deck was the Promenade Deck, with 24 more two-berth cabins, a large observation room finished in maple, located forward, and a smoking room and bar located aft in a separate deck house. Below the

Promenade Deck was the Awning, or Lower, Deck, where the majority of the passenger accommodations were grouped. Forward was a small social hall, and aft were the dining room, galley, and pantry. The spacious dining saloon, one of the most important features of any vessel in the coastal trade, was finished in mahogany with maple panels and had seating for over a hundred passengers. Twenty-six of the Awning Deck staterooms were outside rooms and 16 inside, while below them was the Main Deck, used mostly for cargo space. At the aft end, however, it was fitted with bunks for 84 second-class passengers, and the crew's quarters were on this deck too, along both sides of the vessel amidships. Mail and express rooms were located near the bow. Lower still was the Orlop Deck, containing the main cargo hold, ahead of which was space described as being intended for 'Orientals'.[15] As the *Victoria Daily Colonist* noted with approval, 'the whole vessel shows that nothing has been left undone to provide for the comfort of the traveller, in keeping with CPR methods.'[16]

A man who sailed on the *Princess Sophia* in the summer of 1915 remembers her as 'a strong ship';[17] she had a large mast and boom on the forward deck capable of lifting heavy loads into the freight hold. Originally designed as a coal-burner, she was soon converted to oil, which burned more cleanly and saved a great deal of labour. When full she carried almost 2,900 barrels of oil in two large double-bottom tanks in her hold, of which she consumed 240 barrels per day. She was not a particularly fast vessel–top speed was between 12 and 13 knots–but she was sturdy and comfortable, and handled well in all weather.[18]

The *Princess Sophia* went into service on the west coast of British Columbia in 1912 and plied the route between Vancouver and Skagway for six years. Her service during that period was marked by two potentially serious accidents. On 12 April 1913, en route south from Skagway, she ran onto Sentinel Island reef–only a few feet from the spot where her sister ship the *Princess May* had grounded three years earlier–and almost knocked the light on the reef into Lynn Canal. The ship's bow was seriously damaged, but the water was contained by the bulkhead, and after about two hours she was floated off and continued south. Then in January

1914, less than a year later, she ran ashore in a snowstorm at Mountain Point in Johnson Strait, below Alert Bay. Her passengers were transferred to the American steamer *Al-ki* and taken to Vancouver, while the *Sophia* reached home port under her own power.[19] As Captain Troup had planned, the *Sophia* was also used on the Vancouver-Victoria run during the winter, when traffic to the north was greatly reduced. During the First World War she served on occasion as a troop carrier, ferrying hundreds of men from Victoria to the mainland on their way to Europe, but it was still her primary mission to link the south and the far northwest. It was on that mission that she prepared to leave Vancouver harbour on Saturday, 19 October 1918 on her regular run to Skagway.[20]

In one respect this was the most important trip of the year for the *Princess Sophia*. Because navigation had ceased on the Yukon River, the ship was bound to be full to capacity.[21] For this reason, special arrangements had been made for this trip and the previous one. Lewis H. Johnston, the Canadian Pacific Steamship agent in Skagway, kept track of would-be passengers arriving from the interior. When the *Sophia* had docked in Vancouver on 17 October, it was reported that 600 to 700 people were waiting in Skagway for passage south.[22] As more and more arrived via the Yukon River sternwheelers and the railway, Johnston became alarmed at the congestion, and advised the Vancouver office that he could easily sell another hundred tickets for the voyage.[23] On her previous run south she had carried 268 passengers, and the company expected that the 23 October trip from Skagway would be just as full.

Company officers, pleased at the prospects of a profitable run to Vancouver, immediately arranged for extra space on the ship. Marine regulations in force in that era dictated that extra passengers could not be brought aboard without sufficient 'buoyancy appliances' for them; one lesson of the *Titanic* disaster only six years earlier was that there must be enough boats, rafts, or other floating devices to accommodate all passengers. Complying with these regulations, the CPR added six such appliances–buoyancy tanks, with ropes attached so that people floating in the water could hang on–to the *Princess Sophia* before she left Vancouver, enabling the company to increase the number of passengers from the usual 250 to a temporary limit of 350. Officials of the Canadian Department of Marine and Fisheries certified the company's compliance with the regulations and authorized the increased passenger load.[24]

This arrangement caused extra work for the crew, since the ship lacked the facilities to look after so many people. As the *Sophia* steamed north towards Skagway, crew members erected makeshift berths in the staterooms, squeezing five or six into cabins designed for four. The expansion of the *Sophia*'s capacity pleased those waiting in Skagway for passage south; it also promised a sizeable contribution to the company's revenues.[25]

At the helm of the *Princess Sophia* was Captain Leonard Locke, a veteran of the Canadian Pacific's north-coast run. Born in Halifax in 1852, Locke had joined his father at sea as a boy of sixteen. He served on ships around the globe, most notably in the service of the Red Star Line out of Liverpool. After moving to Vancouver in 1895, he worked for the Dunsmuir family, the wealthy British Columbia coal magnates, on the tug *Lorne*, and in 1901 he joined the Canadian Pacific fleet. He commanded a number of CPR steamers along the coast, and by 1918 had a solid, though not exceptional reputation as a navigator and captain.[26]

The records give but a scant portrait of Locke as a person. He seems not to have made a strong impression on the men he worked for or with, although after his death there was considerable speculation from his colleagues on his competence as a sailor. He was described as 'very fastidious and punctilious, and [in] his ideas of discipline somewhat of a martinet'[27]–probably not a bad thing in a ship's captain. He had had some sort of personal difficulty at one time, and the CPR had laid him off 'for his actions in his private life'. Later, it was also suggested that he was eccentric and erratic, with an intense hatred of Americans that was said to indicated 'senile decay'. There was no proof of these allegations, which seem to have been merely lawyers' ploys, and the CPR vigorously denied them.[28] One man who served under him remembers Locke as strict; he also recalled that the captain wore a toupee, which a member of the crew once threw into a bucket of water (how he got it off Locke's head is not recorded).[29]

Locke's schedule permitted little time for family life. He did, however, marry; his wife lived in Victoria, and the couple had five children. By 1918 the children were all grown and living away from home: one son and one daughter remaining near their mother in Victoria, the other daughter married and living in New Westminster, one son in Salonica, Greece, and the last on active service with the Canadian Engineers in France.[30]

Locke was of medium height and build, his round face framed by heavy white mutton-chop whiskers and divided horizontally by a thick moustache. He was not a legendary 'character' of whom salty or ribald stories were told; rather, he was a workmanlike captain who gave a competent day's work for a day's salary. Somewhere beneath the uniform was a sense of humour and perhaps the heart of a frustrated poet. His burlesques of Robert Service's verse were well-known to his friends, and a story is told of him that gives a glimpse of a romantic streak. During a voyage north on the *Princess Sophia* in 1917, a young girl passenger remarked to Locke that no one had said goodbye to her. Touched, he wrote a poem–beginning 'The good ship sails, I go to sea; but no one says good-bye to me'–and that night at dinner the verse appeared beside her plate. He later gave a copy to J.L. McPherson of the Seattle Chamber of Commerce, who preserved it.[31]

Locke's second-in-command was Captain Jeremiah Shaw,[32] the *Princess Sophia*'s first mate and pilot. Jerry Shaw was born in Glasgow in 1875 and had moved with his family to Vancouver Island as an infant. He joined the Canadian Pacific Navigation Company at the age of sixteen, and stayed on when the company was bought by the CPR. Having worked his way up from deckhand to skipper, he was captain of a number of CPR boats, including the *Beatrice* and the *Macquinna*. In April 1918, while commanding the *Tees*, a 165-foot salvage vessel, he had run ashore on the reef surrounding Zero Point, near Sidney. Passengers and mail were taken off safely, high-pressure pumps were put aboard, and the ship was towed into port. 'We were on our return trip to Victoria and everything was going fine,' explained Shaw. 'A strong current setting inshore took the *Tees* a few points off her course, and before we knew it she was on the submerged reef. We were going at about 12 knots, counting tide and wind, at the time. It was entirely unexpected.'[33] The company apparently did not blame him for the accident, for he was given further employment. In October 1918 he was making his second trip on the *Princess Sophia.*[34]

The *Sophia*'s wireless operator was David M. Robinson of Vancouver. Also from Glasgow, born in 1898, he had arrived in Vancouver with his family in 1912. As soon as he turned 18 he got his radio operator's licence and went to work for the CPR. In May 1918 he was assigned to the *Princess Sophia.*[35]

One of the youngest members of the crew was Francis Burke, a Vancouver native born in 1901, who was a student at King Edward High School. He had what used to be called 'hustle', and from an early age delivered the Vancouver *Province* door to door. As well, he sold candy and popcorn at the hockey arena on Saturday nights, delivered telegrams for Western Union on weeknights, and on Saturday afternoons manned an ice-cream stand at the entrance to Stanley Park. Sunday mornings he would hike up to the CPR dock to pick up the Sunday papers from Seattle, which he sold to regular customers. In the fall of 1918 the influenza epidemic in Vancouver became so severe that the schools were closed. Never one to miss an opportunity to make a dollar, Frank Burke, along with a school friend, Lionel Olson, set off to look for jobs. They soon found places–as porters on the *Princess Sophia.* Frank's father congratulated him, 'saying that not only had he chosen a comfortable ship, but that Captain Locke was the best skipper on the coast'.[36]

The ship left at least two of her crew behind. One was Walter Gosse, a lookout and the younger brother of her second mate, Frank Gosse. Natives of Victoria, the Gosse brothers were sons of the man who had piloted the *Karluk* north of Siberia to Wrangell Island for Vilhjalmur Stefansson during the Canadian Arctic Expedition of 1913.[37] Frank Gosse, like his father, had served the CPR for many years. Joining the company at the age of 17, he had worked his way up through the ranks, and by 1918 had his captain's papers,[38] was married, and had a young son. Before each voyage he would cross the street separating his house from that of his parents and say goodbye to his mother. That October, as usual, he did the same, and then for some reason went back and said goodbye to her again, which struck his mother as odd. The day the ship left Vancouver the two brothers were at a dance. They cut things rather short and had to sprint for a streetcar to reach the dock. Frank, who was the better runner, outdistanced his brother, and made the ship just as she was pulling out of the dock. Walter was left behind.[39]

The first engineer, Archibald Alexander, also missed the trip. Just before the *Sophia* was due to leave Vancouver, his wife telephoned from Victoria to tell him that both their children were seriously ill with influenza, and that his younger daughter was not expected to live. He asked permission to miss the voyage. He rushed to Victoria, and was relieved to find that both children were improving.[40] The three remaining officers, Charles Waller, Duncan Ross, and James Massey, offered to cover Alexander's shift, even though this meant more work for them. The absence of the first engineer was not a serious problem, since ships the size of the *Sophia* often ran with three engineers, and sometimes only two. Captain Locke and his officers were forced to change work schedules, watch duties, and assignments, but such reshuffling was a standard part of most trips.[41]

While Locke busied himself with administrative matters of this sort, the crew readied the ship for the voyage northward. The task of overseeing much of this work fell on Jerry Shaw and the purser, C.G. Beadle, who supervised the crew and the longshoremen as they loaded the ship.[42] The wireless officer, 20-year-old David Robinson, had been with the *Sophia* for only six months, having served earlier on the *Princess Adelaide* and the *Empress of Russia*. While on shore he doubled as freight clerk and checked the supplies as the longshoremen filled the hold.[43]

For Set Yip and the other porters and service crew, the hard work began only when the passengers boarded. Set Yip was one of twelve Chinese men working on the *Princess Sophia* when it left Vancouver. Born in Chong Shar, near Canton, in 1892, he received an education there, then came to Canada at the age of 20 and found work first at a cannery on the Skeena River, then as a labourer on a ranch owned by another Chinese at McLellan Station. He lived at the 'Sit clan house' on Georgia Street in

Vancouver, and regularly sent money in the form of gold coins to his mother in China.[44] Another Chinese crew member, Chin Yuen, aged about 40, also made regular contributions to support his wife and two sons in China.[45] The steamship companies often hired such men as porters, waiters, and cooks for their coastal ships. Like most of the CPR's Chinese employees, Set Yip remains a shadowy figure. Even his name is in doubt, for the records refer to him as both Set Yip and Sit Yep, while several of his countrymen are identified only as 'unknown Chinamen'. Because of the company's poor records and the general indifference to the fate of the Chinese crew, it is not even known how many of them were on the ship.

Preparations for the voyage continued almost until the moment the ship left dockside. At 5.00 p.m. on 19 October, James McGown, Superintendant of Engineering for the CPR in Vancouver, visited the *Princess Sophia* to carry out a final inspection. He 'went all around the ship and saw the chief engineer and saw the chief officer and saw everything was in order, that oil was aboard and that the water was aboard and everything ready for sea, and everything in order, as it should be.'[46] A few minor repairs had been completed, and McGown authorized the ship's departure. Then at 9.00 p.m., on schedule, the *Princess Sophia* pulled away from Pier D in Burrard Inlet, turned north up Howe Sound, and headed for Alert Bay, the first stop on the four-day run to Skagway.

The trip up the Inside Passage is one of the world's most beautiful, and cruise ships still take thousands of tourists every year to marvel at its cliffs, forests, bays, and mysterious wilderness. Although in 1918 it was more a practical route to the far northwest than a tourist attraction, the CPR took pains in its advertising brochures to emphasize the aesthetic pleasures of the trip:

> From Vancouver, BC to Skagway, Alaska, is a thousand miles through the entrancing Inland Channel, winding between islands and the mainland as through a fairyland. The journey is made in the palatial, yacht-like 'Princess' steamers of the Canadian Pacific Railway.[47]

The company was careful to emphasize that the trip was

perfectly safe, and invited travellers to wonder at the pilot's and captain's skill at navigation:

> Today scarcely a sunken rock exists but it is charted, and big steamers journey with the utmost safety through waters which to the landsman would seem to bristle with dangers at every turn. To realize to the full the miracle of this thousand miles of navigation from Vancouver to Skagway, one should stand for an hour or so looking forward, picking out what seems the channel the ship will take, and finding out how invariably one's guess is wrong. For it is not always the mainland which lies to the east. Often the mountains which tower up to the sky, almost from the very deck of the ship itself, are but islands; and other channels lie behind, with countless bays and straits and narrow gorges running miles up into the mainland, twisting, turning, creeping forward and doubling back, till they put to shame the most intricate maze which Oriental mind ever devised. And of such is the whole route, which finally creeps, as through the neck of a funnel, to the sands of Skagway.[48]

The schedule soon went awry. The *Sophia* arrived on time at Alert Bay, a small port on an island off the north-east coast of Vancouver Island, but there Captain Locke learned that the SS *Alaska*, steaming south from Skagway, had run aground near Swanson Bay and was calling for help. He immediately ordered the ship to steam towards Swanson Bay, about half-way up the coast to Prince Rupert, where he had a scheduled stop. By the time the *Sophia* arrived, however, the *Alaska* had freed herself and limped into the harbour. Her three hundred passengers had to disembark, adding to the confusion and congestion of travellers along the coast.

The grounding of the *Alaska* seems to have rung no warning bells among the *Sophia*'s passengers and crew, for they had confidence in her captain. One of the ship's firemen, W.C. Dibble, wrote to his wife:

> one lady passenger of our boat said to our Captain the other night, 'Captain, do you know where every rock is?' and the Captain replied he was not sure about that, but knew where deep water was and keeps in it if possible, and everybody says that Captain Locke knows every inch up to Skagway, so we are safe as far as that goes.[49]

This incident did not delay the *Princess Sophia* more than a few hours, and in the evening of 22 October she arrived on schedule in the harbour of Juneau, a gold-mining town and the capital of the territory of Alaska. There were few passengers on this leg of the trip, for in October most of the human traffic was heading south, and the *Sophia* carried mostly officials and businessmen whose affairs compelled them north at that time of the year. Such a man was C.D. Garfield, Deputy Collector of Customs for the US government, who was returning with his wife from Vancouver. On the wharf at Juneau he met his superior, John F. Pugh, the Collector of Customs.

The Collector of Customs was from 1868 until 1884 the most important civil official in Alaska, responsible not only for the work of the customs office, but also for a wide range of civil and marine matters. But the office was diminished by the Organic Act of 1884, which created the office of governor, and still more by the Organic Act of 1912, which created a territorial legislature. In October 1918 Pugh was leaving Juneau on a trouble-shooting mission to Skagway as a result of reports of massive congestion of people wanting passage out of the north. He was preparing to assist officials at the northern port, and to prevent potential problems among the hundreds of people increasingly anxious to secure transportation southward.[50] As he passed Garfield on the dock, Pugh told him that his trip to Skagway would likely be a short one, as the imminent arrival of the *Princess Sophia* promised to ease the congestion. He would travel back to Juneau with the ship.[51]

Jack Pugh brought a wealth of local knowledge to his position. His long-time commitment to the development of Alaska stood in marked contrast to the quick in-and-out careers of many northerners. Born in Washington State in 1877, raised in the turbulent turn-of-the-century lumber and shipping town of Port Townsend, he had moved north in 1902 to become customs officer at Ketchikan. He worked his way up the ranks of the civil service, moving to Skagway, Sulzer, and, in 1909, to Juneau, where in 1914 he was made Collector of Customs. Early in 1918 he was given a second term in that office. Pugh was one of the survivors of the wreck of the Pacific Coast Steamship Company's steamer *State of*

California, which in August 1913 had struck a rock in Gambier Bay, 90 miles south of Juneau, and went down with the loss of more than thirty lives.[52]

At 1.00 in the afternoon of 23 October the *Princess Sophia* reached her destination. Signs of winter were already present; early risers that morning saw snow on the ground, though with the temperature a few degrees above freezing, it did not stay long. At this season the tops of the surrounding mountains were shrouded with fog and low-lying clouds, where the dampness of the coast met the dry chill of the interior. The mood of those who had managed to secure passage on the crowded vessel was buoyant; those who had not succeeded lamented their ill fortune.

Departure from Skagway to the south was scheduled for 7.00 p.m. the same day, and Captain Locke was anxious to board the waiting passengers as quickly as possible. The weather threatened to hamper operations, for the morning's light snow had turned to rain. But the barometer was rising, promising fair weather for the voyage.[53]

Much work had to be done before the ship could leave. Frank Gosse and Arthur Murphy, second and third mates, organized the off-loading of the cargo, while Captain Locke visited the office of L.H. Johnston, the CPR's Skagway agent. Locke needed to recruit additional crew members in the northern port, for four of the ship's stewards and two deckhands had come down with the influenza that was raging across North America.[54] He feared that his depleted crew could not handle the extra passenger load.

But there was no shortage of applicants for the jobs. Dozens of crew members from the WP&YR steamers were in town, waiting to head south. Given the meagre wages they were paid for their northern work, and the fact that they were going to Vancouver in any case, many eagerly sought an opportunity to work for their passage. In short order ten men, six of whom were WP&YR waiters, signed on for the trip.[55]

The manpower problem solved, the officers now turned their attention to loading the ship. The difficulty here was not in the amount of cargo waiting in the freight sheds at Skagway–though there was a great deal of it–but in its diversity. Many of the people leaving the interior of Alaska and the Yukon in the fall of 1918 were doing so for the last time. People like the Tackstroms, the O'Briens, and Charlie Castleman, who were quitting the north forever, were taking with them as many of their worldly goods as they could afford to ship. Two tons of household effects, including clothing, sewing machines, and small pieces of furniture–some 266 individual items–were destined for the hold of the *Princess Sophia.*[56] The crew also had to load hundreds of Christmas parcels, forwarded from Dawson and destined for the troops fighting on the western front in Europe.[57]

The cargo also included twenty-four horses. Thirteen of them were heavy draft animals belonging to Herb McDonald, a long-time freighter in the Dawson City area. McDonald had sent the horses to Skagway in the care of James Kirk, a pioneer of the 1898 gold rush, who was working as a carpenter in Dawson when he took on the job of seeing the horses safely to Vancouver, after which he planned to return to his wife in Dawson.[58] McDonald was on the *Sophia* as well. He was a native of Portage la Prairie, Manitoba, born in 1878, who had come as a young man to the west coast and then moved on to the Yukon in 1899. He worked for a number of years as a freighter, driving mule teams over the Ridge road to the creeks, and then went into business for himself in 1905, the year he married Emma Carlyon. He gained a considerable local reputation for a feat of freighting: 'He moved Milvain's Walker's Fork dredge over the divide, up Poker creek, down Little Gold onto Sixtymile, thence up Miller's creek, which was a great undertaking, in 1912.'[59] The McDonalds had three children. Eunice was a Girl Guide, 'an exceedingly bright and cheerful worker', and a great knitter; Russell was 'an exceedingly rugged boy', and both he and 'little Ruth' were 'bright and lovable children'. Emma McDonald, nine years younger than her husband, was a pillar of the Martha Munger Black chapter of the IODE.[60] Though they seemed a typically happy and prosperous Dawson family, by 1918 they had had enough of the north and announced their intention of leaving for Vancouver, where McDonald planned to use his draft horses as a base for re-establishing his business. The Dawson newspaper regretted the news, calling McDonald 'one of the greatest hustlers in the freighting business in Dawson and vicinity' and remarking that 'should he not return, the Klondike will lose one of its most valued and enterprising citizens'.[61] The McDonalds left Dawson shortly after Kirk, and they met in Skagway in time to help with loading the horses aboard the *Princess Sophia*.[62]

McDonald's horses were not the only ones on the ship. There was also an old white horse named Billy whose owner, Walter Barnes, had been a miner in the Dawson area for eighteen years. He was born in Wiltshire, England, around 1870, and came to Vancouver in the early 1890s. Joining the rush to Atlin in 1899, he moved to Dawson in 1900 and since then had prospected on Hunker Creek and elsewhere, all over the region. His brother Fred was the principal owner and chief operator of a large hydraulic property on Lovett Gulch, and when he died in 1913 Walter Barnes took it over. It was a substantial operation:

> The properties are among the most productive in the Yukon. During the last ten years an enormous quantity of gravel was handled on the property. The hill was tapped by a tunnel running 1,700 feet back into the hill, and the pay dirt was worked largely with use of cars, operated on a small iron track.[63]

These ore cars were pulled by old Billy, who worked faithfully summer and winter and was known as a 'real horse-miner';[64] his owner claimed that he had hauled at least $500,000 in gold from the mine. Each fall Barnes came out to Vancouver, where he maintained a family home on Nicomen Island, near the city, but in 1918 he was bringing with him two companions–his brother Allen and his horse. Billy had given loyal service for many years, but he was now too old for work. Rather than abandon him in the north or ship him to the knackers, Barnes arranged for Billy to retire in the greener pastures of southern British Columbia.[65]

L.H. Johnston, the CPR agent, also checked at least five dogs aboard ship. Two of them, dark, handsome creatures with white blazes, belonged to John Colver, a miner in his fifties from Chicken, Alaska, who had come in with the rush of 1898. Like so many of his generation, Colver had had a varied career in the north, working sometimes as a prospector and sometimes as a road-house operator. He was born near Albany, Oregon, and had managed a hotel in that state. After mining on Bonanza and other creeks for several years, he eventually built an establishment known as the Cliff Roadhouse, a landmark for many years at the Bear Creek bluff. Later he went to Chicken Creek near Fortymile to manage some mining properties for Frank Davidson and Associates, investors in Toronto and Rochester, New York. On this trip he was travelling with his niece, Mrs Olive Pinska, and her husband Albert, to visit his family in Oregon's Willamette valley.

Throughout the afternoon of 23 October the Skagway dock buzzed with activity. The arrival at 5.30 of the daily train from Whitehorse added to the noise and confusion as it discharged more people wanting to board the ship. Jack Pugh and his officials hurried about trying to establish some order among the crowd.

Among the lucky ones who had booked their passage in advance were Captain James Alexander and his wife Louise, on their way to Toronto to negotiate the sale of the Engineer Mine. On 23 October the Alexanders arrived by train from Carcross and joined the other passengers awaiting permission to board the *Sophia* for the scheduled 7.00 p.m. departure. Some passengers were allowed on board early: Ilene Winchell, for instance, even weaker after the long journey from Iditarod, was taken to her stateroom, number 35, while the families with small children were assisted in boarding by the porters and stewards. Finally, in the early evening all the passengers were allowed to board. It was later reported that in the confusion several men had scrambled aboard without tickets as stowaways, and were soon absorbed in the crush.[66] The whirl of people, baggage, and crew seemed chaotic, but in a surprisingly short time order was restored. The passengers settled in, the crew completed their dockside tasks, and the ship was ready to depart.

CPR agent Johnston completed his work on shore. He walked the short distance from his office to the *Princess Sophia*, conferred briefly with the purser, Charles Beadle, and then climbed to the bridge to talk to Captain Locke. They exchanged pleasantries–the boarding had gone smoothly, loading was complete, and Locke was anxious to leave, since it was now past 10.00 and the ship was already three hours behind schedule. Johnston said his goodbyes and returned to shore. Five minutes later, at 10.10, the *Sophia* pulled away from the Skagway dock, turned slowly down the channel and, in the misty darkness of the late fall evening, steamed southwards down Lynn Canal.[67] A north wind began to gust down the channel, tailing the ship south, and, combining with the cold dampness of the coastal air, chased passengers off the decks and into the warmth of their cabins.

Exactly how many people sailed on the *Princess Sophia* that night will probably never be known. The passenger list published later gave the names of 278 passengers, of whom 27 were travelling second-class.[68] But the names of stowaways, if any, were not recorded, nor can the number of crew members be exactly determined. The best estimate, taking the published passenger list and the lists later printed in the newspapers and the court records, is that there were at least 353 people on board, of whom about 65 were crew.

The voyage promised to be a profitable one for the CPR. The majority of passengers were going the entire distance to Vancouver and Seattle and paying the full first-class fare of $37.50; children were charged $18.75 and infants $2.50. So substantial was the annual migration of riverboat crews that the company also gave a special discount to employees of the White Pass & Yukon Route river steamers; their fare of $25 made it even easier for them to take the annual trip south. The second-class passengers, almost all of whom were going to Seattle, paid $22. The total ticket sales for the voyage, as recorded in the official passenger list, came to $7,968.35.[69]

Once settled below decks, the passengers prepared for the trip to Vancouver. The ship's motion was no problem, since the waves and wind coming from astern gave the decks at most a gentle roll. The children would naturally have wanted to try their sea legs, running up and down the passageways, but it was late and their parents soon bundled them into their bunks.

While the children slept, the adults pursued business and pleasure. Lulu Mae Eads had decided not to give her jewellery to the purser for safekeeping; instead, she found a hiding place in her cabin. Some passengers headed for the saloon to resume the convivial gatherings that had begun on the riverboat from Dawson. Old friends who had travelled on different boats and trains found to their delight that their paths had crossed on the *Sophia*. John Maskell, on his way to England for his wedding, met Louise Davis on board. They were friends, having worked together at the Cascade Laundry in Dawson City, but had left there on different boats. Captain John Green of the WP&YR steamer *Yukon* met other riverboat men, two of them fellow-captains, and together they discussed the past season on the river and the prospects for the region's future.

Some of the passengers gathered in the smoking room, where they learned from the purser and his staff the schedule of the next day's meals and entertainments. The *Princess Sophia* and other CPR ships published daily menus, complete with mildly risqué drawings–the sort that would have caused criticism on shore, but that in the holiday atmosphere of an ocean voyage were taken in good spirit by all aboard.

Not long after 11.00 p.m., just after the *Princess Sophia* passed Battery Point, a small headland 16 miles out of Skagway, the weather suddenly worsened, and a blinding snowstorm overtook the ship from the north. A strong north wind, gusting up to 50 miles per hour, whistled over the mountains that rimmed Lynn Canal, blowing heavy snow before it. The water turned rough, boiling with heavy rollers and whitecaps. It was a bad storm, but Captain Locke had faced worse, and coastal mariners were used to running through white-out conditions. He decided not to slow down. Keeping the ship at regular speed, he continued to run before the wind and snow down Lynn Canal.

A few miles south of the *Princess Sophia*, William Stokes, captain of the small fishing boat *Electo*, was feeling the full effect of the blizzard. Battling the wind and gusts of driving snow, he reached shore, tied a line to a rock, and prepared to wait out the storm. The frantic tossing of his boat kept him awake, and about half an hour after midnight he heard in the distance a low, groaning sound–the foghorn of a large ship coming from the north. For over an hour he lay awake following the sound, which approached, passed him, and faded to the south as the *Princess Sophia* made her way at speed down the channel towards Juneau.

4. Vanderbilt Reef

The blinding snow that swirled around the *Princess Sophia* as it steamed down Lynn Canal in the early hours of 24 October was no novelty to Captain Locke and his crew. Although the Inside Passage–the twisting, narrow route from Skagway to Prince Rupert–protected ships from the worst of the north Pacific storms, blunting the wind that swept in from the open sea, they were vulnerable to the winter storms blowing down over the mountains to the north. These northerly storms often came up without warning, playing havoc with visibility and navigation, and winds of 80 miles per hour were not uncommon.

Over the years the Inside Passage had claimed its share of victims, and more than one steamship had already come to grief in its waters. The *Islander* disaster of 1901 was followed nine years later by the *Princess May* episode. Four feet longer than the *Princess Sophia*, though only about half the tonnage, she was following the same Skagway-to-Vancouver route. Steaming south down Lynn Canal in heavy fog on 5 August 1910, she struck a reef off the north end of Sentinel Island, about 50 miles from Skagway. At low tide she was balanced precariously on the rocks, her hull entirely out of the water and her bow pointed awkwardly at the horizon. A photograph taken of her in that predicament became 'the most spectacular and famous shipwreck photograph in the history of the Pacific coast'.[1] All eighty passengers and sixty-eight crew were landed safely on the island and the ship was later salvaged. Though this episode was more of an embarrassment than a tragedy, the waters south of Skagway had once again earned their reputation as tough and dangerous, to be approached with care, particularly in bad weather.

While the driving wind and snow caused Captain Locke and his pilot, Jerry Shaw, some concern, they kept the *Princess Sophia* at full speed. As the ship steamed past Berners Bay, Locke took comfort in the fact that the channel was nearly seven miles across, wide enough to permit some margin for error. It was ahead, at Favourite Channel, that he would be compelled to proceed cautiously, for there the passage narrowed considerably as it began to wind through the islands towards Juneau. In the best of weather ships had to move carefully between Poundstone Rock, a small reef in mid-channel, and Lincoln Island. In a storm the last miles into Juneau would have to be taken with extreme caution. But such navigational problems were ahead; in the small hours of 24 October Locke had no hesitation in maintaining speed.

The only potential danger in the main channel of Lynn Canal lay at Vanderbilt Reef, where the shipping lane narrowed to two and a half miles. The reef was named in 1880 by Captain L.A. Beardslee of the United States Navy–not after Cornelius Vanderbilt, the notorious 'robber baron', but after Captain J.M. Vanderbilt, the man who discovered it. Vanderbilt, who had gone to Alaska about 1875, was the captain of the Northwest Trading Company's ship *Favourite*, which as well as carrying trade goods did surveying work for the US Navy.[2] The reef, a rock about half an acre in area, was three-quarters covered at high tide: it might show a little above the water's surface, or it might be awash with the swell, depending on the strength of the wind. At low tide it looked like a rocky table rising a few feet from the water, its highest point at extreme low tide about 12 feet above the surface.[3]

It was in fact the small, flattish top of a considerable underwater mountain rising a thousand feet from the deep bottom of Lynn Canal. The reef lay about two and a half miles from the east and four from the west shore; at its southern end a small red and black marker buoy was anchored–easy enough to see by daylight, but useless as a warning at night.[4] Coastal navigators and travellers had for years been asking the American government to put a proper lighted buoy on the reef,[5] but, as was typical of Washington's treatment of Alaskan complaints, the requests had been ignored.[6] Officials saw little reason for alarm, for despite the potential danger, the existence of only one obstruction in the channel seven miles wide seemed to give enough room for manoeuvre to make a warning device unnecessary.

Navigation in Lynn Canal in the First World War era was more art than science, particularly in foul weather. In daylight or on a clear night there was of course no difficulty. But on a cloudy night, or in fog or blowing snow, it was another matter. The *Princess Sophia*'s last voyage took place a full generation before the invention of radar, when the skill of the navigator was crucial, particularly in waters as tricky as those of Lynn Canal. Though it is not now considered a difficult passage–the *U.S. Coast Pilot* says that it is 'nearly free of dangers'[7]–there are more warning lights in Lynn Canal now than in 1918.[8]

The canal is a long, narrow arm of the sea, stretching nearly 85 miles from the junction of Chatham Strait and Icy Strait to Chilkat and Chilkoot Inlets. It is about 90 miles from Skagway to Juneau, through a passage that is never more than 10 miles wide, and often less. The technique that ship's captains used to navigate this passage in bad weather was to take compass headings from known positions and stick to them as closely as possible. Pilots would take a bearing as they passed Point Sherman Light, about 15 miles north of Vanderbilt Reef. Of course, an error in this bearing could be catastrophic, since there was not much margin for error, and in 15 miles a mistake of a few degrees could run a ship onto the reef or, indeed, onto either shore. A backup technique was to sound the ship's whistle and listen for echoes from the shore, which would give a reasonable estimate of where in the channel the ship was. A man who once crewed on the *Princess Sophia* remembers the pilot sounding the whistle, then shifting his weight from foot to foot to count the seconds–'a thousand and one, a thousand and two'–until the echoes came back.[9] It was not a bad technique, and had served Captain Locke for many years. He had no reason to think that it would fail him now.

But Locke was wrong. Despite several extensive investigations, the reasons for what happened in the minutes after 2.00 a.m.[10] on 24 October 1918 were never made exactly clear, nor was it established who was on watch at that unlucky hour. Certainly the snowstorm obscured the view of those charged with navigating the *Princess Sophia*. Captain Locke was intimately familiar with the waters of Lynn Canal; he knew that the reef was ahead of him, and that a point was approaching at which the channel narrowed. The most likely explanation for what happened next was that either Locke or Jerry Shaw, the pilot, made a miscalculation as the ship passed Point Sherman. A few degrees of error in a course set there would take a ship out of the deep channel and place it on a collision course with the reef. Perhaps the howling of the wind obscured or distorted the whistle's echoes. It is also possible that the tides, noted for their volatility in this region, could have combined with the driving north winds to push the *Sophia* off course.[11]

For whatever reason, by 2.00 a.m. the ship was steaming down the centre of Lynn Canal, when she should have been closer to the east side. Instead of clearing it by hundreds of yards, she was heading straight for Vanderbilt Reef.[12]

At 2.10 the unthinkable happened. The *Princess Sophia*, steaming at her regular cruising speed of 11 or 12 knots, ran directly onto the middle of the reef. Because the reef was so low in the water, the effect was not like that of running directly into a cliff or an iceberg, which would have stopped the ship dead and crumpled its bow; rather, the bow lifted out of the water and, with a horrible grinding and tearing, slid up and onto the rock. The rapid deceleration–from 11 knots to a standstill in a few yards–threw passengers from their bunks and the crew to the deck.[13] Supplies and furniture crashed about, and the men on the bridge were tossed violently into the bulkheads. The turmoil lasted only a few seconds. Then there was silence, followed by commotion as the passengers and crew picked themselves up. For a time the ship's twin screws continued to turn, feebly grasping for water, until the main engines were stopped and their comforting throb was replaced by the ominous howl of the wind.

The *Sophia* hung suspended; the hull, partly afloat in the shallow water, scraped against the rocks, each creak and groan increasing the passengers' alarm. As a precaution, Locke ordered the lifeboats swung out on their davits. But it soon became evident that the ship was not going to shift off the reef, and those aboard, reassured for the moment that they were not about to sink into an icy grave, took stock of their situation.

Despite the terrific force of the impact, there were few if any injuries, probably because most people were in bed. Yet the passengers, many of whom were familiar with stories of earlier disasters, were not easily calmed. John Maskell described their feelings in a letter to his fiancée: 'We struck a rock last night which threw many from their berths, some were crying, some too weak to move, but the life boats were swung out in all readiness, but owing to the storm would be madness to launch.'[14] US Army Private Auris McQueen wrote of the confusion around him: 'There was some excitement but no panic. Two women fainted and one of them got herself into a black evening dress and didn't worry over who saw her putting it on. Some of the men, too, kept life preservers for an hour or so and seemed to think that there was no chance for us.'[15]

As the crew moved about the ship assessing damage and checking for injuries, Captain Locke sent word of the accident to his superiors by wireless. Because of the severely limited range of the instruments of that era, it was impossible for him to communicate directly with Canadian Pacific headquarters in Victoria; he would be lucky to get a clear signal through to Juneau, twenty miles away in a straight line over the coastal mountains. He sent a message to the *Cedar*, anchored near Juneau harbour, reporting the accident and asking for help, and also made contact with the CPR agent in Skagway: '*Princess Sophia* ran on Vanderbilt Reef Lynn Canal at 3 o'clock [BC time]. Ship not taking any water unable to back off at high water fresh northerly wind ship pounding assistance on way from Juneau.' This message was relayed to CPR headquarters in Victoria, but because of communications difficulties did not reach Captain Troup until later that afternoon, more than twelve hours after the accident.[16]

The news came as a complete surprise in Juneau. The wind and snow that had engulfed the *Princess Sophia* had not yet reached the territorial capital. Frank Lowle, the CPR ticket agent there, was sound asleep when his phone rang at 3.15 a.m. (Alaska time) Someone at the harbour was calling to relay the message, just received, that the *Princess Sophia* had run aground on Vanderbilt Reef. Lowle immediately called an assistant to start preparations for the reception of the crew and passengers, then got dressed and headed for his office to begin arranging a rescue.

It was not an easy task. There was no ship anywhere near Juneau that was large enough to take on all the *Sophia*'s passengers at once. Lowle had no choice but to recruit as many small vessels as he could contact, and ask them to go at top speed to Vanderbilt Reef. He remembered that the *Peterson*, an 85-foot long US Army harbour boat, had been in Juneau the previous evening and was now on its way back to Fort Seward, at Haines.[17] He telephoned the cable office and asked that Haines be telegraphed immediately. Though Lowle knew this was a long shot, for the Haines cable office was closed in the evening, he had heard that the operator slept in the office, and hoped that an emergency call might wake him. But one ship would not be enough; the *Peterson* could carry an absolute maximum of only 125 people. So while he struggled to make contact with Haines, he told his assistant, named Smeaton, to run down to the docks and recruit additional rescue boats. The sense of urgency was beginning to grow, for the radio operator in Juneau had now relayed a second message to the effect that the *Princess Sophia* was being pounded heavily against the rocks, and was trying to lower its boats.

As word spread along the waterfront and into the town, coastal mariners docked in Juneau harbour responded quickly to Smeaton's call for help. James P. Davis, master of the *Estebeth*, was awakened at 3.30 a.m. by Mrs Kaser, wife of the ship's owner, and the two agreed that the ship should go immediately to assist with the rescue. The *Estebeth* was a 65-foot mail and passenger boat that worked the coastal waters between Juneau, Sitka, and Skagway. She was virtually brand new, having been launched on 10 June, but Davis, who had worked in the Lynn Canal area for seven years, did not hesitate to take her out into the heavy seas around Vanderbilt Reef.

Just over an hour after learning of the accident, Davis and his crew of six pulled out of Juneau harbour. The first part of the journey went smoothly, for the snow was light and the wind little more than a sharp breeze. Then, as the *Estebeth* cleared Outer Point, at the northwestern tip of Douglas Island, and headed up the main channel of Lynn Canal, it ran into heavier snow and the first signs of a strong north wind.[18]

Other captains also headed to the *Princess Sophia*'s assistance. Edward McDougall, master of the *Amy*, was awakened near dawn by a night watchman. Lowle had asked her owner, Mr Roberts, superintendent of the Alaska Juneau Gold Mining Company, to lend his vessel to the rescue. In the absence of a larger ship the *Amy*, a 65-foot freight and passenger boat, might prove useful. McDougall contacted Lowle, protesting that she carried no food or supplies. Lowle exclaimed, 'I wish you would go right out and not wait for that [food], as it is blowing a north gale, and the passengers are all on the boat.'[19] A few minutes later, McDougall piloted the *Amy* out of Juneau harbour.

Lowle continued his efforts to draft vessels and crews for the rescue attempt. By 6.30 that morning he had persuaded Charles Duffy to take his small fishing boat, *Lone Fisherman*, to Vanderbilt Reef, but as dawn broke he was still searching frantically to secure enough shipboard space to take off all the *Princess Sophia*'s passengers and crew. Meanwhile he waited anxiously for the first word from the rescue vessels, which were then nearing the stricken ship.

While Lowle and Smeaton worked at organizing a rescue fleet, the earlier attempt at contacting the cable office at Haines finally succeeded. The agent who supposedly slept near his equipment was not there that night, but fortunately for Lowle someone happened by the office as the distress call came in. The quartermaster at Fort Seward informed Captain Cornelius W. Stidham, master of the *Peterson*, that the *Princess Sophia* was 'driving to pieces' on the reef, and that the lifeboats had been swung out. Stidham recruited two more men to bring his crew to nine and loaded fifty extra blankets aboard. At 4.45 a.m., only an hour and a quarter after Lowle's message from Juneau had come in, the *Peterson* set out for Vanderbilt Reef.[20]

For those aboard the *Sophia* the news of their impending rescue, transmitted from Juneau, brought considerable relief. By daybreak they had been on the reef for several hours, and although they did not seem to be in immediate danger of sinking, their situation was still serious. The wind and waves continued to beat the hull against the reef, and at 6.00 a.m., high tide, there was alarm when, as one passenger recorded, 'it was thought she might pound her bottom out on the rocks'. But the crisis passed, and 'everybody settled down to wait for help'.[21] In Juneau Lowle had wired this information to Captain Locke, asking him if he had any further requests. Locke replied that he had none;[22] it was comforting to know that several ships were on the way.

After giving the question more thought, however, Locke decided that the rescue flotilla was inadequate for its task. Although four ships were en route to Vanderbilt Reef–the *Estebeth*, *Amy*, *Lone Fisherman* and *Peterson*–they were all small vessels, collectively able to hold the *Sophia*'s passengers and crew but lacking the size and equipment required to take them off in the midst of a driving north wind. Locke wired Lowle again, asking for more assistance–in particular, that the *King and Winge*, a local fishing vessel, be sent to the scene. This boat had pulled into Juneau harbour early that morning and its crew were busy unloading the catch when Lowle ran along the wharf with his request.

Lowle was desperate to enlist the *King and Winge* for the rescue operation. Her captain, James J. Miller, was at the age of 36 a veteran of north coast waters, and his crew, skilled dory fishermen, were the most experienced sailors in the region. His vessel was a hundred feet long, 140 gross tons, and capable of holding 150 people if they were packed in as tightly as the fish that usually filled the holds. Although she was not a perfect solution to Lowle's requirements–he would have preferred a full-size coastal steamer, like the Alaska Steamship Company's *Jefferson*, then several hundred miles down the coast–the assistance of the *King and Winge* would make an orderly evacuation more possible. Lowle ran up to the side of the ship and, in Miller's words, 'ordered me out there'. Miller balked, telling Lowle that he needed the permission of the ship's owners before such a voyage could be undertaken. Lowle harangued Miller for some time, and then left in an unsuccessful search for a company officer. After several hours Miller gave the matter further thought and approached Lowle. 'Do you want us to go to the wreck?' he asked. 'Yes, I certainly do. And every boat I can get,' Lowle replied. 'Captain Locke says to send out all the boats we can, and he thinks he can get off the reef at high water.'[23] Miller finally relented, and at 11.00 a.m. he left with his crew to join the rescue fleet.

The *King and Winge* was given a particular task in the rescue attempt. The plan was to let the smaller boats take off the passengers, while the larger vessel used its 140-horsepower Corliss gas engine to pull the *Princess Sophia* off the reef.[24] The *King and Winge* also carried J. Clark Readman, a Juneau accountant and amateur reporter who would take notes of the day's events for the local newspaper,[25] and E.P. Pond, a professional photographer from Juneau who hoped for some dramatic pictures. Shortly after the *King and Winge* left Juneau, Lowle also dispatched two small cannery tenders, the *Excursion* and the *Elsinore*.[26] Lowle then wired Captain Locke that help was on the way and sent a message to L.H. Johnston, his fellow CPR agent in Skagway, in which he optimistically stated that the *Princess Sophia* was 'expect[ed to] float [at] high tide'.[27]

For the passengers and crew aboard the stranded ship, the wait was excruciating. Daylight came late on the morning of 24 October; the sun at that time of year was rising well to the south, its rays fighting to penetrate the grey mist and intermittent snow swirling above the waters of Lynn Canal. Shortly before 9.00 a.m. those on deck heard a welcome noise above the wind–the steam engine of the *Peterson*, ending a four-hour trip in rough seas down the channel from Haines. As she drew close to the *Princess Sophia* the skies brightened and the snow stopped blowing. Captain Stidham noted that the *Sophia* 'sat upon the reef, almost on an even keel, if anything with a little bit of a list to starboard'. Bringing the *Peterson* 75 yards upwind of the *Sophia*, as close to the reef as he dared, Stidham had one of his crew call through a megaphone to Captain Locke, asking for instructions. Locke requested that Stidham stand by until the next high tide, when he hoped to remove the passengers.

By full light the seas were somewhat calmer. The *Peterson* bounced in the chop as she waited for a signal from Locke. Stidham allowed his boat to drift downwind, past the *Sophia*. As he passed the stranded vessel, he noticed crew members lowering lifeboats. He immediately approached the *Sophia*, thinking that Locke had decided to remove his passengers. The lifeboat nearest him had four or five men in it, pushing hard against the hull of the ship to keep from crashing against it. Men on deck handled the boats' lines.[28]

But this was not an attempt to escape from the *Princess Sophia*. When the lifeboats had dropped almost to the water, the men on deck stopped lowering, and it became evident that Locke had ordered them down to assess the damage to the hull. Though the storm had let up enough to enable the lifeboats to be lowered without too much danger, there was another difficulty. The *Sophia* was sitting almost squarely in the middle of the reef. At low tide there was exposed rock on both sides of her; as the tide rose, most of this rock was covered with water–but not enough to float a lifeboat safely in a heavy swell. It was decided to wait until the next high tide and calmer seas, and then try again.

As the crew of the *Princess Sophia* were lowering the boats, the *Estebeth* arrived at the reef. James Davis, her master, saw that the stranded vessel was almost completely out of the water, even though it was just past high tide. As he described her condition:

> forward she had a big rent in the bow, fore and aft, and the water was pouring out of her in a big gush–running out say probably two or three hundred gallons a minute–something like that–probably a 4 or 6 inch seam. Her propeller was just showing aft, resting very easy–probably wasn't two feet off of her natural water line, that is fore and aft, and listing maybe five to ten per cent to starboard.

Like Stidham, he pulled near the *Sophia* and called across the water to Captain Locke. In answer to Davis's questions about the passengers, Locke replied that his crew 'had examined the rock and they were resting securely in a cradle on the reef, the vessel was in no danger whatever, and he wanted me [Davis] to stay around until the wind went down and then come up on the port side and take the passengers off.'[29] Locke warned Davis to keep his vessel well clear of the *Sophia*, lest he too end up on the reef. Davis complied. Tying the *Estebeth* to the marker buoy in the calmer water to the lee of the reef, he awaited Locke's instructions.[30] He did, however, make one further effort to help. Believing that a light boat could reach the *Sophia* without grounding on the reef, he lowered a small skiff, intending to row over to her. He pulled a few yards in her direction, then realized that the cold, waves, and spray made the idea suicidal. Abandoning his plan, he returned to the *Estebeth* and raised the skiff.[31]

Some months later, reflecting on the day's events, Stidham and Davis questioned Locke's optimistic view of his situation. The ship seemed firmly stuck on the reef, but there were no guarantees that it would stay there indefinitely. She had a huge hole in her hull, and the weather, though moderating slightly, was still bad and could get worse. The *Sophia* was still in serious danger. But it seemed there was little that could be done. The exposed reef, though partly awash, would not permit lifeboats to be launched in the swell. For now, the *Peterson* and *Estebeth* had no choice but to toss about in the increasing chop and await their chance.

While the two ships waited by the reef, the rest of the rescue flotilla fought its way against the surging waves of Lynn Canal. The *Lone Fisherman* ran into a strong northwesterly wind about 10.00 a.m. as she reached Portland Island. Bouncing violently in the rough waters, she finally put in at Sentinel Island, where her master, Charles Duffy, learned from the watchman at the lighthouse that the ships at Vanderbilt Reef had been prevented by heavy seas from taking the passengers off the *Sophia*. Rather than risk a vicious pounding at the reef, Duffy chose to keep his boat at the lighthouse dock.[32] Others too decided that there was little they could do to help. Robert Lucy, piloting a small gas boat down from Skagway and Haines to Juneau, passed Vanderbilt Reef at 10.00 a.m. He noticed passengers on deck and other ships nearby. With his boat already filled to capacity and other vessels standing by, Lucy felt no need to stay, and continued on to Juneau.[33] Niels P. Madsen, master of the *E.A. Hegg*, a 46-foot gas boat docked at Juneau, also made the trip up to the reef that day, and stood by for a time before running for shelter.[34]

While these smaller vessels headed for safety, the larger ships continued to steam towards the *Princess Sophia*. The *Amy* arrived at the reef about 10.20 a.m., and joined the *Estebeth* near the buoy, rocking gently in the lee of the reef. Her master, Edward McDougall, hoping to get some food, tried to call over to the *Estebeth*, but the howling wind blew his words away. He then crossed over to the *Peterson*, lying at anchor 250 yards off. There he learned that no immediate rescue was planned.[35] As the other captains had done, he then circled the *Sophia* several times, examining the ship's condition and pondering his course of action. And, like the others, he concluded that there was little to do but wait.[36]

For the passengers and crew of the *Princess Sophia*, the sight of the would-be rescuers made their position less frightening; on the other hand, the impossibility of crossing the short distance to the safety they offered generated anger and frustration. More ominously, as the crew and a few passengers realized, their sense of security was a false one. The ebb tide brought new dangers, described by Auris McQueen:

> We had three tugboats here in the afternoon, but the weather was too rough to transfer any passengers. The most critical time, nobody but the ship's officers, we soldiers and a few sailors amongst the crew and passengers were told about it, was at low tide at noon, when the captain and chief officer figured she was caught on the starboard bow and would hang there while she settled on the port side and astern. They were afraid she would turn turtle, but the bow pounded around and slipped until she settled into a groove, well supported forward on both sides.[37]

John Maskell was less sanguine about his prospects. Convinced that the *Sophia* was about to sink, he wrote out his last will in a letter to Dorothy Burgess, his fiancée in Manchester: 'I made my will this morning, leaving everything to you, my true love, and I want you to give £100 to my dear mother, £100 to my dear father, £100 to dear wee Jack, and the balance of my estate (about £300) to you, Dorrie dear. The Eagle Lodge will take care of my remains.'[38] The letter did not arrive until six months after the disaster, and since her address was published in the press, she got a number of letters from Canadians. She never received the £300; Maskell's father claimed that there had been no witnesses to the signing of the will, and kept the money himself.[39]

For the Canadian Pacific agents in Skagway and Juneau, and the company's executives in southern British Columbia, the hours were painfully long. The lack of direct contact with the *Princess Sophia* was infuriating. Information dribbled in hours after events, relayed second- or third-hand to and from Vanderbilt Reef, Juneau, and Victoria; it took Lowle in Juneau seven hours to get a coded message about the accident through to the provincial capital.[40]

In Victoria, hundreds of miles from the scene, and unable to establish regular communication either with the ship or with his agent in Juneau, James Troup struggled to organize a proper rescue. A constant source of frustration was the uncertainty of wireless communication. At 9.45 on the morning of the accident Troup attempted to send a message to Lowle in Juneau, but could not get through. A second attempt two hours later was equally unsuccessful.[41] There were several reasons for this confusion. Wireless messages directed towards the northern towns of Sitka, Skagway, and Juneau had to compete with local traffic, which was particularly heavy just then because the cable between Sitka and Juneau had been severed on 21 October and was not yet repaired.[42] The Ketchikan station had great difficulty getting through to Juneau, as the capital's wireless operators were constantly busy with messages from Sitka. E.J. Haughton, District Superintendent of the Dominion Government Wireless Service, and the man who bore the brunt of Troup's frustration, tried several times to clear all local wireless traffic in order that messages concerning the *Sophia* could be transmitted quickly, but he was unsuccessful,[43] largely because he had no authority over American operators. Thus the international character of the incident added its share of difficulties to the rescue attempt.

While Lowle in Juneau and Troup in Victoria fumed at their inability to get fresh news, more boats were heading toward Vanderbilt Reef. Shortly before 2.00 p.m. the wireless operator at Juneau contacted the lighthouse tender *Cedar*, telling Captain John Leadbetter: '*Sophia* aground near Sentinel Island. Peterson and several gas boats have arrived at wreck but can do nothing account of northerly wind.'[44] The *Cedar* was then 66 miles south of the *Princess Sophia*, steaming up Stevens Passage near Midway Island. Leadbetter established wireless contact with the *Sophia* and offered his assistance, estimating his time of arrival at 8.30 p.m., despite the weather. Locke accepted, glad to have the large vessel–which could carry four hundred people in an emergency–join the rescue flotilla. He informed the *Cedar*'s captain: 'Impossible to get passengers off tonight, as sea is running too strong; will probably be able to get them off early morning; strong tide.'[45]

At about 4.00 p.m. there was a flurry of activity on the deck of the *Princess Sophia*. J.P. Davis, master of the *Estebeth*, saw several people getting into one of the *Sophia*'s lifeboats. Believing that this signalled the beginning of an emergency unloading, Davis started his engines and cast off from the marker buoy to which his ship had been tied. But as he approached the *Sophia* he saw that the crew had abandoned the attempt and was raising the lifeboat. He manoeuvred the *Estebeth* close to the stranded ship and called across to Captain Locke, who asked him to stand by and wait until the wind moderated, at which time another attempt would be made to off-load passengers. Davis noted in his log: 'He will be lucky if the damn wind don't come up. He says he is secure on top of the rock.'[46] At the same time Captain Stidham, cruising around the reef on the *Peterson*, saw passengers lined up on deck, many clutching suitcases. There had been people on deck all through the day, but now, in the late afternoon, there were many more, and it looked as if they were preparing to leave. Stidham also assumed that Locke was intending to abandon ship.[47]

If Locke had ordered an evacuation based on the hope that the afternoon high tide would permit the boats to be launched, and that the winds would continue to drop, he was disappointed. As the captains watched and waited, the storm increased in intensity. Those passengers who had been on deck went below, and by 5.00 only a few stragglers remained.[48]

In fact, the afternoon high tide posed a serious threat. If it were to float the *Sophia* free of the reef in the increasing wind, there could be sudden disaster. Fortunately, though the high tide did move the ship somewhat, it did not shift her dangerously; as one report put it, '*Sophia*'s stern lifting with sea but does not seem to be pounding very hard.' Locke and his officers, who had paced the deck as the tide rose, now retired to the pilot-house, removed their greatcoats, and relaxed with a smoke. An observer noted that 'they seemed to be quite well satisfied.'[49]

Locke's belief that the *Princess Sophia* was safe showed in his concern for his would-be rescuers, particularly the small vessels–the *Amy* and the *Estebeth*–which were taking an increasingly severe pounding in the rising swell. Through a megaphone Locke called to the *Estebeth*: 'We are perfectly safe; you better go into harbour until morning.'[50] A similar message was passed to the *Amy*. Reassured by Locke's confidence, and aware of their own vulnerability to the increasing force of the north wind, Captains Davis and McDougall obeyed, and headed for shelter. Davis took the *Estebeth* to anchor at Mab Island, from where he could still see the *Princess Sophia*.[51] McDougall and his men, having left their home port without food or supplies, were by now cold and ravenously hungry. Assured that there was little more they could do, McDougall headed back to Juneau.[52]

Standing by at Juneau, Frank Lowle was delighted to hear that Captain Locke saw no real danger in the *Sophia*'s predicament. He had done what he could to help the ship, and now he could plan to take care of the passengers on their arrival in Juneau. He made sure that either he or his assistant, Smeaton, was never far from the telegraph office in case new information came in. All through the afternoon of 24 October Lowle raced about town, visiting all the hotels and boarding houses, trying to secure suitable lodging for the passengers. Rooms were at a premium in Juneau, for the town, like Skagway, was crowded with people travelling south. The Zynda and Alaskan Hotels were already full. Lowle did find room for 80 at the Gastineau, 25 at the Bergman, 30 at the Occidental, 50 at the Circle City and 35 at the Orpheum. But 220 beds were not enough; he needed nearly 130 more. Lowle then turned to boarding houses and private homes. He sent news of his arrangements to Captain Locke and asked him to draw up a list assigning passengers to the rooms–reserving the best ones, of course, for the first-class ticket holders.[53]

Locke passed this task on to a purser and continued to plan for the rescue. At 6.20 pm the *King and Winge* arrived. Heavy seas from the northwest had slowed her from her usual speed of 8 miles per hour to 5. As her captain, James Miller, did not have a wireless he could not contact Locke. Instead he circled the reef, hoping the presence of his vessel 'would give a certain amount of comfort and assurance to the passengers on board'.[54]

Two more boats arrived at about the same time. The *Excursion* and the *Elsinore*, both cannery tenders, got to the reef between 6.00 and 7.00 p.m. and steamed around it for several hours until, realizing they could be of little help until a proper rescue effort was mounted, they finally retreated to the safety of Bridget Cove for the night.[55]

The *Peterson*, which had been on the scene since early morning, continued to circle the stranded ship until 8.00 p.m. Then, coming close to the *Sophia*, Captain Stidham had one of his crew ask Locke through a megaphone if he wanted them to stay through the night. Locke asked him to stay close until a steamer–the *Cedar*–arrived on the scene. Shortly afterwards the *Cedar* arrived, and Stidham left for anchorage at Shelter Island.[56]

By then it had been pitch dark for several hours.[57] Captain Leadbetter took the *Cedar* as near to the reef as he dared, closing to within 200 yards. He turned his searchlights on the *Sophia* and assessed the situation. Learning from Locke over the wireless that nothing was planned for the evening, and receiving Locke's permission to leave, he took the *Cedar* to the west shore of Sentinel Island, but failed to secure an anchorage there. He then moved on to the Sentinel Island lighthouse where, protected by Benjamin Island from the force of the wind, he anchored for the night.[58]

Those aboard the *Princess Sophia* viewed the departure of all vessels except the *King and Winge* with mixed feelings. It was reassuring to know that Captain Locke considered the situation sufficiently stable to permit the others to leave. But the sight of them circling the reef and bobbing at anchor in its lee had added a measure of comfort. Now all but one had gone, leaving the *Sophia* to pass the cold and windy night almost alone. On board, the ship John Pugh, the Juneau Customs Collector, wired his wife: 'High and dry on Vanderbilt Reef; perfectly safe and happy.'[59] His message expressed more optimism than most on board felt, for the waves continued to strike the *Sophia*'s hull, causing it to groan as it moved over the reef. Shortly after 8.00 p.m. Locke sent a coded message to Troup in Victoria that spoke more directly to the danger: 'Ship sitting firmly on reef, unable to transfer passengers on account strong N.W. sea pounding heavily; cannot get off without assistance salvage gear.'[60]

Suddenly, at 8:30, the *Sophia*'s lights went out and the ship lay in complete darkness. The men aboard the *King and Winge*, assuming that the worst had happened,

> prepared for an emergency rescue: Thinking of no explanation for this except that the ship was taking on water and that the fire room had been abandoned, we feared that this was the beginning of the end and accordingly crept up even closer than we were and redoubled the vigilance of the look-out for anything which might come our way from the wreck.[61]

Locke wired to the other vessels that a steam pipe had broken, causing a failure of the electrical system.[62] Then a handful of feeble lights began to gleam, first in one place, then in another–flickering lanterns that showed the watchers on the *King and Winge* that the *Sophia* was still on the reef.[63]

In Victoria, Captain Troup fumed until 4.30 p.m., when a message from Juneau informed him that the *Princess Sophia* was in no immediate danger of sinking. Reassured that unless there was another catastrophe the passengers would be able to leave the ship in safety as soon as the weather improved, Troup began to arrange for their passage. He sent several messages to Lowle in Juneau, trying to discover what rescue measures had already been taken, and whether the passengers could be taken off in the forty-eight hours before the *Princess Alice*, a Canadian Pacific steamer in service between Vancouver and Victoria, could arrive. At the same time, he arranged for the salvage of the *Sophia*. He contacted Captain Logan, an agent of Lloyds of London, one of her insurers, and arranged to have him accompany the Canadian Pacific's salvage vessel *Tees* to Vanderbilt Reef.[64]

All that day Troup did what he could to facilitate the rescue and salvage operations, but his task was complicated by poor communications from the north. He kept sending messages to Lowle in Juneau and Locke on board the *Sophia*, but for hours he had no reply. At 11.00 p.m. the *Princess Alice* left Vancouver, disrupting the Vancouver-Victoria service,[65] and at midnight the *Tees* also left Vancouver, heading for Ladysmith on Vancouver Island for coal and other supplies. As the *Tees* left port, Troup finally received a message from Locke, asking him to ship salvage gear to the reef, thus reassuring him that his preparations had been in order;[66] Locke did not know that the *Tees* and *Princess Alice* were already on their way north.

By midnight on Thursday, 24 October, the *Sophia* had been stranded for nearly twenty-four hours. Troup in Victoria and Lowle in Juneau had done all they could to help. Rescue vessels were on the scene, and a salvage boat and large passenger ship were on their way. Preparations had been made to receive passengers and crew in Juneau. Late in the day, the wireless stations along the coast had finally been persuaded to give priority to messages concerning the *Sophia*; this promised to alleviate the confusion that had plagued rescue efforts since the beginning. At the same time, the Standard Oil tanker *Atlas* arrived in Juneau. Lowle wired Locke, asking if he wanted her sent to his aid. Locke asked that the *Atlas* join the rescue flotilla, adding that an attempt would be made at the next high tide–early on the morning of the 25th–to take the passengers off.[67]

After that, it was a matter of waiting. Lowle and his assistant Smeaton camped in their Juneau office, sleeping in shifts through the night, making sure that one of them would be near the wireless at all times in case conditions on the *Sophia* should change. Troup in Victoria stayed close to a telephone. The crews of the rescue ships–*Amy*, *Estebeth*, *Cedar*, *Peterson*, *King and Winge*, *Lone Fisherman*, *Elsinore*, and *Excursion*, and the two steaming north from Vancouver, the *Tees* and *Princess Alice*–all maintained a state of watchful readiness.

Locked in the grip of Vanderbilt Reef, battered by the rising seas and the bitterly cold north wind, their hopes raised by the sight of rescue crews only a short distance away, but undermined by the constant grinding of the ship's hull as it moved on the reef, the passengers and crew of the *Princess Sophia* waited: some slept, some prayed, some wrote letters to their loved ones, some comforted their children. For them, the wait was the longest.

5. The Sinking of the *Princess Sophia*

In the early hours of Friday, 25 October, the north wind howled relentlessly down the Chilkoot Pass, along Lynn Canal, and over Vanderbilt Reef and the ship it had captured. The *Princess Sophia,* though firmly stuck for more than a day, moved with the waves that pounded against it. The grinding of her plates on the reef added to the passengers' apprehension. Because of the power failure, the darkness was total, except for the occasional lantern that marked the preparations being made for the rescue attempt. Captain Locke directed the crew to give out life-jackets, assign passengers to lifeboats, and explain the rescue procedure. Nearby the *King and Winge* had stood watch all night, its engines turning steadily. It had no wireless, so it was unable to maintain contact with the stranded vessel. But its captain, J.J. Miller, felt that at least one ship should stay near the *Sophia* in case of a sudden emergency.[1]

A few miles away, the men aboard the *Cedar*, tossing lightly in the lee of Benjamin Island, prepared for their part in the impending drama. Their plan was simple. The next high tide, due at about 5.00 a.m., would cover Vanderbilt Reef with several feet of water. If the wind abated sufficiently, the *Sophia*'s lifeboats could be lowered and the passengers transferred to safety. There were enough vessels in the vicinity to take all the passengers and crew, and Lowle had arranged for their reception at Juneau. Still, there was nothing routine in taking over 350 people off a stranded ship, particularly in total darkness.

The rescue effort began at 4.00 a.m. Aboard the *Cedar*, Captain Leadbetter weighed anchor and steamed slowly up the channel, bucking intermittent squalls of wet snow and a strong northwest wind that was increasing at times to a moderate gale. The trip took about half an hour. At 4.35 the *Cedar* approached the *Princess Sophia* and the *King and Winge*, which still hovered nearby.

When Leadbetter ordered the *Cedar*'s spotlights turned on the *Sophia*,[2] the sight was disquieting. The ship hung like a faint image in the snow-filled darkness, the spotlights partially breaking through the snow and spray to reveal details of her structure. Despite the tide, now almost at its peak, she was still helplessly stranded. Her bow was completely out of the water; Leadbetter claimed that he could almost see her keel. The ship was facing south by east, which meant that the wind, now increasing to gale force, was striking her between midship and stern.[3] Nearby, on the *King and Winge*, Captain Miller noted that the *Sophia* was lying 'just as she would be in dry-dock, not a particle of list on'.[4]

Leadbetter soon realized that the rescue attempt would have to be postponed. He circled the *Princess Sophia* several times, taking comfort in the fact that there at least seemed to be no sign of damage. But as the north wind continued to rise, dashing breakers against her hull, Leadbetter, Miller, and Locke all agreed that the planned evacuation was too dangerous, and that though the passengers' position was precarious, they were safer aboard the *Sophia* than they would be in the lifeboats. Leadbetter wired Frank Lowle in Juneau to say that nothing could be attempted until at least dawn.[5]

Daylight came slowly on Friday, 25 October, the weak sun of

late autumn penetrating with difficulty through the blowing snow and heavy clouds that hung over Lynn Canal; the north wind showed no sign of abating. By 8.00 a.m. the *Sophia*'s crew had fixed the broken steam pipe and restored electrical power. Captain Locke immediately established radio contact with Leadbetter. The first message he received was from Captain Troup in Victoria. Sent at 9.00 the previous morning, it had been stalled along the line before being passed on to E.M. Miller, wireless operator aboard the *Cedar*. Troup had asked, 'Do you think she will back off at next high water?'–an ironic question, given the long night the ship had just passed on the reef.[6]

Leadbetter, Miller, and the other captains anxiously awaited news of the *Sophia*'s condition. The news from Locke was bad, but not as serious as had been feared. Water had entered the forward compartment, but the engine room, fire room, and afterhold remained dry. The exact extent of damage remained unknown, although the limited flooding suggested that the hull was not badly torn.

As he circled the reef, Leadbetter noticed that Locke had again ordered the lifeboats swung out on their davits in anticipation of the rescue attempt. Several of the crew were loading small parcels into them; Leadbetter assumed they were provisions placed there in case of a forced evacuation. The lifeboat covers were still on, in deference to the snow that continued to swirl about the ship.[7] The boats dangled invitingly, seeming to offer safety and freedom to the few passengers who braved the wind to stand on deck. But the hope was false. Below them the breakers crashed over the sharp rocks of Vanderbilt Reef, promising almost certain disaster if they were lowered.

As dawn broke, the passengers aboard the *Princess Sophia* tried hard to keep their spirits up and establish some semblance of normality. The hours dragged on, the sense of danger waxing and waning with the wind. The repeated false starts–Locke's confident assertions that the next high tide would provide the opportunity for escape–added to the tension fueled by mixed fatalism, frustration, anger, and hope. The cold wind and driving snow kept most of them indoors, but from time to time the waiting rescuers saw a couple venture out on deck and, arm in arm, make their way around the ship. For the watchers, the scene was filled with pathos–endearment contrasting with imminent peril.

While they waited, some of the passengers wrote letters to friends and relatives, mostly messages of hope rather than despair. Auris McQueen wrote to his 'Mama':

> It's storming now, about a 50-mile wind and we can only see a couple of hundred yards on account of the snow and spray. . . . [S]he is now . . . on the rock clear back to the middle and we can't get off. She is a double-bottom boat and her inner hull is not penetrated, so here we stick. She pounds some on a rising tide and it is slow writing, but our only inconvenience is, so far, lack of water . . . I reckon we will be quarantined as there are six cases of influenza aboard. The decks are all dry, and this wreck has all the markings of a movie stage setting. All we lack is the hero and the vampire. I am going to quit and see if I can rustle a bucket and a line to get some sea water to wash in. We are mightly lucky we were not all buried in the sea water.[8]

The flurry of activity in the waters surrounding the *Sophia* no doubt brought some reassurance to her passengers. Early that morning, the *Sitka*, a small halibut fishing boat, arrived at the scene, and like the others began to circle the reef.[9] Other vessels were kept away by the foul weather. The *Estebeth*, *Peterson*,[10] and *Lone Fisherman*[11] had gone to anchor the previous evening, and now found conditions in the channel too rough to leave their shelters.[12]

Ominously, by mid-morning the wind, already strong, was picking up and shifting to the northwest, so that it struck the *Sophia*'s stern more directly. Soon it was blowing a full gale. The *Cedar*, which had arrived as planned before dawn, was having increasing difficulty maintaining her position near the reef. About 9.00 a.m. Captain Leadbetter moved to the lee of the reef and attempted to find anchor about 500 yards downwind of the *Sophia*. He hoped to run a line to the stranded ship and use it to transfer passengers to safety by way of a breeches buoy. But the effort failed. Twice he cast anchor, and twice it would not hold. He remained at the mercy of the wind.

Watching the *Cedar*'s struggle, Captain Locke realized that the rescue attempt would have to be postponed once more. At 10 a.m. he wired Leadbetter, 'No use, too rough, wait until low water.' Leadbetter replied, 'I cannot make anchors hold, could not row boat to you at present, believe your passengers are perfectly safe until wind moderates, will stand by until safe to make transfer.'[13] Although conditions were getting worse rather than better, the two men believed–they had no other choice–that the passengers were better off aboard the *Princess Sophia* than risking a dangerous transfer across the reef. At 11.30 a.m. Leadbetter wired the decision to Juneau: '*Sophia* resting even keel on high part Vanderbilt Reef, blowing strong northwest wind, will transfer passengers as soon as possible to *Cedar*.'[14]

It was around the same time that E.P. Pond, the photographer on board the *King and Winge*, took his dramatic photographs of the *Princess Sophia* sitting on Vanderbilt Reef.[15] Though badly seasick, Pond managed to capture the helplessness of the ship's situation and the danger she was in. The photos show a heavy swell, and the smoke cutting abruptly off at the ship's funnel indicates the force of the wind.[16] The ship is perfectly level and looks at first glance as though she is steaming safely towards Juneau, but the sharp peak of Vanderbilt Reef just forward of the bow reveals her true situation.

Leadbetter's progress report was only one of many messages exchanged between Juneau and the rescue scene that Friday. With the *Cedar* to relay messages, Frank Lowle in Juneau was able to get regular reports on the condition of the *Sophia*, a welcome change from the confusion of the previous day.[17] For Captain Troup, isolated in his Victoria office, the communication problem eased more slowly. On Thursday the 24th he had ordered Lowle to 'send all possible assistance to *Sophia*'. Lowle had done so, but he did not receive the message until 7.50 the next morning.[18] The tangle in communications up the west coast had all but cut Juneau off from the south, and messages continued to flow in both directions at a frustratingly slow pace.

Early on the morning of the 25th, Lowle received a first-hand report on conditions at Vanderbilt Reef. The *Amy*, its crew without water or food for twenty-eight hours, arrived in Juneau harbour at 7.00 a.m. She had left the *Princess Sophia* the previous evening, had anchored for several hours at Tee Harbour, and had then pushed on to Juneau. Edward McDougall, master of the *Amy*, passed his log on to Frank Lowle, provided a short description of events, and departed in search of a long-overdue meal.[19]

In Juneau Lowle did what he could to help the stricken ship.[20] For the most part he accepted the optimistic forecasts he received from Locke, Leadbetter, McDougall, and others that the *Sophia*'s passengers would soon be removed, probably on Friday afternoon. With that in mind he continued his preparations for their arrival, arranging to have the water, heat, and light in Juneau's abandoned Orpheum building connected and laying on a hot meal for them.[21]

Meanwhile, Captain Troup in Victoria was becoming increasingly frustrated. For a man of action, the lack of precise information and the impossibility of influencing events was maddening. He sent several messages, each one more abrupt, demanding that Lowle let him know the condition of the *Sophia*. On Friday morning he telegraphed: 'You have not replied to my wires. Please make every effort to get suitable boats to *Sophia* for transferring passengers moment it is safe.'[22] Cut off from events in Juneau, and receiving no answer to his enquiries, Troup thought that Lowle might be in Skagway, where he regularly travelled on official business, leaving no one in charge of the necessary preparations in Juneau. He thus wired John Pugh, the US Collector of Customs in Juneau, asking for the assistance of United States ships.[23] His message was answered by an assistant, for Pugh was on board the *Princess Sophia*. The first message from Lowle to Troup did not arrive in Victoria until 12.29 p.m. on the 25th, more than twenty-seven hours after it had been sent. It bore the news that evacuation plans were in place, and asked if tranportation could be arranged to bring the passengers south from Juneau after the expected rescue.[24] Troup would rather have learned that the danger had passed and all aboard were safe in Juneau; however, it was encouraging to know that something was being done.

Many along the coast shared Troup's desire for more information. On the morning of 25 October the regional papers carried the first news of the accident. 'Passengers Still on Board' read a page-one headline in the Vancouver *Daily Province*, with a sub-head noting 'Wind in Lynn Canal Prevents Transfer from the *Princess Sophia*'. The story conveyed little of the drama and no sense of the impending tragedy, ending with the comment that the *Sophia* was 'resting easily as far as can be gathered, and there is no danger to the passengers unless the weather becomes worse'. In the article, Captain Troup attempted to soothe worried friends and relatives: 'The passengers are our first consideration, and we have done everything in our power to relieve them, even to the extent of disorganizing our gulf service.'[25] Most newspapers in the coastal towns repeated the optimistic predictions of an early rescue.[26]

Aboard the *Sophia* many of the passengers and crew, realizing that word of the accident must have spread along the Pacific coast and farther, tried to reassure their friends and relatives that rescue was imminent. David Robinson, the wireless operator, telegraphed his mother in East Vancouver, 'Still ashore, all well.' He then passed on the same report for Charlie Beadle, a purser, and for second officer Frank Gosse, third officer Arthur Murphy, and one or two others. There was no time on the wireless for the passengers' messages, and with the exception of Customs Collector Pugh, no one other than the crew was able to send word out. It mattered little, for none of these reports reached its destination.

David Robinson had his hands full with messages to and from Captain Locke. Because of power outages and problems with the storage batteries, the *Princess Sophia* did not communicate directly with the outside world. Robinson sent his messages the short distance to Elwood Miller, wireless operator on the *Cedar*, who then relayed them to Juneau or to Victoria, often by way of other ships. For instance, at 1.00 on Friday afternoon Miller wired a message from Captain Locke to Troup in Victoria, telling him that the ship's bottom was 'badly damaged but not [t]aking water. Unable to back off reef; main steam pipe broken.'[27] At the same time he forwarded a message to Lowle in Juneau: the Captain of the *Sophia* 'cannot do anything until the weather moderates. *Cedar* and *King and Winge* standing by. How is weather at Juneau?' The message reached the *Cedar* at 1.00, was relayed to the *Atlas* at 4:45, and finally arrived in Lowle's hands at 7:30 that night.[28]

But in the end none of this helped. The weather did not improve. Some time before noon the barometer began to drop, and the wind, already strong, blew even harder. Some later estimates put it at 100 miles per hour; by the next morning, the barometer at Sitka had dropped to 28.92 inches-proof of a major storm.[29] Captain Leadbetter, worried about the safety of the *Cedar*, saw that he could be of little use to the passengers of the *Sophia*, and asked Locke if he could withdraw to anchor behind Sentinel Island.[30] He promised to return to Vanderbilt Reef later in the day if the weather improved and again stand by during the night. Locke agreed and said he would call at 4.30 p.m. The *Cedar* then ran for shelter, reaching anchorage at 1.45 p.m.

For Robinson and Miller, the wireless operators on the *Princess Sophia* and *Cedar* respectively, the break was a chance for some much-needed rest. Robinson had been battling with power problems on the *Sophia* and struggling to maintain contact with the rescue ships. Both men had been at their posts for nearly forty hours. They agreed to break off contact until 4.30. Robinson returned to work on his batteries. Miller lay down with his headphones on, but could not sleep. After half an hour he tried unsuccessfully to establish contact with the *Sophia*, and then began to pass a backlog of messages via the *Atlas* to Juneau.[31]

Captain J.J. Miller of the *King and Winge* followed the *Cedar* to anchor and safety. He brought his ship alongside her and shouted up to Leadbetter for instructions. Leadbetter told him that Locke had postponed the transfer of passengers until the weather improved.[32] Later in the afternoon, Captain Miller crossed to the *Cedar* in a dory to discuss the rescue plans with Leadbetter. The two agreed that it was safer to leave the passengers on board the *Sophia* than to risk their lives attempting a rescue in such foul weather. In more than a day on the reef the ship had shifted hardly at all, and they believed that even in the worsening storm it was not likely to shift much more. As J.J. Miller later testified,

> she had stayed on all the morning, which was a higher tide than the afternoon, and she had never moved on the reef, according to the message that the captain of the Cedar had received. As she hadn't moved with the higher tide at that time, I didn't figure she would

pound off with the smaller tide, unless the sea would get some enormous hold of her.[33]

On the *Cedar* Leadbetter and Miller laid new plans for the evacuation. As the *Cedar*'s anchor had failed to hold after several attempts, it was agreed that the *King and Winge*, carrying a 350-fathom cable, would anchor to the northwest of the *Sophia*. The cable would be slowly let out until the *King and Winge* got as close as was safely possible to the stranded ship. A line would be run between the two vessels while the *Cedar* stood off to windward, making a lee for the lifeboats. The passengers would be lowered into the *Cedar*'s waiting lifeboats–the *Sophia*'s boats would not be needed–and then be transferred, through the relative calm created by the *Cedar*'s windbreak, to the waiting *King and Winge*. The plan seemed workable, but it required a moderation of the weather.[34]

Through the afternoon everyone waited and watched the skies. Lowle in Juneau and, particularly, Troup in Victoria still had problems getting up-to-date information. Lowle continued his preparations for welcoming the passengers. He contacted the CPR agent in Skagway, Lewis Johnston, asking for a breakdown of first- and second-class passengers, assuring him at the same time that although the seas were too high to remove them, ships were standing by: 'everybody happy'.[35] Not far from Lowle's office, however, there were those who knew better. The oil tanker *Atlas* left Juneau harbour and retreated to Taku Inlet, a safer sanctuary in a really bad storm. This augured ill for those aboard the *Princess Sophia*.

For Captains Miller and Leadbetter, the darkening skies and gusting winds meant that the rescue would have to wait until the next morning. Around dusk Miller prepared to return to the *King and Winge*. Just as he climbed into his dory, he heard the clatter of *Cedar*'s wireless. Knowing that Robinson on the *Sophia* had agreed to call the *Cedar* twenty minutes earlier, he assumed that all was well and, without waiting to hear the latest news, continued back to his vessel. His assumption was wrong.

It was 4.50 on the afternoon of Friday, 25 October. 'Ship Foundering on Reef. Come at Once.' The message from Robinson spelled out the impending disaster briefly and dramatically.

Elwood Miller scrawled the message on his note pad and passed it to Captain Leadbetter, who immediately prepared to steam to the reef. Miller wired the *Atlas* and asked her to join the rescue, then re-established contact with Robinson on the *Sophia*.[36]

On the *King and Winge*, Captain Miller, just back aboard, heard two whistles from the *Cedar*, indicating that the ship had weighed anchor. Unsure of what Leadbetter was up to, Miller went below for a quick meal, confident that the *Cedar*'s captain would let him know if there was an urgent problem.

Aboard the *Cedar*, wireless operator Miller waited anxiously for further word from the *Princess Sophia*. Nothing came for half an hour. Suddenly, at 5.20 p.m., the static broke with a horrifying message: 'For God's sake hurry,' David Robinson pleaded, 'the water is coming in my room.' There was more, but Miller could not follow it. He told Robinson to conserve his meagre battery power, and to come back on air only if absolutely necessary. 'Alright I will,' Robinson replied, adding anxiously, 'you talk to me so I know you are coming.'[37] That desperate plea for reassurance was the last word heard from the *Princess Sophia*.

Meanwhile, Captain Leadbetter took his ship alongside the *King and Winge* and shouted over the storm to Captain Miller: 'I am going out there to try and locate him. If the snow should clear up, you come out and relieve me.' Miller responded, 'I will give you an hour to find him.' With this understanding and, in the face of a worsening storm, considerable trepidation, Leadbetter ordered his ship out of its shelter behind the island and into the full force of the northwesterly gale.[38]

It was a brave but hopeless effort. As soon as the *Cedar* emerged from its shelter it was battered by heavy seas and snow that blew almost horizontally across the water. Leadbetter knew that his ship was within 500 yards of the Sentinel Island lighthouse, but in the whiteout and the screaming wind he could neither see the light nor hear the blast of the foghorn. For thirty minutes he battled with the weather, pushing very slowly northwards towards Vanderbilt Reef. The farther he went, the greater his danger, since he had only a rough idea of his actual position. Finally, and with great reluctance, he had to admit that the effort was in vain. He wired the *Atlas*: 'We can't do a thing now–thick weather, heavy sea running and gale. Can't even see the *Sophia* or get out boats to her. Will have to stand by until weather clears.'[39]

Now Leadbetter's main concern was the safety of his own ship. Captain Dibrell, the Lighthouse Inspector for that part of the coast, was on board, and advised him either to steam north to Port Hilda or to try and return to his safe anchorage. Leadbetter chose the latter option, though neither was a particularly safe bet. Navigating more by intuition than observation, he headed south again, sounding his whistle repeatedly in an attempt to locate his position. Eventually J.J. Miller on the *King and Winge*, still at anchor behind the island, heard the whistle and responded repeatedly with his own, guiding the *Cedar* back to safety. The storm and darkness were such that Leadbetter took his ship to within 20 feet of Miller's before he saw her.[40] As he told Miller, 'I was in danger of losing my boat and crew out there tonight.' Much as they hated to do so, they were forced to admit defeat and wait for better weather before renewing the rescue attempt.[41] He wrote in his log: 'terrific seas were running together with a blinding snow storm. Made it impossible to see our bow. Green seas were continually breaking over bow of *Cedar*.'[42]

The two ships rested safe at anchor, their captains desperate to learn the fate of the *Princess Sophia*. Frustrated by his inability to act, Leadbetter wired the *Atlas*: 'Attempted to reach *Sophia* five p.m. blinding snow storm, could not make her. Will advise you soon as weather permits. Blowing a gale and snow.'[43] Others in the area, though unaware of the present emergency on the *Sophia*, feared for the safety of those aboard her. J.P. Davis, master of the *Estebeth*, had passed much of the day circling Vanderbilt Reef, but, like the others, he had headed for shelter as conditions deteriorated. After dragging anchor several times behind Mab Island, he decided to retire further to the safety of Bridget Cove for the evening. At 7.00 p.m. he recorded that a heavy blizzard had descended on the region, obscuring all vision and making navigation all but impossible. He noted in his log book, 'God help those aboard the wreck.'[44] But by that time it was too late.

Among the *Sophia*'s passengers the tension had mounted throughout the morning and afternoon.[45] The repeated delays in the rescue effort, the increasing wind and snow, and the disappearance of their rescuers to shelter added to their anxiety. They were not poised by the lifeboats, however, nor did all of them have life-jackets on. It was obvious that rescue would be delayed, and since all aboard believed that the ship was secure on the reef, there was no sense of acute peril.

A few minutes before 4.50 p.m., when Robinson wired his first desperate message to the *Cedar*, the final disaster struck. For nearly forty hours the *Princess Sophia* had sat firmly wedged on Vanderbilt Reef, her stern pointing approximately north into the wind and her bow in the general direction of Juneau. Now the wind and waves began to lift the stern off the reef. Under their force the *Sophia* rose, then swung slowly around in a 180-degree turn, as if on a pivot. The weight of the ship as it turned ground the rocks beneath it 'white . . . as smooth as a silver dollar'.[46] Now her bow faced up the channel, into the storm, and the *Princess Sophia* began inexorably to move off the reef into deep water. As she began to turn, passengers and crew ran to the lifeboats. Several were launched, others partly lowered, and a number of passengers clambered into them.

Slowly the *Sophia* turned and then, twisting and grinding, slid backwards off the reef. The rocks ripped gaping holes in her hull, tearing out virtually the entire bottom. Heavy bunker oil poured into the sea and frigid water rushed in, flooding the engine and boiler rooms. The boilers exploded, devastating the lower decks. A number of passengers who had sheltered from the storm below decks were killed by the explosion and the flying debris.[47] Portholes were shattered, allowing the sea to enter even faster. The explosion pushed upwards as well, blowing off part of the deck.[48] As the ship settled and began to slide beneath the waves, the wounds in her hull releasing thousands of gallons of oil into the sea, the dark, cold waters of Lynn Canal reached up to claim their victims. In a matter of minutes–just long enough for Robinson to send his last, panicked message–the water had reached the pilot house. And then the entire ship was engulfed.

The exact sequence of events aboard the *Princess Sophia* that dark afternoon will never be precisely known. Some of the passengers and crew were dressed for an evacuation, and many were wearing life-jackets. Others, however, were in their cabins, some even in bed. Clearly Captain Locke had not called a general alert, and there was no planned abandonment of ship underway at the time she sank. The uneven preparation shows how quickly the final crisis had developed.

Many of the passengers were caught unawares. Ilene Winchell had remained in her stateroom with Sarah O'Brien, but some of her belongings were scattered about the ship: her pocketbook was found in a man's coat and–here was the stuff to titillate rumour-mongers–her baggage was found in another man's room.[49] The rest of the O'Brien family were separated in the chaos.[50] Louise Davis was trapped between the saloon and the social hall. W. Lidgett, second cook on the WP&YR steamer *Yukon*, grabbed 4-year-old Sidney Smith and in a desperate attempt to save the child from the rising water, hoisted him onto his shoulders. They died together. Some parents tied their children with lengths of rope to the additional 'flotation devices' that had been provided. The children either drowned or suffocated.

Many seemed entirely unprepared. Several children were found carefully tucked in their beds. Five people, perhaps confused by the noise and tumult, were found in the washrooms, fully dressed.[51] In all there were almost a hundred people trapped below decks. The reason is not easy to ascertain. There was, after all, half an hour between the first SOS, at 4.50 p.m. and Robinson's last despairing plea at 5.20. Most of the watches found on the bodies had stopped around 6.50, or 5.50 Alaska time,[52] indicating that another half hour passed between the last message at 5.20 and the time when the watches were stopped by oil and sea-water. This evidence suggests that it took as much as an hour for the *Princess Sophia* to sink: first the tide and waves gradually lifting her stern so that she bumped on the rocks, then the terrifying pivot so that her position on the reef was reversed, then the slow slide backwards. With thirty minutes, and possibly as much as an hour, to get on deck, it is difficult to understand why anyone was found in a stateroom. Perhaps the boilers exploded before the ship sank, trapping people below. It seems that Captain Locke either left the order to abandon ship until the last moment, or never gave it at all. Over the previous two days there had been several false alarms; perhaps those below deck believed the shifting of the ship's position was no cause for alarm. Yet at 4.50 it must have been evident that they were in grave trouble. It has been suggested that some people realized they were doomed, and composed themselves calmly, in their cabins, for the end–but such resignation is rare in human nature. This part of the episode is the greatest mystery of the disaster.

It is clear, however, that the majority of the passengers had feared the worst. These may have been the ones who had been seen on deck many times, ready to take to the lifeboats with or without Captain Locke's order. Those who did get off the ship were, almost without exception, wearing life preservers. Several of them had evidently made preparations in expectation of the worst. Lulu Mae Eads, the former 'Queen of the Klondike', had placed all her jewels– later valued at some $5,000–in a chamois bag and strung it around her neck.[53] Like her, most people had their valuables with them, usually in a coat pocket. Several women had dressed in overalls, abandoning fashion in favour of protection against the frigid ordeal they faced.[54] John Maskell tucked his will and some last-minute letters into his pocket; Auris McQueen carefully pocketed a letter to his mother. Yet there was no organized evacuation. Several of the lifeboats were lowered, but later examination of the davits by divers suggested that this was done in the final desperate seconds, as the *Sophia* slid from her resting place into the sea.[55]

As the ship started to sink many aboard panicked, either jumping directly into the water or scrambling into one of the few lifeboats freed from the davits. Most surely paused for at least a second to consider the odds. To stay on the ship meant certain death, but their chances in the sea were little better. Visibility in the driving snow was scarcely twenty feet, and the shrieking wind and the crash of the waves breaking against the doomed vessel emphasized their peril. All semblance of order lost, passengers and crew jostled at the rail–mothers separated from children, husbands from wives. Now, singly at first, and then in larger numbers as the *Sophia* began to slide down, people leapt off the deck. What they could not see was the bunker oil pouring from the shattered hull, covering the water with a viscous mass that already stretched many feet from the reef.

Death came quickly for most who jumped. The water was

bitterly cold. Jack London, in his most famous story, captured the essence of a plunge into the north Pacific:

> The water was cold–so cold that it was painful. The pang, as I plunged into it, was as quick and sharp as that of fire. It bit to the marrow. It was like the grip of death. I gasped with the anguish and shock of it, filling my lungs before the life-preserver popped me to the surface.[56]

This natural gasping reflex filled the mouths and lungs of the victims with oil congealed by the cold. Blown by the spray and the wind, it stuck to clothes, weighing them down. Those who may have made it into the lifeboats were no better off, for as the captains of the rescue ships had predicted, the boats were immediately swamped on the reef, throwing their human cargo into the water. The two wooden lifeboats capsized and floated upside down; the eight steel ones sank. The extra flotation devices–simply hollow rectangular wooden buoys with ropes attached to them–were useless; the idea that people could cling to them until they were rescued was practical in the Caribbean, perhaps, but absurd in the Lynn Canal. One of these devices was later found smashed on the rocks of Lincoln Island with the bodies of four women tied to it.[57] Mercifully, whether by drowning or choking and suffocating on the oil, within a few minutes nearly all were dead. Some were in the steel coffin that the *Sophia* had become; others floated inert in their life-preservers, an oily mass coating their lungs, mouths, and nostrils. The howl of the storm echoed over Vanderbilt Reef. The *Princess Sophia* was gone, only a few feet of its forward mast visible above the water.

Some had behaved heroically in those last moments. James Kirk of Dawson, travelling in charge of Herb McDonald's horses, had been heading for Vancouver to consult a specialist about his eyes. A native of Wentworth in Cumberland Country, Nova Scotia, he was 50 in 1918, but apparently still a strong swimmer. During the *Sophia*'s last moments, he tied himself to a younger man, wrist-to-wrist, evidently in an attempt to save him from drowning. The newspapers later acclaimed him as 'one of the most heroic, if not the most heroic man, of the *Sophia* wreck.'[58]

And at least one man probably survived those first few moments after the ship went down. Frank Gosse, the ship's second officer, clambered into a life boat that somehow did not swamp, but made it to shore. The boat grounded, and the first rescuers on the scene claimed to have seen footprints leaving it. Gosse, they speculated, might have landed safely and, in climbing the rocks to shelter, slipped and cut his head; it was badly gashed, and he was found with his coat covering the wound. Perhaps he had lain down to wait for rescue, and died of exposure. Others claimed that no one could have made it to shore, that the footprints belonged to rescuers, and that his body had floated to shore with the rest. But if Gosse did not make it to safety, he likely came closer to doing so than anyone else.[59]

In fact, there was one survivor. An English setter–who had owned it was later hotly debated, though it likely belonged to Captain Alexander–did get to shore. Half starved and covered with oil, the dog must have swum to Tee Harbour, eight miles from the reef. From there it struggled another four miles to Auk Bay, where residents discovered it, terrified but alive, two days later.[60]

Unaware of the catastrophe, Lowle and Smeaton at Juneau persevered in planning for a rescue that would never happen. Knowing only that the weather had deteriorated, Lowle tried again to contact the *Princess Sophia* and Troup in Victoria. The same evening he received messages from both. Troup's had originated a full day earlier; the one from Locke, sent via the *Cedar*, was six and a half hours old.[61] If Lowle was out of touch with events, Troup was even more so. In the early hours of 26 October, just after midnight, he received a wire from Captain Locke: 'Steamer *Cedar* and three gas boats standing by unable to take off passengers account strong northerly gale and big sea running–ship hard and fast on the reef with bottom badly damaged but not [t]aking water. Unable to back off reef. Main steam pipe broken–disposition of passengers normal.'[62] By the time Troup received it, they were all dead.

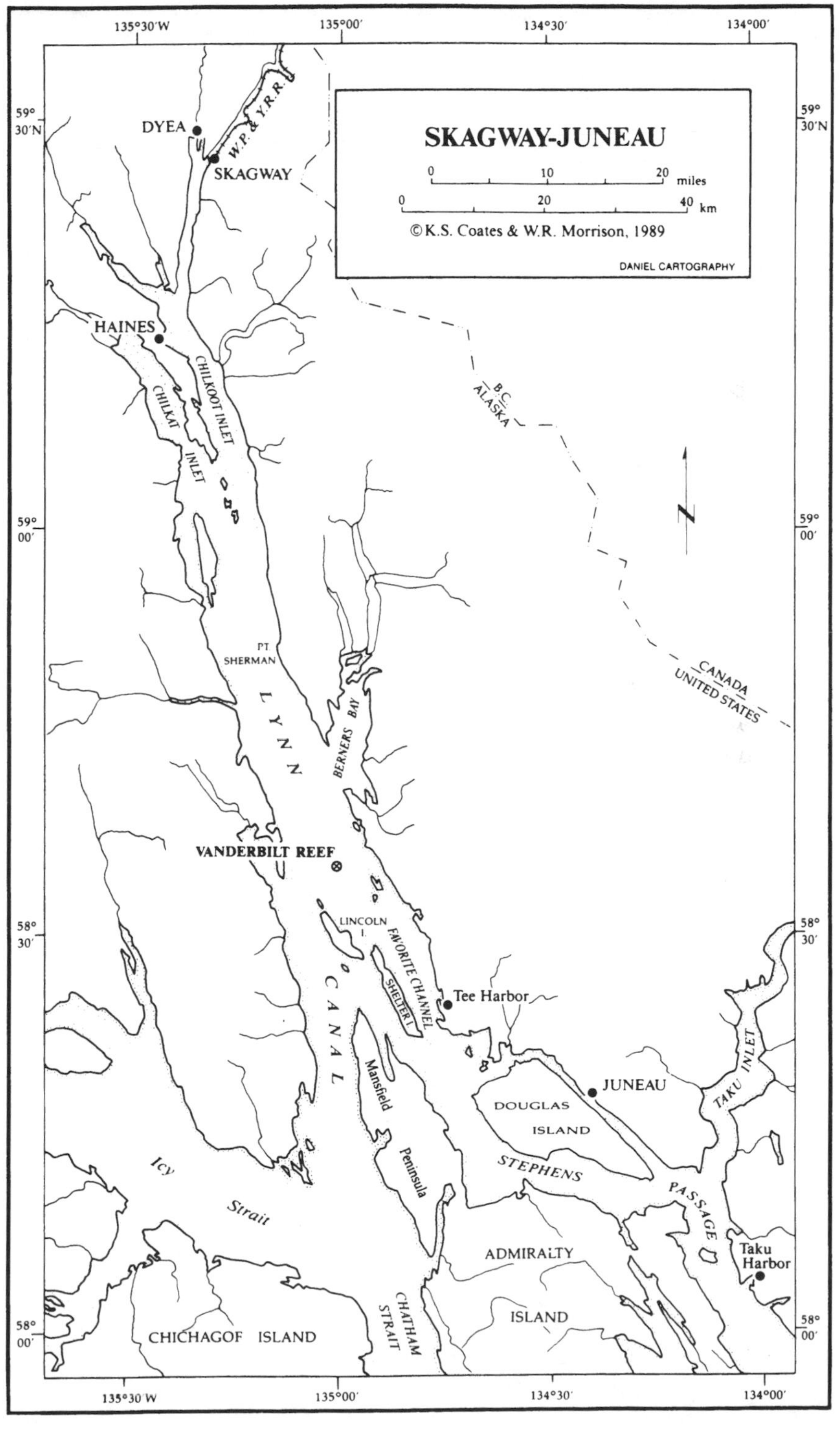
SKAGWAY-JUNEAU
0 10 20 miles
0 20 40 km
©K.S. Coates & W.R. Morrison, 1989
DANIEL CARTOGRAPHY
135°30′W
135°00′
134°30′
134°00′
59° 30′N
59° 00′
58° 30′
58° 00′
DYEA
SKAGWAY
W.P. & Y.R.R.
HAINES
CHILKOOT INLET
CHILKAT INLET
B.C.
ALASKA
CANADA
UNITED STATES
PT. SHERMAN
LYNN CANAL
BERNERS BAY
VANDERBILT REEF
LINCOLN I.
FAVORITE CHANNEL
SHELTER I.
Tee Harbor
JUNEAU
DOUGLAS ISLAND
TAKU INLET
STEPHENS PASSAGE
Mansfield Peninsula
Icy Strait
ADMIRALTY ISLAND
Taku Harbor
CHATHAM STRAIT
CHICHAGOF ISLAND

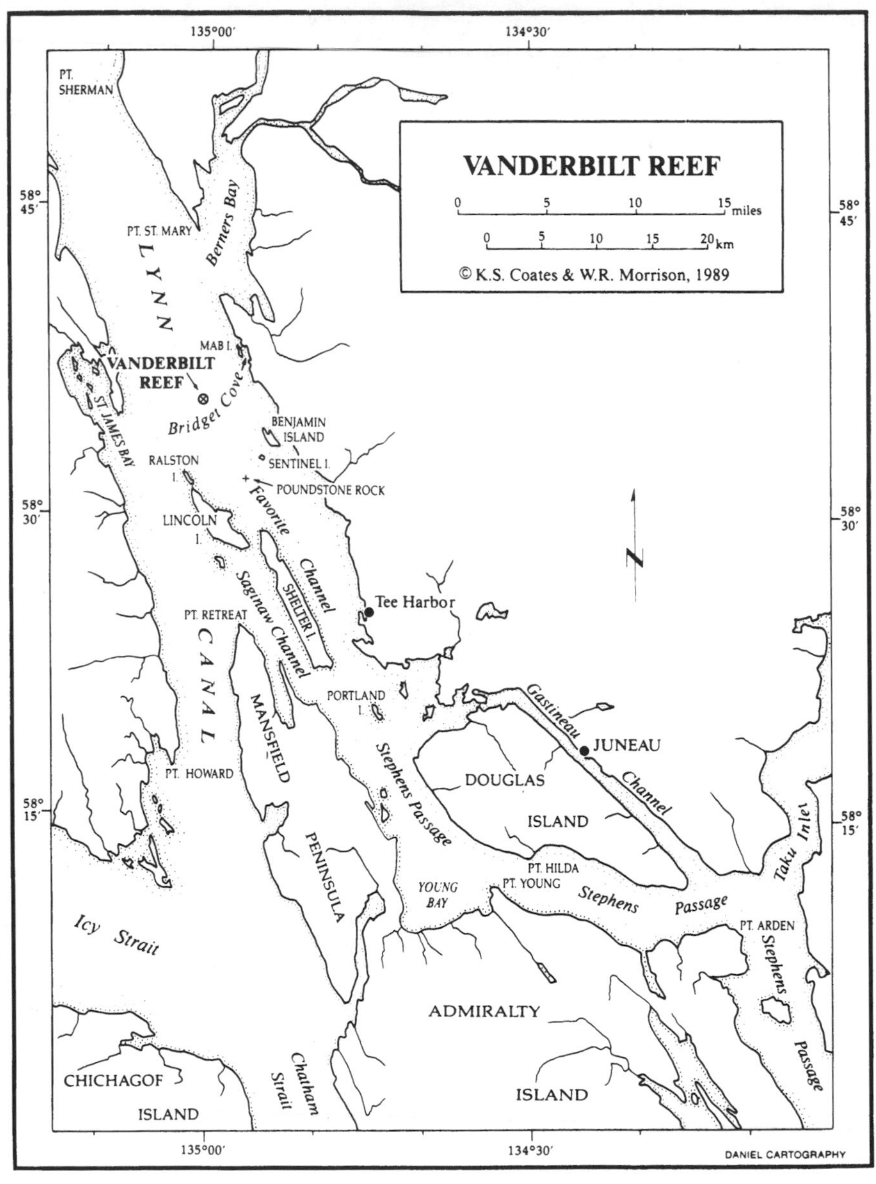

ABOVE RIGHT: *The* Princess Sophia, *built 1911, sunk 1918.*

RIGHT: *During the First World War, the* Sophia *carried troops from training camp on Vancouver Island to the mainland.*

BRITISH COLUMBIA ARCHIVES AND RECORD SERVICE HP 70213

BRITISH COLUMBIA ARCHIVES AND RECORD SERVICE HP 45735

ALASKA HISTORICAL LIBRARY, JUNEAU

ALASKA HISTORICAL LIBRARY, JUNEAU

The Sophia *aground on Vanderbilt Reef, photographed by Capt. Davis of the* Estebeth *about 11 a.m. on 24 October, facing to the northeast. The marker buoy is in the foreground.*

Twenty-four hours later the wind has risen and the sea is rougher. The ship has half a day to live.

Two postcards depicting the last trace of the Princess Sophia– *the ship's cargo mast.*

6. Finding the Victims

None of the men on the rescue boats slept much that Friday night. Though all had found shelter from the storm in the lee of islands and in the small inlets off Lynn Canal, the wind allowed them little rest as their vessels rocked and jostled in the heavy swell. Far worse than their discomfort was their concern for the crew and passengers of the *Princess Sophia*. The men of the *Cedar*, the *Estebeth*, and the *King and Winge* knew that if she had foundered there would be few survivors. They continued to hope, but as the hours passed and their wireless calls to the *Sophia* were answered with silence, they realized that the ship must have been lost.

The *Cedar* was lucky not to have shared the *Sophia*'s fate. Captain Leadbetter's foray into the snowstorm in response to the *Sophia*'s emergency call had put his vessel at serious risk; through the night he remained at anchor, waiting for the first chance to return to Vanderbilt Reef. His counterpart aboard the *Atlas*, still in Taku harbour, asked him if there was any point in going to the scene. Leadbetter's reply, transmitted by the wireless operator, was a mixture of hope and despair:

> Capt. says another vessel might be needed. We are going to try to make her as soon as light enough and may get in trouble ourselves. We are only boat out here except couple gas boats. It is a Lynn Canal blizzard blowing here now. Capt. didn't want to send you away when he couldn't get any news of Sophia.[1]

At 7.21 on Saturday morning, 26 October, Captain Leadbetter weighed anchor and headed for Vanderbilt Reef. Snow was falling heavily, but a lull in the wind had improved visibility somewhat, allowing the *Cedar* to make good speed. At 8.30 the rescuers arrived at the reef.

The sight that greeted them confirmed their worst fears. Vanderbilt Reef was bare, covered only by the waves. Off its southern end the top twenty feet of a ship's foremast protruded from the water. There was no sign of life or of wreckage. Leadbetter sent a message to the *Atlas* with the first news of the catastrophe to reach the outside:

> Guess it's all over. We made out the Sophia which has slid off and only mast showing. Rough sea breaking over reef, and gale and thick snow. Unable to get close so far. Looks like she must have broken in the middle as there is only one mast showing. Pretty hard time finding our way now.[2]

The *Cedar*'s wireless officer, Elwood Miller, then sent the terrible message on to the Customs Office in Juneau, where Lowle and others had been standing by for hours, and to the lighthouse office in Ketchikan; from there it was quickly passed up and down the coast. Leadbetter ordered the *Cedar*'s steam whistle blown as a signal to the other craft lying to nearby. In response to its scream, distorted and partly muffled by wind and snow,[3] slowly the other ships came from their shelters and gathered at the reef.

At least one of the captains already knew what had happened. Captain J.P. Davis had anchored the *Estebeth* in the lee of Mab Island. At first light, when visibility improved, he walked across the small island to see how the *Sophia* had weathered the storm. Looking over the two miles of open water to Vanderbilt Reef, he saw only a mast above the waters of the canal. He quickly returned to his ship, and was already heading for the reef when he heard the *Cedar*'s whistle.[4] The *King and Winge* was also en route to the reef when the whistle sounded. The vessel had difficulty bucking the swell and the wind, taking over an hour to make the four-mile journey from her refuge at Sentinel Island. The men aboard her were unprepared for the sight that greeted them at the reef. As one wrote a few days later:

> We could not bring ourselves to believe that the vessel we had seen a short time before, apparently so secure, could have met disaster . . . We were simply dumbfounded to see no sign of the Sophia, except fifteen or twenty feet of one of her masts sticking out of the water, close to the buoy. Our feelings were hardly describable. It seemed to strike us numb and cold, so that we could scarcely credit the evidence of our own eyes. It was incredible.[5]

At first the rescue crews spent little time speculating, for there was reason to hope that some had survived. The *Princess Sophia* had plenty of lifeboats, though not enough for all on board, and life rafts to make up the difference. If the crew had had time to launch them, there might well be dozens of people alive, tossing in the rough waters of Lynn Canal. The captains therefore now turned their efforts towards organizing a search. It would not be an easy task, for the shifting tides and strong winds of the previous night could have taken boats or bodies considerable distances in almost any direction, along hundreds of miles of coastline and inlets.

There was no reason to stay at Vanderbilt Reef. The foredeck mast was the only visible sign of the tragedy. A quick search revealed no bodies, no wreckage, not even an oil slick. The north wind that had torn the ship off the reef had blown away all traces of its handiwork.[6] Posting look-outs to watch for any signs of survivors, bodies, or wreckage, the two ships moved away from the reef.

That they searched for more than three hours without discovering a single victim, alive or dead, says more about the difficult conditions than about the efforts of the searchers. Snow continued to fall heavily, the wind was intermittently strong, making visibility poor at times, and the ships' captains were understandably reluctant to make much speed.

At 11.30 a.m. a look-out on the *King and Winge* made the first sighting–a lifeboat, beached and overturned on the northwest end of Shelter Island. Soon other lifeboats were found in the area. The crew lowered the ship's boats and headed for shore. A few minutes later one returned bearing the body of a woman.[7] Then more corpses were found. The *Peterson*, steaming offshore a short distance away, sighted another body in the water and sent two men in a dory to collect it.[8]

All ships in the immediate vicinity–the *Peterson*, the *King and Winge*, and the *Cedar*–congregated near the discoveries. It was clear by now that this was to be a search for bodies, not a rescue mission.[9] Even the collection of the dead would have to wait for better weather. Leadbetter wired Captain Thomson aboard the *Atlas*: 'Don't believe you can do any more[.] When weather moderates can walk beaches for bodies.'[10]

For Stidham and the crew of the *Peterson* the search was ending. After two days in the area, they had no drinking water, were running low on other supplies, and were due to pick up a party that had been hunting in the region. Stidham sent a farewell message to Captain Leadbetter and headed south.[11]

The *Atlas* and *Cedar* remained into the early afternoon. In a cove near the north end of Shelter Island the crew of the *Cedar* sighted a life raft and a piece of the *Sophia*'s skylight. Prevented by rough water from landing, Leadbetter steamed a mile along the shore and put off a small crew, including his second officer, who walked back along the beach to the site of the discoveries. At 1.30 p.m. they found the bodies of four women and a man, but were prevented by the waves from loading them aboard the ship. The men returned to the *Cedar*, and at 2.45 Leadbetter decided to continue searching in that area, hoping to finish before dusk.[12]

Later that afternoon Captain Miller of the *King and Winge*, who had been in the area for more than forty-eight hours, left for Juneau.[13] Supplies were running low, and Miller needed to call in at home port to restock in order to continue the search. He turned his vessel southward at 3.30 p.m. On the way to Juneau he met a number of small gas boats, sent out from the territorial capital to help with the rescue. These boats, including the *Amy*, *Adolphus*, and *Sitka*, had found plentiful signs of the disaster around Point Hilda on Douglas Island, about thirty miles south of Vanderbilt Reef. A number of capsized lifeboats had been sighted, and the crew of the *Sitka* reported that they had already brought six bodies on board and were still picking up more. The *King and Winge*, running short of fuel, could not stop to help, and continued towards Juneau.[14]

The gas boats that Miller met were the first of a flotilla organized in Juneau by Frank Lowle when he heard of the final disaster. Between 8.15 and 9.00 a.m. on 26 October, as soon as word reached him that the *Princess Sophia* had sunk,[15] Lowle abandoned his efforts to find food and lodging for her passengers and began instead to organize a full-scale search and rescue operation.

News of the sinking had spread quickly through Juneau that Saturday. Mrs Pugh, who only hours earlier had received reassuring words from her husband that he was perfectly safe, now joined the crowd gathered outside Lowle's office, anxiously awaiting further details. In Vancouver, Seattle, and Victoria the news was passed by telephone among the relatives of passengers and crew. The shock of receiving it is fresh in the memory of people still living. Kitty Cousins was the wife of Charles Cousins, a member of the Victoria firm of Cousins Brothers, which had built two boats for the White Pass & Yukon Company for use on Tagish and Atlin Lakes. Her husband was working in Alaska during the summer of 1918, and she had travelled north to visit him. Like many other wives, she took the last boat outside. Her niece remembers the terrible anxiety in the home as her mother, Kitty Cousins' sister-in-law, waited two days for news from Vanderbilt Reef. Word of the sinking arrived in the middle of the night:

> It is one of my most early and vivid memories–to see my mother with her head resting on the wall telephone as she kept in touch with other relatives and then her blood-curdling shriek which woke my Dad and me and then her terrible wailing.[16]

It was a scene repeated in scores of homes that October weekend in 1918.

In Victoria the news of the final disaster was first received as a 'scoop' by the *Times*. Working on the paper as a 17-year-old police court reporter was Bruce Hutchison, later to become one of Canada's most respected journalists. The arrival of the news gave rise to one of the best anecdotes in his memoirs, *The Far Side of the Street*–a memorable clash between the paper's editor, Benny Nicholas, and the city editor, T. Harry Wilson, a cultured but vapid Englishman:

> Benny had been given a world scoop on that disaster through an unauthorized phone tip from a friendly wireless operator and, calling me to his telephone, waited while I took the message down in shorthand. Since I could not be trusted to write such a momentous story, for which the press of America was already panting, Dick Freeman, the experienced shipping editor, wrote it, in about five minutes, smack on the afternoon deadline. Wilson carried the copy up to the composing room, persuaded the peevish old foreman to set it in type, and told Benny that it would reach the street immediately.
>
> Of course, said Benny, the news would be splashed all over the front page. Why no, said Wilson, it had been placed where it properly belonged–in the marine column at the back of the paper, for obviously it was shipping news. But, he added proudly, it had been given the special distinction of a two-column headline.
>
> With that, Benny exploded in a mighty oath, ordered the presses stopped, ran puffing and screaming up the stairs, watched the printers set a huge eight-column headline, and managed to get the story on the front page, an hour late but still a world scoop. Though Wilson's feelings were hurt, he merely complained, out of Benny's hearing, that it had been a mistake, a breach of journalistic rules, to move a shipwreck out of the marine department.[17]

On Saturday and again on Sunday, newspapers up and down the coast, then all over North America and the rest of the world, reported the dreadful story. The Toronto *Globe* carried the news on Monday, 28 October, under the headline 'Worst Marine Tragedy on the Pacific Coast'; the London *Times*–too dignified for anything so vulgar as a headline–on 30 October under 'Imperial and Foreign News Items'. In Glasgow, Archibald Alexander's mother was riding on a bus when she saw a newsboy's headline: 'Terrible Disaster at Sea: Princess Sophia Lost'. Horrified to learn that the ship on which her son was first engineer had been sunk, and assuming he was dead, she rushed home. A day later a cable arrived from Victoria with the news that her granddaughter's influenza had kept him at home and saved his life.[18] In Seattle, the destination of many of the White Pass & Yukon Route steamboat crews, the company's purchasing agent, C.J. Rogers, went personally to dozens of houses that weekend to tell wives and children that their husbands and fathers had perished on the *Princess Sophia*. One of his saddest encounters came at the home of Elof A. Wendt, a 40-year-old deckhand on the river steamer *Washburn*. As Rogers came up the walk of the Wendt's home, a 14-year-old girl leaned out the window. 'Does E.A. Wendt live here?' Rogers inquired. 'I'm his little girl,' said the child. 'Papa's up in Alaska.' 'Your father was on the *Sophia*,' Rogers said. The girl ran crying to her grandmother, and a moment later he was forced to repeat the sad news to Wendt's mother. She had read of the disaster in the newspapers, but did not know that her son was coming out to Seattle and had no reason to believe he was in danger.[19]

Rogers had an equally sad task at the home of Mrs A.E. Schutt. She was the sister of Frank M. White, aged 37, first mate on the steamer *Yukon*. The two were natives of Carlisle, North Dakota, about as far from salt water as it is possible to get in the United States. Frank had gone to sea at the age of 13, had served in the US Navy, and had worked on Yukon riverboats for many years. His name did not appear on the first lists of victims, and while the *Princess Sophia* was heading for Vanderbilt Reef, his sister had received a letter from him saying that he was frozen in on the Tanana River and would not reach Seattle for some time. She therefore believed that her brother was not on the ship: 'The arrival of Rogers, with the news . . . came as a double shock and plunged the household into sorrow after it had rejoiced over White's escape.' Adding to the hideous irony of the situation was the arrival, some days after Rogers' visit, of a wireless message sent by White from the *Sophia* saying that the ship had run on to Vanderbilt Reef but that he was safe.[20]

At first, relatives got little co-operation from the authorities in their desperate search for news. Elizabeth Hitchin of Victoria, mother of Henry John Hitchin, a waiter on the ship, related that her daughter went to the port steward to try to find out if he was on the ship, but he could tell her nothing:

> So on the Monday I was like a raving woman and I went down with my papers to the port steward place and I said I wanted to know if my boy was on that boat or was he off with the flu. He says, 'No, there was quite a few off with the flu and I cannot tell you. Wait until the paper comes out at night.' And I was all that time from Friday until Monday night when the paper came out and I saw that my boy was on it and Tuesday night it was in the paper that he was picked up.[21]

While families of the victims grieved, the grim labour continued in Juneau. Lowle worked closely with Governor Thomas Riggs and Acting Collector of Customs Garfield; together, they agreed to recruit as many boats as possible and to divide the search area–the waters, channels, inlets and islands–so as to ensure a complete survey of the region. It took most of that day to put the plan together, and their task was hindered by bad weather; the storm that had sunk the *Sophia* had blown down the telephone line to the CPR office in Juneau, forcing the three men to move to the Customs Office and leave an assistant to tend to the Company headquarters.[22]

The plan was to search the entire Lynn Canal from Haines in the north to Admiralty Island in the south, a straight-line distance of 90 miles. To carry this out, Lowle called a meeting at the Customs House of seamen with experience in local waters, explained the situation, and called for volunteers. He promised that the Canadian Pacific Company would offer a fair wage to the searchers and pay for all supplies.[23] Late in the afternoon of Saturday 26 October the first boats left Juneau; the rest would leave on the 27th.

Captain Troup's uncertainty was dispelled the same day. Waiting impatiently in Victoria for news from Juneau, he received a message from Lowle at 3.38 on Saturday afternoon, forwarded from Bremerton Navy Yard in Seattle. In five sentences it told the whole terrible story:

> Princess Sophia driven across reef last night. No survivors. Had two hundred and sixty eight passengers seventy five crew. Everything done here to help. Nothing could be done owing [to] terrible rough weather.[24]

Troup immediately ordered Lowle to organize search efforts

and a shore patrol, unaware that this was already being done.

The residents of Juneau spent most of that weekend in a state of apprehension; they knew that over three hundred people had died at Vanderbilt Reef, but there was no physical evidence of the catastrophe until the *King and Winge* arrived in Juneau harbour at 6.30 Saturday afternoon with the first victims, followed closely by the *Peterson* with more. After docking, Captains Miller and Stidham met in Lowle's office for the first of many unofficial post-mortems. In the course of the discussion, which did not last long, Miller apparently said that 'it was possible to take those passengers off that boat [the *Sophia*].'[25] But there was little time for such speculation, since Lowle was anxious to get both vessels to sea again to continue with the search. Stidham, however, had been scheduled to pick up the hunters south of Haines. Governor Riggs tried to arrange for other boats to do so, but was unsuccessful.[26] So Stidham and the *Peterson* did not rejoin the search.

Riggs had been involved in the rescue effort from the beginning, but with the news of the sinking he assumed a more active role. The disaster required him to act in his official capacity as territorial Governor, and it was he who helped clear the wireless channels for quicker transmission of rescue messages after the *Cedar* reached Vanderbilt Reef.[27] Riggs, like many of the *Princess Sophia*'s victims, was a veteran of the far northwest. Born in Maryland and trained as a civil engineer, he had joined the Klondike stampede in 1897 and had prospected and mined for three years in the Klondike. He was appointed a member of the Alaska Boundary Survey of 1911, and in 1917 he joined the commission supervising the construction of the Alaska Railroad.[28]

Governor Riggs also assumed the role of official spokesman for the Alaskan administration in matters relating to the sinking. He answered requests, such as the one from the Skagway *Alaskan*, for details of the tragedy, sending a preliminary passenger list to the newspaper for publication.[29] His message to Secretary of the Interior Lane in Washington contained more details:

> Report most ghastly accident in history of Territory. Canadian Pacific steamer Princess Sophia, southbound from Skagway with two hundred sixty-eight passengers and seventy-five crew, struck Vanderbilt Reef,

unlighted rocks in Lynn Canal morning of twenty-fourth. Unable take off passengers owing to rough weather. Terrific storm night of twenty-fifth and sixth. Lighthouse tender Cedar standing by forced to seek shelter. Reported this morning at eight-thirty that Sophia driven over reef during night and only masts showing. No survivors known.[30]

Riggs also recognized that this was neither a Yukon nor an Alaskan tragedy, but one that transcended boundaries and struck at the heart of society in both territories. He telegraphed George P. Mackenzie, the Yukon Gold Commissioner,[31] 'Wreck of Princess Sophia has cast great shadow over all Northland. Alaska grieves with the Yukon.'[32] At the same time he issued a formal proclamation:

Whereas, It has pleased Almighty God to visit the Territory with a calamity which has reached in and touched the heart of each and every citizen through personal bereavement either of beloved family or cherished friend; and Whereas, the wind-swept waters of Alaska have closed over the gallant steamship Princess Sophia, leaving no known survivors of passengers and crew; and Whereas, Death has brought untold sorrow to all Alaskans unable yet to realize the far-reaching effects of the disaster; Therefore, I, Thomas Riggs Jr., Governor of Alaska, do request that as a mark of respect to our beloved dead and to the crushed and broken families, all flags in the Territory shall be placed at half-mast for a period of three days; that all churches shall hold memorial services and that each person believing in a just and merciful God, knowing how little and helpless are we all, shall ask for guidance and strength to be of such service as can be given.[33]

But Riggs' Yukon counterpart, Commissioner Mackenzie, was not at his post to receive this telegram. He too had gone outside for the winter, spending four months in the south, partly on official business in Ottawa. He was in Nova Scotia when news of the tragedy arrived, and did not learn of it for many days, when mail forwarded from Ottawa reached him. He did not feel that the fate of his fellow Yukoners required an immediate return to Dawson, and he stayed outside until the end of January 1919.[34] Isaac Stringer, Anglican Bishop of the Yukon, and Mr Justice Macaulay of the Yukon bench were in Toronto at the time. The fact that the leading figures of state, church, and bench were all wintering in the south emphasizes the transient nature of the territorial society.

The Governor had worked all through the day of the disaster at Lowle's side, co-ordinating search efforts and beginning plans for reception of the bodies. As messages continued to arrive from the *Cedar*, now anchored at Shelter Island, Riggs decided on the morning of Sunday, 27 October, to leave Juneau, join the rescue flotilla on the lighthouse tender, and supervise the search in person.[35] In the meantime there was not much more that could be done. Perhaps a new day would bring an end to the driving wind and snow that continued to hamper the search.

A few days after the disaster, the letters of inquiry from friends and relatives of the victims began to arrive in Juneau, and it was Riggs' unhappy duty to deal with them. His involvement, and that of other Alaskan officials such as Assistant Customs Collector Garfield and Deputy Marshall Harry Morton, proved vital to the search effort. As Lowle later reported, 'It was the moral influence of these men of affairs that helped considerably in our being able to report not a single instance of looting.'[36] The three men divided the main tasks at hand. Morton took charge of the field work, accompanying the small gas boats to the search area, and co-ordinated the recovery of bodies and wreckage. Garfield took over much of the work previously undertaken by Lowle, for the sinking of the *Sophia* had changed the episode from an internal affair of the Canadian Pacific Company into a civilian disaster; working from Juneau, he checked men and boats in and out of the harbour, requisitioned supplies, collected the log books of the ships' captains, and ensured both a steady stream of searchers to the target area and a proper management of affairs in Juneau.[37]

Thomas Riggs left Juneau at 5.00 a.m. on 27 October aboard the *King and Winge*. Nearing Young Bay, 26 miles down Lynn Canal from Vanderbilt Reef, the ship passed a number of small boats, including the *Estebeth*, *Monaghan*, *Sitka*, and *Lone Fisherman*, all collecting bodies from the middle of the channel. Fearing that some might be washed right out of the coastal waters into the open Pacific, Riggs ordered Captain Miller to abort his scheduled run to Shelter Island and stop to help collect them. Miller manoeuvred his ship into position about a mile north of the other boats, and his crew began fishing bodies out of the water. Within two hours they had taken thirty victims from Lynn Canal. They also received five bodies from the *Elsinore* that had been picked up earlier.[38]

Throughout the grey daylight hours of Sunday the gruesome work continued. The searchers found plentiful evidence of the disaster–patches of thick bunker oil and wreckage from the ship drifted aimlessly about, and bodies could be made out floating all over the channel, some rocking in eddies at the shoreline.

The arrival of Governor Riggs on the *King and Winge* transformed the role of the *Cedar* and its crew. Accompanying Riggs was a wireless operator, H. Wallace, to relieve the ship's regular operator, Elwood Miller. Miller had been awake at his post transmitting and receiving messages since shortly after the *Sophia* ran aground, and was so exhausted that he could hardly move his key. Riggs had come to co-ordinate the search effort, and the *Cedar* was to be his base of operations. He had brought with him a large chart, showing all the ships participating in the search, assigned to specific sectors.[39] Having delivered the Governor to the *Cedar*, Captain Miller returned with the *King and Winge* to Juneau, carrying a load of corpses.

Nothing more could be done that day. About mid-afternoon the wind picked up again, and another snowstorm descended on Lynn Canal, forcing the searchers once more into shelter. Captain Leadbetter took the *Cedar* back to the south end of Shelter Island and by 3.00 p.m. was safely at anchor.[40] The night passed slowly for the men on the waiting vessels, for they knew that the delay, compounded by the rising wind and the tides, meant that the bodies still in the water were floating farther down the canal in the direction of the open sea, a hundred miles away. With each hour that passed, the search area had to be enlarged, and the likelihood of finding all the dead decreased. The delay did give Riggs a chance to interview Captain Leadbetter and the other members of the *Cedar*'s crew, giving him a better picture of the disaster. But for all of them it was a long night.

In Juneau, that Sunday evening, Garfield wired a report to Governor Riggs that nine search vessels[41] had located 160 bodies, and that seven of the boats were going out the next day to continue the search. The *King and Winge* would concentrate on

Young Bay, while a new addition, the *Osprey*, would patrol from Point Young to Point Arden. All the boats would report to Riggs on the *Cedar* and would operate under his instructions. Best of all, Garfield was able to tell Riggs that the weather was moderating; for the first time in nearly five days, since the *Princess Sophia* pulled out of Skagway, the forecast called for calm seas and diminishing snowfall.

The prediction proved correct, and on the morning of Monday, 28 October, no longer facing a heavy swell and driving snow, the searchers could proceed quickly and safely with their job. For the crew of the *Cedar* work began at 6.45 a.m. Leadbetter moved his vessel slowly along the coast of Shelter Island, picking up bodies as he went. All the other boats, under Governor Riggs' direction, scoured the coastline for bodies and wreckage. There was much for him to contend with: 'We were keeping track of where they were working, and seeing . . . that there was no pilfering by Indians, or anything of that sort.'[42]

Not content with giving orders and watching the progress of the search, Riggs decided to take a more active part. At 7.30 a.m. he and Captain Leadbetter went on shore to help look for victims. Struggling through waist-deep snow, after a short time they found five bodies washed up on the shore near a broken lifeboat. They hailed the launch *Amy* and had the bodies put aboard, then continued their search. Soon they found ten more, which in their haste and shock they recorded, incorrectly, as 'ten bodies, which were four children, two men and six women'.[43] These victims, along with ten trunks found on the scene, were also placed aboard the *Amy* and subsequently the *Cedar* for shipment to Juneau.

The discovery of bodies so close to a lifeboat raised an important question about the disaster. Had some passengers got safely into the boats, only to be swamped by the turbulent seas? Could others have clambered aboard a boat and got safely to shore, perhaps to wander a distance and then freeze to death? A quick investigation scotched both these ideas. As Captain Leadbetter later testified, 'there was no evidence that they [the passengers] had ever been in the boats.' The canvas covers had been removed from the boats that were found, but the oars and painters were undisturbed, and though they had evidently been prepared for launching, there was no indication that they had been used. None of the bodies was found aboard a lifeboat.[44]

The deep snow lying on the shoreline made the search more difficult, as did the low tides. On the evening of the sinking, the tides had been running very high–one of the reasons why the *Princess Sophia* was carried off the reef. But over the next two days, tidal shifts remained comparatively small. As John Lund, Jr, the Game Warden for Juneau, noted: 'The bodies were probably carried high onto the beaches and were then covered with snow as the tide receded. There has been about two feet of snow along the beaches, and it has drifted in places higher than that.' Hence any bodies hidden beneath the snow would be uncovered only by a thaw, or by a series of high tides.[45]

At noon on 28 October Deputy Marshall Morton arrived on board the *Monaghan* and Riggs asked him to reassign the search boats to ensure that the investigation would be as complete as possible. Work continued throughout the afternoon. Dr Sargeant, brought to the area the previous day to assist survivors, was clearly not needed, and went back to Juneau on the *Amy*, which also carried a load of corpses.[46] By nightfall over 180 bodies had been delivered to Juneau.

The CPR steamer *Princess Alice*, originally sent to collect passengers from the stranded *Sophia*, had also just arrived in the territorial capital. She was now scheduled to continue to Skagway the next day to pick up men and equipment and take them to Juneau to assist in handling the corpses; she would wait in Juneau until most of the bodies were cleaned, identified, and embalmed, then would take them south to Vancouver, Victoria, and Seattle.[47] The *Alice* brought to Juneau two members of the Mounted Police: Inspector A.L. Bell, commander of the Whitehorse detachment, and Sergeant Mapely, the assistant immigration inspector. Under orders from R.S. Knight, the RNWMP commander at Dawson,[48] their mission was to safeguard the interests of relatives of the victims and to assist in the identification of bodies. In addition, the ship carried Bert Whitfield, an undertaker from Skagway, E.R. Strivers from the Customs office in Skagway, and J.J. Hillard of the Customs office in Eagle to help with identification, and

Lewis Johnston of the Skagway CPR office with the booking records.

A number of private citizens also came to Juneau to identify their friends and relatives. Reginald Brook, a partner in Captain Alexander's Engineer Mine, travelled from the mine to catch the train at Carcross, then went on the *Estebeth* to Juneau to identify the remains of Alexander and his wife. 'Luckily,' he later recounted, 'there were four of us to identify Mrs Alexander, as there was Mrs Christina Dunn of Vancouver there who had already identified her as her sister. We had a photo taken of Mrs Alexander to avoid complications and for future reference.'[49]

The officials worried that the Natives of the Lynn Canal region might attempt to loot the bodies and scavenge the wreckage along the coast. Riggs and Morton had kept a sharp eye out for any evidence of such activity, and Garfield had gone further. With the permission of the Indian Department, he had authorized all patrols to 'warn under authority [of] this office [that] all Indians found [were] to leave adjacent waters immediately and not return under severe penalties.'[50] There was not the slightest indication that this concern was warranted, for there was no sign at all of looting or pillaging; their apprehension over the Indians' behaviour did the officials little credit.

Juneau was a beleaguered town in the fall of 1918. The first signs of the dreaded influenza epidemic, which had so devastated the lower forty-eight states and, indeed, most of the world, had appeared in October, despite attempts to keep it out of the north. When the crew of the *Princess Alice* arrived in Juneau on 28 October to lend what help they could, they were not allowed to leave the ship lest they spread infection. At the beginning of October, the town had been devastated by a flood caused by the heaviest rains ever recorded in the region. Now, at the end of the month, it was about to be turned into a charnel-house.

Few at that time paid any attention to the ecological damage that accompanied the disaster. The *Princess Sophia* had released thousands of gallons of bunker oil, which the frigid sea had congealed into a viscid sludge lying in patches on the surface of Lynn Canal. Wave and tidal action washed the heavy tar up on the beaches and coves, where it quickly fouled miles of coastline. As hundreds of seabirds, particularly ducks, settled in the mass, their oil-soaked feathers lost their buoyancy and insulating ability. The birds froze or drowned, and within two days thousands floated, dead or dying, in the fouled waters of the canal.[51]

Throughout the last week of October and the first week of November the grisly work continued. While politicians sent formal messages of condolence, and northern communities staggered under the enormity of their loss, the seamen of Juneau continued the thankless task of collecting bodies. They found dozens. More would be found in the following days, weeks, and months; others, never. Now the burden shifted to the people of Juneau, then a town of just over 3,000.

The task that faced them was daunting. Between the last few days of October and the middle of November, nearly two hundred bodies were brought in from the sea, all of which had to be identified and prepared for burial. Juneau responded magnificently. Under the direction of Governor Riggs–who at the same time had to deal with the hundreds of messages of condolence and inquiry that flooded in from all over North America–an organization was set up to handle the job that involved practically every adult in town.[52]

Most of the bodies were delivered to Juneau in the first week after the disaster–about 180 by 1 November.[53] During that time the residents, almost all volunteers, were formed into teams that would work almost like an assembly line. Several teams were on call twenty-four hours a day to meet ships at the dock, take bodies off, and carry them to a warehouse set aside as a morgue; another team guarded this warehouse round the clock. There the bodies were handed over to four businessmen[54] and given numbers for identification purposes, then searched for personal effects; these were catalogued by another four businessmen, put under the care of the coroner, Judge H.L. Burton, and sent to the vaults of Behrend's Bank. Most of the victims were readily identified: of the first 179 to be brought in, all but 21 were identified by their personal effects, by local residents, or by people who had come on the *Princess Alice* to help with the work. The lifebelts were cut off those who were wearing them, and clothes were removed–by a male team for male victims and a female team for women and children–and cleaned as much as possible.[55] The bodies were carefully examined for identification marks, then given to another team, who scrubbed them thoroughly with gasoline. This task was made particularly unpleasant by the state of the bodies, many of which were so covered with oil that when 'first brought in [they] could not be recognized as human bodies at all. They looked more like a huge liver.'[56]

Particularly ghastly were the remains of a young girl, described by Inspector Bell of the Mounted Police:

> The head was in horrible condition, eyes, lips, nose and interior of head completely gone, eaten by gulls and ravens, and the face had been 'made up' artificially by the embalmer, so that while the body answers the description of Joy Vifquain, and it is the only child the description would fit, there is, as I have said, an element of doubt. Positive identification is impossible even by the father.[57]

Bell also noted that of the first 162 bodies to be recovered, only two had drowned; the rest had been suffocated by the oil that covered them.

Once they had been cleaned, most of the bodies were embalmed. This job, which required some skill, was too much for the local undertakers, and embalmers who had been summoned from Skagway were joined by others from Ketchikan and Seattle, along with a large quantity of embalming fluid. The local supply of coffins ran out overnight, and there was neither time nor enough finished wood on hand to build more. Every town from Skagway to Ketchikan was ransacked for extra supplies. The bodies were then ready for burial locally, or for shipment south.

The aftermath of the tragedy brought out the best in the citizens of Juneau, as Inspector Bell found:

> the Juneau citizens–bankers, professional and businessmen–were simply wonderful. They put aside self entirely, worked night and day, and there was not the slightest attempt on the part of anyone to profiteer, and that is something which, I think, could only happen in this northland.[58]

The problem remained, however, of what to do with the bodies of those who were residents of the Yukon River valley. Since it was impossible to ship any of them back to the far northwest until navigation on the Yukon River reopened in the spring of 1919, the CPR rented a cold-storage plant in Juneau to hold the bodies until their disposition could be decided upon. The company also announced that it would pay the cost of shipping bodies anywhere on the continent, as well as $250 each for funeral expenses. It also announced a reward of $50 per body to those who found more. The *Princess Alice*, which had been sent north to take the passengers off the *Sophia*, was now readied to take the bodies of the victims remaining back to Vancouver, except for those whose relatives had requested burial in Juneau, and a few that were still unidentified. A number of people from the Yukon River valley–Charley Castleman and Mr and Mrs Walter Harper–were among those buried in Juneau, and at Archdeacon Stuck's request the Harpers' grave was marked for the later erection of a substantial monument.[59]

The tragedy was made particularly real for the residents of Juneau when the body of John F. Pugh, the Customs Collector who was the only resident of the town to perish on the *Sophia*, was brought in. His body was found on 29 October at Tree Point on the north end of Douglas Island. He was well-liked in the community; on the day of his funeral it was said that 'the towns on Gastineau channel are filled with gloom, as "Jack" Pugh was one of the most popular men holding office in the territory, and his friends were legion'[60]:

> news of the arrival of his body spread like wildfire throughout the town, and while it caused sighs of relief, it emphasized the feeling of personal loss to the hundreds of friends of the popular official and citizen. Minds that had been stunned by the awfulness of the catastrophe reverted to introspection and permitted grief that had been held in reserve to find expression.[61]

On 31 October, when the town buried this favourite son, the banks closed for the afternoon, and all the flags in town were flown at half-mast. The funeral was conducted by his fellow Masons, and it was requested that only Masons attend, 'on account of the precautionary measures being taken to prevent the spread of the influenza epidemic now apparent in Juneau'.[62] He was survived by his wife and daughter, a student in the Juneau high school.

Governor Riggs had presided over an energetic and largely successful search effort. About 180 bodies had been found in three days of searching, and 155 of them identified.[63] He had done what he could to facilitate the search for victims, and had also spent time interviewing witnesses and reading the logs of lighthouses in the area to get a sense of the events. In a statement he prepared for the press, outlining the disaster, he gave his opinion that it was an act of God, and that Captain Locke was one of the most competent mariners in the north-west:

> I wish to reiterate that everything possible had been done for the safety of the passengers that could be done, not only by the captain of the Princess Sophia, but by the captains of all the vessels in the vicinity. The accident . . . is no more due to any fault of these men than was the damage done in the recent flood at Juneau. There should be no unjust criticisms of what uninformed people think might have been done, as nobody could foresee what Providence had in store.[64]

A few days after the sinking of the *Princess Sophia*, the CPR vessel *Tees* arrived in Juneau. On board were two professional divers, John Donaldson and Thomas Veitch, as well as Walter Gosse, the lookout who had missed the *Sophia* in Vancouver. The *Tees* had come north to see if the wreck could be salvaged. The divers were to locate and, with the help of the *Tees*' crew, raise the *Sophia*'s Wells Fargo safe–which was rumoured to be carrying a substantial quantity of gold–and if possible to locate the bags of mail that she had been carrying. Since the front part of the ship was lying in water so shallow that the foremast was still well above water,[65] the job might not have appeared particularly difficult, but the aft three-quarters was off the reef, hanging at an angle over much deeper water. This meant that the divers had to go to a depth of 70 feet to get the safe. Because the *Sophia* was now in the lee of the reef, protected from the prevailing winds, there did not seem much danger of her falling off the ledge on which she was perched. The divers reported, however, that the after part of the vessel was badly damaged, and in their opinion she was likely to break up. They went down to the wreck in their heavy diving suits, linked by an air hose to pumps at the surface, and shivering in the near-freezing water. They worked for four hours on Monday, 4 November, but the seas remained heavy, and they could not stay down for long. They did find the safe, however, from which was recovered $62,000 in gold bullion. They also found one body on the upper deck.[66]

The victim was George Paddock, a 62-year-old resident of Dawson City. He was born near Malone, NY, the eldest of eight children of a 'progressive farmer' who operated a 250-acre farm and had trained his son to succeed him. Until he was 54, George Paddock worked at home almost all his life. He had the equivalent of a grade-nine education. In 1882, at the age of 26, he had married a girl ten years younger than himself, and the couple had two daughters. Two of his younger brothers went to Alaska at the time of the gold rush, and for several years wrote home urging George to come north and make his fortune. Finally, in 1910, he succumbed. The first year he worked at mining, and then at farming and gardening; for some time he was in charge of the Faulkner ranch, near Dawson. He also worked as a carpenter on one of the big dredges. It was later reported that though he was a hard worker, he 'was not always careful with respect to his expenditures, and as a result did not accumulate much property . . . [he] was more interested in having a good living for himself and family than in hoarding property'; the description suggests a man fond of a good time and perhaps the occasional spree. Though he seems to have remained on good terms with his wife, who stayed in New York State and ran the farm, she never came north, nor did he visit her once in eight years. He sent her money regularly, however, and in the fall of 1918, when one of his daughters became seriously ill, he decided to return home to visit her. He had the bad luck to secure passage on the *Princess Sophia*.[67]

The most startling result of this examination of the wreck was the divers' statement that there were probably no more bodies to be found on board. This assertion, which for a time the CPR accepted, was reasonable if one assumed that all passengers and crew had been on deck (and presumably wearing life-jackets) when the ship went down. But since over a hundred were still missing, it suggested that there must still be dozens of bodies floating in hidden places along Lynn Canal or out in the open ocean.

All through the first week of November the grisly task of cleaning, identifying, and embalming the dead continued in Juneau. Meanwhile, the influenza epidemic reached its peak, and for several days the volunteers in the temporary morgue wore gauze masks to protect themselves from infection. Inspector Bell took the precaution of taking a shot of a new anti-flu serum that had just been developed. By 2 November 180 bodies had been found, but a week later the flood of corpses coming to Juneau had slowed to a trickle. More would be found floating in the canal or cast up along its shore, but not in large numbers. In response to an inquiry, Governor Riggs said on 20 November that the results of the search for the previous two weeks had been 'so discouraging as to not warrant its continuance beyond the end of this week. The waters in this vicinity are of such a low temperature as to discount to a minimum the chances of any bodies being floated to the surface through the effects of decomposition.'[68] It was time to take the dead south for burial.

7. In Memoriam

On 9 November the *Princess Alice*, dubbed the 'Ship of Sorrow' by the press, left Juneau quietly, without a whistle or sound except the Captain's command, 'Let go.'[1] It carried 156 bodies–62 destined for Vancouver, 25 for Victoria, and the rest mainly for Seattle, with a few heading for other points. Elaborate arrangements had been made for the handling of the bodies in Vancouver. The freight shed on Pier D was set aside as a temporary morgue. Members of the clergy, nurses, doctors, and undertakers were told to be ready for the ship's arrival. It was arranged that the bodies–those that had been identified–would be laid out alphabetically. Relatives could enter and claim them on presentation of suitable identification.

But one of the most hideous ironies of the entire episode lay ahead. By unhappy coincidence, the 'Ship of Sorrow' pulled into Vancouver harbour late in the evening of Monday, 11 November. It was Armistice Day–a day of general rejoicing. Thomas H. Kirk, acting mayor of Vancouver, had just issued a proclamation:

> In commemoration of the victorious Armistice which has been officially announced, and in order that the Citizens generally may participate in appropriate celebrations, I hereby declare Monday, November 11th, 1919, as a Public Holiday within the City of Vancouver, and would request that the same be observed by all.[2]

The citizens of Vancouver needed no urging to celebrate. 'Surging Thousands' turned the city into a 'Maelstrom of Laughing, Jubilant, Flag-bedecked Humanity', with 'Every Variety of Noise-making Apparatus Brought into Play' to 'Celebrate the Glorious Victory and Demonstrate Their Affection for [the] Gallant Boys Who Made It Possible.' According to the Vancouver *Sun*, it was 'the Most Extraordinary Scene in [the] City's History'.[3] At 11.00 on the evening of 11 November, just as the celebrations were reaching a peak, the *Princess Alice* arrived in Vancouver with its cargo of corpses.

W.H. D'Arcy of Winnipeg, the general claims agent for the CPR, was in charge of the arrangements. Since it was too late to take the bodies off the ship, they were kept aboard overnight and unloaded onto Pier D at 7.00 the next morning. Then, while most of residents of Vancouver, and of North America, were still celebrating the end of the Great War, or sleeping off the celebrations of the day before, a few score people went to the docks to claim the bodies of their friends and relatives. Out of respect for the dead of the *Princess Sophia*, the Vancouver City Council asked that, in the midst of the cheering and singing, all the flags in the city–and there were thousands of them flying on 12 November–should be lowered for an hour, from 1.00 to 2.00 p.m.[4]

One of the bodies taken off the *Princess Alice* on the grey morning of 12 November was that of Frank Burke, the high-school student from Vancouver. His father went down to the pier to claim his son's remains. There was a sizeable crowd on the sidewalk, looking towards the pier. The people stood in hushed silence, the men with their hats removed in respect for the dead. To get inside the shed, which was decorated with flags, crêpe hangings, and flowers, friends and relatives had to identify themselves to a CPR policeman. One young woman immediately ahead of Frank Burke's father could not provide satisfactory identification. He took the guard aside and spoke a few words, which persuaded him to let the lady enter. Frank's brother remembered that

> Mother was pleased to hear this, and ever alert to point up a good example to us kids, asked Dad what he had said to the guard. His answer was not exactly what she had had in mind. Dad, it seemed, had offered to 'knock his block off'.[5]

After unloading its cargo, the *Princess Alice* steamed to Victoria to deliver its share of bodies, and to transfer the rest to vessels heading for Seattle and other American ports. At 3.00 p.m. on 12 November the *Alice* came through the mist and rain to the wharf at Victoria harbour, and there the scene was repeated. A warehouse had been fitted out as a mortuary, crêpe had been hung, and a doctor and nurse were present to attend to grieving friends and relatives. Twenty-five bodies were unloaded and placed in alphabetical order in the warehouse; then relatives were admitted to claim them.[6]

Most of the crew of the *Princess Sophia* and those who had worked on the Yukon River steamers were buried privately in Victoria, Vancouver, or the Seattle area. Because there were so many funerals in the Pacific northwest the week of the Armistice, and because the influenza epidemic was still raging, graves couldn't be dug fast enough to meet the demand, and some Vancouver burials had to be delayed for several days.[7] Other bodies were taken off at Vancouver for trans-shipment to other points. The bodies of Oscar and Crissie Tackstrom and their daughter Margaret–their son George had not been found–were delivered at Vancouver into the care of Mrs C.J. Pfrang, Crissie's sister. She took them home with her to Oakland, California, and had them cremated.[8]

The body of 26-year-old Orton M. Phillips, an American-born waiter on the *Princess Sophia*, was identified by the Victoria police. In August he had been arrested and convicted there on a charge of driving a motor vehicle while under the influence of liquor and, unable to pay his fine, had spent a week in jail. His only relatives were in the United States, so two policemen who remembered him from his term in prison were asked to make the identification.[9]

In Portland, Mrs M.E. Brown was preparing for her marriage to Joseph Santine, a marine engineer who spent his summers with the American-Yukon Navigation Company in Alaska and his winters working in Portland's Willamette Iron Works. Santine, a 38-year-old native of Florence, Italy, was a member of the Portland Lodge of Elks, and it was to the Elks Hall that Mrs Brown went for news of her fiancé. When she entered the hall and saw his photograph displayed in a place of honour, she collapsed and had to be hospitalized.[10]

The remains of Albert and Olive Pinska were shipped to St Paul, Minnesota, at the expense of the CPR. It was reported that 'both bodies arrived in good condition and were easily recognizable by the family and old friends'.[11] They were buried beside Albert Pinska's mother and sister, who had died earlier that year, in the family plot at Oakland cemetery in St Paul, 'one of the most beautiful cemeteries of the state'.[12] Edmund Ironside and his mother Mary were given a double funeral at Nanaimo, where his brother Charles lived, and buried side by side amid 'profuse and magnificent floral tributes' sent from various parts of Canada and the United States.

The reaction in Dawson City to the news of the *Sophia*'s fate was one of numb shock. The first word that had come to the Yukon River valley on 24 and 25 October was that the ship was aground but there were no casualties. When the news arrived on the 26th and 27th that all passengers and crew had been lost, Dawsonites could hardly comprehend the magnitude of the disaster–perhaps as many as one in ten of the town's citizens had died. The first issue of the Dawson newspaper published after the truth became known ran an editorial entitled 'Keep Heart', but there was little consolation to be had. The newspaper was correct in saying that the 'hand of sorrow' had fallen heavily on the town:

> Few tragedies, indeed, take at one fell stroke such a heavy percentage of those so well known in a community. In few places are the residents so

> closely knit by common interests and so well acquainted and so deeply concerned in the welfare one of the other as in this remote locality. The intimacy and the esteem of those who were called and those who remain was like unto that of a family.[13]

For over a week the *Dawson Daily News* carried practically nothing but accounts of the *Sophia* tragedy. The hunger for details was so great that the paper put out a special 'memorial edition' on 7 November; advance orders were taken, and readers were asked to supply biographical details about the victims for inclusion in it. It was hard to find any silver lining in an event so damaging to the community, but an editorial in the memorial issue suggested a strengthened bond between the communities of the far northwest:

> Yukon and Alaska suffered in common; they grieve in common, and they will sustain one another in common. Ill could they afford to lose such sterling citizenry, and never will the scar be effaced from memory. But over it will rise a hallowed vision in love for those who have gone. . . . In each name of that long list of absent ones there is a friend, in each absent friend a star to point the better way.[14]

Further comfort was drawn from the certitude that the victims of the *Sophia* had behaved nobly in the face of death:

> memory enshrines them in Yukon's hearts as of the best of the breeding of a land whose signal trait is dauntless courage in the face of greatest trials.
>
> The tradition of the Yukon, it can be depended upon, suffered no tarnishment but rather was glorified by heroic acts in those last moments. If the tale of the individual considerations could be recited, if the stories of refusals of opportunities to be first to take the best facilities for attempting to make shore through those wild seas could be told today, no doubt they would reflect as true tokens of heroism as ever came from the seas.
>
> Yukoners will cherish the belief that not even the magnificent valor of the men of the Birkenhead, nor the supreme sacrifices of the noble souls who stood back and perished when the Titanic went down could have been more noble than that of the un-named heroes and heroines of the Sophia. No doubt the tradition of honor and courage which signalize the people of the Northland was theirs until the end, and if the tale were known in full it would crown an epic theme. Now that

> they have passed through the storm to the large portals of another world, Yukon can cherish the conviction, earth knew no nobler souls.[15]

James Parkin Harris of Last Chance Creek contributed a poem entitled 'At Rest':

She was loaded to the gunwales,
  On her journey south was bound;
She was just the boat for Klondikers,
  A Princess of renown.

They waited long in Skagway,
  Until she hove in sight,
And the joy of those old timers
  Made Skagway ring that night.
They left the dear old Klondike–
  Their hearts all filled with glee,
With the thoughts of friends and loved ones
  And old homes they longed to see.
Some were going to old mothers,
  Some to sweethearts, some to wives;
Some were going out for country
  And the freedom of our lives.

Some weathered many stormy gales–
  Brave captains were there, too,
Who always landed safe in port,
  And again it still is true.
Some had bags of gold in plenty;
  Some with nothing but their fare;
But you could not tell the difference,
  Once you breathe the Yukon air.

They'd suffered cold and hunger–
  Reverses were not new–
And if you ever needed help,
  Their gold sack emptied, too.

There were fathers, there were mothers
  With their children on that boat,
And the love of those old timers
  Was the same as when Christ spoke.

But, ah, the good Sophia
  Through darkness lost her way,
And now she's at the bottom
  Of Lynn canal this day.
A host of friends have left us,
  But they've gone to join the blest-
Praise God that all those noble souls
  Have won eternal rest.[16]

Throughout the week following the disaster, messages of condolence and sympathy came in from the south. Prime Minister Sir Robert Borden assured the 'sorely bereaved people' of the Yukon of his deep sympathy: 'The shocking completeness of the great tragedy has deeply moved and touched the citizens of the entire Dominion.'[17] In Cobalt, Ontario, the Mining Corporation of Canada shut down its operations for the day on 28 October 'as a mark of respect for their chief, Chas. Watson, manager of the Corporation', who had been travelling with Captain Alexander and his wife on the *Princess Sophia.*[18] The news was received by Ottawa's 'Yukon Colony' with horror.[19] Dr Alfred Thompson, the Yukon's MP, wired that he was 'simply overwhelmed':

> I knew personally a great many of the passengers on the ill-fated ship and have been hoping against hope that some of them would be saved. I have journeyed on the Sophia many times, and knew Captain Locke well, but I also know the terrible snowstorms that occur on that coast at this time of the year.[20]

A committee of 'Northerners in Vancouver', made up of Yukon businessmen and river captains who had been lucky enough to take a different boat out, wired Dawson City offering their services in the matter of disposition of bodies and other business arrangements: 'Don't hesitate to ask for any service, large or small.'[21] Residents of the town of Courtenay, on Vancouver Island, read that Christmas parcels destined for Yukon troops in Europe had gone down on the *Princess Sophia*, and informed the postmaster in Dawson City: 'If you will wire names and addresses of boys at front whose parcels were lost on Sophia the people here will forward them parcels for Christmas.'[22] The White Pass & Yukon

Route was devastated by the disaster, which had killed 'a great many employees . . . among whom were some of our most capable officers, some being with this Company since its inception'.[23]

The majority of the victims' families, of course, lived in the south, so funeral arrangements posed no difficulty. But this was not the case for all. What was particularly painful for the friends and relatives in the far northwest was that there could be no funerals in the region. It was simply impractical to ship bodies to the Yukon River basin in the winter: they would have had to be brought in over land to Dawson or Fairbanks one or two at a time, and it was not desirable to leave them unburied until navigation resumed in the spring. Thus although memorial services could be held in Dawson, the remains of the victims were all buried 'outside'.

Marie Vifquain, for example, had traveled on the *Princess Sophia* with her brother and 5-year-old daughter to visit her parents in Ladysmith, BC, where she planned to stay until her husband came from Dawson City to join her in December. When the bodies of Marie and her daughter Charlotte Joy were recovered, they were taken to Vancouver to await her husband, who could not leave the Yukon until the overland trail had frozen, making winter travel possible. A mass was celebrated for them in Dawson City, but the decision on what to do with the bodies was delayed until his arrival in the south. Eventually her sister-in-law came from California to the temporary morgue at Juneau to identify and claim the bodies. Difficulties of this kind meant that for many people, the grieving process was not completed for months. And for those whose dead were never found, it remained incomplete forever.

On Saturday, 2 November a public service was held in the Arctic Brotherhood hall in Dawson City to honour the dead of the Yukon and Alaska. The service was international; the only decorations in the hall were 'the gently draped forms of the Union Jack on one side of the proscenium arch and that of the Stars and Stripes on the other'.[24] It was also a notable example of the importance of fraternal organizations in the life of the north. Groups such as the Moose, the Eagles, the Order of Pioneers, the Masons, the Eastern Star, the Arctic Brotherhood, the Odd Fellows, the Scouts, the Girl Guides, and the IODE were central to the social life of the Yukon River valley. It was rare for a northerner not to belong to one or another of them, and many belonged to several. They were all hard hit by the disaster–the fraternal lodges of Fairbanks alone lost over twenty men and women, not counting family members[25]–and they played a prominent role in the memorial services, which, rather than focussing on the individual, took on a group character. The Dawson lodges assumed responsibility for much of the work of locating next-of-kin and informing them of the disaster, of making arrangements for those who wished their relatives to be buried in Juneau, and of raising money for those temporarily in need. Fairbanks' lodges did the same.[26]

On 24 November, the Yukon Order of Pioneers in Dawson held a memorial service at the Pioneer Cemetery in honour of those members who had died both on the *Princess Sophia* and on the battlefields of France:

> The members of the lodge assembled at Pioneer Hall . . . and a line of march was formed, with Past Grand President R.L. Gillespie leading and carrying a beautiful large crown of flowers to which were attached long black ribbons . . . a large glass frame containing the names of the departed members and their families . . . Then came the gold pan, with the golden letters 'Y.O.O.P.' on the bottom . . . the members formed a large circle around the prepared place, where a temporary headboard had been erected . . . A large crown was placed on the board. The gold pan was buried with mourning cards from all members present. The regular burial service of the order then was held.[27]

It was a significant measure of the disaster that whereas three members of the order had died in France, fully nineteen members and fourteen of their wives and children had perished on the *Sophia*.

Perhaps one of the most heartfelt funeral tributes was written for George J. Milton. He was a native of St Paul, Minnesota, where he had operated a large milk and dairy business there before going to the Yukon in 1898. For a number of years he operated claim 35 on Hunker Creek. Later he bought an interest in a coal mine near the Five Finger Rapids on the Yukon River. He was married and had two daughters, but as was the case for so many men in the north, his family lived permanently in St Paul, and he paid frequent visits to them.[28] After his death, Milton's 'lifelong friend'

B.C. Matteson wrote a dramatic version of the *Princess Sophia* disaster and sent it from St Paul to be published in the Whitehorse *Star* as a tribute:

> It was autumn; the snow line was gradually creeping down the Alaskan mountain sides, and into the cavernous mouths of the various mines on their slopes and down into the fertile valleys at their base.
>
> From these romantic mountain and picturesque hamlet scenes of this northland clime there wended their way with joyous tread three hundred and forty of our friends towards that welcoming ship, from whose masthead the national emblem streamed abroad as though to extend the hand of greeting to her passengers. They crowded aboard. Never had the Princess Sophia borne such a host of passengers and accumulation of wealth as now were upon her decks.
>
> The hour was come. The lines that bound her to the rocky harbor were now on her deck. The signals were given, her wheels revolve, and turning her prow to the winding channel, she begins her homeward run.
>
> The pilot stood at her wheel. Men saw him. Death sat upon her prow and no eye beheld him. He never revealed his presence or whispered his errand, and so was hope effulgent. Life and gaiety were in every guest. Amid any inconvenience all murmurs were hushed with the thought that home and friends were awaiting us.
>
> Four hours had passed with roaring wheels and rushing prow, beating an echo on the rocky structures along the shore and re-echoing the sound back to the more distant mountains, and so she glided along in her gayer hours.
>
> But a great change now comes. Consternation has come aboard and is now prevailing on her decks as a northern blast is now disputing her passage of the channel. But the Princess Sophia boldly plunges into the icy winds which wrap her about. She will never emerge, the last sunlight has flashed upon her decks and the last voyage is done for ship and passengers, as there arose from those mysterious depths dreaded and fatal instruments of destruction that rended her steel plates asunder. And now death reveals itself, when with a reel and shiver along her mighty hull as the deadly and mortal wounds were being inflicted, and down, down, down she sank and the quick return water [sic] allowed the unbroken waves in ghoulish glee to pass as though she had not been, and on their way to the rocky shore to loosen the frail hold of those who would anchor there.
>
> Oh! what a burial was here! Not as when one is borne amid a

> weeping throng to the green fields and laid peacefully beneath the turf and flowers. It was an ocean grave.
>
> Morning dawns! The wind and the waves have sunk to rest, and in their ebb and flow as on they go, under a cloudless sky, seemingly without a wail or murmur of what has been, but those rocky monuments that surround this sad abode bear no memories of those who perished there.[29]

The far northwest did not grieve alone that November. Memorial services were also held in Seattle, Victoria, and Vancouver, and two services were held in Toronto. At Bonar Presbyterian Church, Bishop Stringer, who, like the Gold Commissioner, George P. Mackenzie, had come south with his wife and family on the *Princess Sophia* earlier that fall, spoke of the importance of the tragedy:

> Were it not for this world conflict the loss of the Princess Sophia, with all on board, would be chronicled around the world as one of the greatest disasters in marine history. The losses in this disaster may seem to the general public trivial, but to us who know many of the victims it is not so. One-tenth of the population of a town like Dawson, comprising 2,000 people–what would it be to have them all taken at once.[30]

He read aloud a letter his 9-year-old son had received from Bobby O'Brien, written a few days before the entire O'Brien family was lost on the ship. 'Clasped tight in his father's arms,' said the bishop, quoting a report that proved later to be untrue,[31] 'Bobby and his father were among the first to be picked up.' Sobs could be heard from the congregation.[32] Bobby O'Brien's body in fact was not found for several weeks. It was carried by the tides and currents nearly 50 miles back up Lynn Canal in the direction of Haines. When discovered, by a soldier from Fort Seward, it was in bad condition, but was identified by the little Mounted Police uniform with the sergeant's stripes on the sleeve that had belonged to the boy.[33] His father, not found until the summer of 1919, was buried in Vancouver.

Some of the *Sophia*'s victims had no relatives or friends to claim their bodies, and others were never identified. The disposition of the remains of the Chinese crew members was not recorded;

apparently they were all buried in Juneau, but they were not considered important enough to be mentioned in the newspapers. There were twenty-four burials in Juneau immediately following the disaster, and more later on as more bodies were found. Some were never claimed; others were people whose relatives did not want to bring the bodies south, or could not take them farther north for burial.

Anna Lenez was one of these. The miner's wife from Dawson City who was on her way to the Rochester Clinic in Minnesota for treatment of her rheumatoid arthritis,[34] she was a devout Roman Catholic, and a mass was said for her in St Mary's chapel, Dawson City. Because she had a sister in Juneau, however, it was decided to bury her there.[35]

One of the unclaimed bodies was that of Frank Brown. He had lived in the Yukon for about ten years, working as a miner for the Yukon Consolidated Gold Company in the summer and finding work in the south each winter. He was a Bohemian by birth, what later would be called a Sudetan German. A hard worker who kept to himself, he seems to have been extremely thrifty: he was paid $150 a month plus board, and saved $100 of it. When he died he had almost $4,500 on deposit in various Seattle banks and in War Savings Certificates–a substantial sum for those days. It was not until the fall of 1921 that his father came forward to claim his estate, which was held in trust by the Yukon government, and the truth about Frank Brown became known. His real name was Frank Brandstaetter, Jr, and his father was living in Newark, New Jersey. Frank Jr, born in 1876, was one of three sons. His mother died young, and in 1884 his father emigrated to America, leaving his children behind. He found a job as a cement worker, and over the years sent back to Europe for his sons. In America the family adopted the name Brown for the sake of convenience; as the father said, Brandstaetter 'is a very difficult name to be spoken or written in the business'. Frank Jr came to New Jersey in 1905. He and his father had 'a slight argument', and he left home, appearing at Dawson in 1908. His father had a postcard from him in October 1908 and another in June 1910, but apparently did not hear from him after that. He was unmarried, and when no one claimed his body, the Acting Gold Commissioner in Dawson had wired to

Frank Lowle in Juneau, 'Bury remains Frank Brown at Juneau. He was a Bohemian without relatives.'[36] The Foresters Lodge stepped in, however, and he was buried in Vancouver.

Because some of the bodies were badly damaged in the wreck, or had deteriorated from weeks of immersion in the sea, there were a few cases of mistaken identity. These were particularly sad when children were involved, like 6-year-old Loretta Beaton. In 1918 Florence Beaton was taking her son and daughter outside for the first time. The bodies of Florence and Loretta were found and identified soon after the disaster by Gilbert Bates, a business partner of Beaton's, who came up from Seattle to take charge of the bodies. But when John Beaton himself travelled from Iditarod to Juneau in the third week of December to arrange for funeral services and burial, he found to his horror that although the woman was indeed his wife, the girl was not his daughter; his partner had made a mistake. Up until Christmas of that year neither his son nor his daughter had been found, and as the Dawson paper noted, 'no other claimant has appeared for the beautiful child whose body is lying at Juneau'.[37]

James Kirk, the powerful swimmer from Dawson who was found tied by the wrist to a younger man, was also involved in a case of mistaken identity. There was no question about who he was, but another James Kirk, a pioneer miner and prospector, lived in the Fairbanks district, and when the local paper published the names of the victims, the friends of the Alaska man gave him up for dead. To their relief, however, 'our Jim blew in from Fish Creek, where he [had] been prospecting of late'.[38]

Some of the crew members who died on the *Princess Sophia* were hardly more than children themselves. Frank Burke was only 17, Lionel Olson was even younger, and Stewart W. Macey was only four months past his sixteenth birthday. Macey was a native of Vancouver, the younger brother of a man who had crewed on the *Sophia* on earlier voyages. He left school at the age of 14 and found work in sawmills, as a construction labourer, a longshoreman, a cook, and a 'swamper', or driver's helper, on delivery trucks in Vancouver. He went to sea on ships operated by the Union Steamship Company, and apparently served as quartermaster on one of them, though he was only 15 and had little or no experience–an indication of the effect that wartime manpower shortages had on hiring practices. His mother later remarked:

> I was surprised, very much surprised, when the boy came home and said he was quartermaster on board, because I didn't think he had been out on the boat very much, and my oldest boy was working at the same time on the same boat, and the boys were laughing at home at him being over my oldest boy–boss over him.[39]

On 17 September 1918 he was hired on the *Sophia* as an able-bodied seaman. The *Princess Alice* unloaded his body in Vancouver on 12 November, and his funeral was held later that day; members of the Navy League attended and draped the casket with the Union Jack.[40]

Within a week or two, depending on how far they had to travel, all of the bodies discovered in the first days of searching had been laid to rest, including two who remained unidentified: one a boy, the other a man, they were buried in an unmarked grave. Most of the Vancouver burials took place in Mountain View cemetery, where for a while it was feared that there would not be enough plots for them all; however, the Masons were persuaded to give up some of their space.[41]

Some of the stories associated with the victims were terribly poignant. Arthur Johnson's in particular reads like a tale from Victorian melodrama. He was 43 in 1918, born in Wallaceburg, Ontario, and had gone north during the gold rush. He had worked steadily in mining, mostly around Dawson, and though he was not much of a letter-writer, he did send $300 a year to his mother. At one time he was injured in a mining accident at Bonanza, and recovered in the Dawson hospital. By 1918 his mother, who had not seen him in twenty years, was urging him to leave the north and make a home with her and a daughter; to make it easier for him to do so, they even moved west to Portland, Oregon. His sister sent a heartbroken letter to St Mary's Hospital in Dawson:

> After persistent urging he decided to leave that country and come to us, and he was . . . a passenger on the 'Princess Sophia'. Can you imagine our grief and disappointment? Fancy waiting twenty years for such a message! On the day before we received the terrible word my

mother had a letter, or, rather, a note from him, saying that his ticket was bought and he was just leaving. She nearly went mad with joy, but the poor, little, delicate mother's time of rejoicing was all too short . . .

He spoke of having to have his picture taken to put on his passport. We would so like to get that picture. I wonder would you be able to give us the name of one of your leading photographers . . . Any information that you could give us at all would be most gratefully received, not only by a crushed and delicate little mother and two sisters in Portland, but by two young brothers in the East as well as one in the King's uniform overseas. We had hoped for a happy and joyous reunion at this Christmas season, but it seems God willed it otherwise . . . I remain, His heart-broken sister, (Miss) Maude Johnson.[42]

Because the bodies were found over a prolonged period, there were instances in which husbands and wives were buried a good many weeks apart. Such was the case with Herbert and Ellen Beatrice Davies, both staunch members of the Salvation Army. He was the purser on the river steamer *Dawson*, and his wife had gone north in 1918 to spend the summer with him and work as a stenographer in the law office of F.T. Congdon.[43] Herbert Davies was 30 years old, a native of Winnipeg, and a member of a large family; he had four sisters and six brothers, of whom one had already been killed in France. He was good at his work and enthusiastic about it. Earlier that year he had written to his father: 'Mr Johnson, the superintendent, said that my boat seemed to be a lucky boat this year, as we have always left Whitehorse with a load of passengers and did more than all the other boats put together, leaving Dawson for Whitehorse.' 'Of course,' commented his father, 'belonging to the Salvation Army you can understand what kind of a life he lived and how he would do good.'[44] Ellen Davies, 25, had been born in England into a Salvation Army family. Her body, discovered early in 1919, was buried in Victoria's Ross Bay Cemetery on 12 January:

The Salvation Army Citadel was filled with sorrowing friends on Sunday to pay their last respects to the late Mrs Herbert Davies, a victim of the Sophia disaster. The army band attended. Commandant Jaynes gave a brief address. The local members of the Salvation Army followed the casket, the women wearing white mourning sashes,

> while the men wore white arm bands. . . . The army band on the march to Ross bay rendered the Dead March in Saul. . . .[45]

Her husband's body, discovered much later, was not buried until 8 June.

A number of the tombstones of *Sophia* victims commemorated the disaster. One marker in the Mountain View cemetery in Vancouver, for instance, is inscribed 'Charles L. Queen / Lost His Life on S.S. Sophia / October 25, 1918 / Aged 73 Years.' Another reads 'In Memory of / My Beloved Husband / Victor C. Whitecross / Who Lost His Life / on the S.S. Sophia Wreck / Oct. 25, 1918 / Aged 29 Years / Christ Will Clasp the Broken Chain / Closer When We Meet Again.' There are four other markers in the same cemetery that mention the *Princess Sophia* specifically.[46] It is not usual for tombstones to carry information as to the cause of death, at least not in this century. Perhaps the relatives took some comfort in the fact that their loss was not isolated–that they had been bereaved in the course of an event of major historical importance.

As far as the CPR was concerned, by Christmas 1918 the episode seemed over. The divers from the *Tees* reported that the *Princess Sophia* had a 70-foot gash in her hull, and that her superstructure was extensively damaged; the ship was essentially unsalvageable. Captain W.H. Logan, who went to the wreck site on the *Tees* as a representative of Lloyd's of London, the *Sophia*'s insurers, said on 9 November that she was a 'total loss' and had only 'sentimental interest'.[47] Although the CPR was still offering a reward of $50 for each body found, Logan said that all the bodies had been recovered that were likely to be–some had presumably floated out to sea, while others were either trapped in parts of the ship that could not be reached by divers, or lying scattered on the floor of Lynn Canal (the water was so cold that they would disintegrate rather than decay enough to float to the surface). On this point, however, one man was determined to prove the CPR wrong, and out of his determination came one of the strangest chapters in the entire story.

Al Winchell was the miner from Flat Creek, near Iditarod, Alaska, who had sent his wife Ilene south to California for her health, promising that if anything happened to her, he would bury her next to her mother. Her fears had been realized, but her body was not among the nearly two hundred found in the weeks after the disaster. The CPR's position–that there were no more bodies on the *Princess Sophia*–was not good enough for Al Winchell. What happened next inspired at least one journalist to a flight of purple prose:

> There are men who have torn the writing of solemn pledges to shreds and drenched the shreds in blood and called it nothing. There are men who have been willing to spend life itself to keep good a promise made. Of the latter is Al Winchell.[48]

When he heard the news of the *Sophia*'s sinking, Winchell waited until it was cold enough for winter travel, then walked the four hundred miles from Flat Creek to Anchorage–an epic journey in itself. He went by steamer to Juneau, and discovered that because of his wife's illness she had been given a stateroom to herself: number 35, in the waist of the ship. Told that the company did not intend to search the wreck any further, he used his life savings to hire a local diver named Selmer Jacobson. On 21 December Winchell and Jacobson went out to Vanderbilt Reef with two assistants to man the air pump. The conditions for diving were terrible: it was the shortest day of the year, the water was bitterly cold, and cakes of ice floating down the canal threatened to cut the air hose to Jacobson's bulky diving suit as he worked 60 feet below the surface. He immediately found the body of a man on deck, and recovered a woman's body–that of Louise Davis–from the observation room. He was able to find stateroom 35, and looking in the window he saw the bodies of two women, one in a berth and the other on the floor. He could not force the stateroom door open, and the wreckage of the superstructure was lying in such a position that he was afraid to break through it. Instead he broke the window and pulled one of the bodies towards him. Her long hair came off in his hand, and she floated away. He could not stay in the water any longer, and when he came to the surface a storm was brewing that forced the men to return to Juneau.

When the weather cleared they went back to Vanderbilt Reef, and this time Jacobson was able to remove rings from the fingers of one of the women. Later identification showed this to be the body of Sarah O'Brien, wife of William O'Brien, the Yukon Territorial Councillor. The speculation was that she had gone to the cabin to help Ilene Winchell during the ship's last crisis. Believing that the other body, the one on the berth, must be Ilene's–like her, the victim had long black hair, and was dressed in a grey coat–Jacobson redoubled his efforts, but still did not succeed:

> One day when it seemed as if but a few hours would see Mrs Winchell's body discovered the diver working below felt smothered. His trembling, half-frozen fingers in their cold-brittled gloves slipped over the handle of the valve in his helmet and closed it, and with the air confined in the helmet he shot to the surface sixty feet above the wreck.
>
> A slug of ice, formed by the moisture of his breath in the air pipe just above his head partially clogged it.
>
> 'That settles it,' he told Winchell. 'I wouldn't go down again for all the money there is in the world.' Winchell remonstrated with him, but in vain.[49]

In all, Jacobson went five times to Vanderbilt Reef, making between three and six dives each time.[50] By then Winchell had run out of money, but he borrowed more, and in March he hired a Seattle diver named J.J. Donovan, who finally succeeded in bringing the body in stateroom 35 to the surface. But it was not Ilene Winchell.

In May 1919 the CPR company, realizing that its earlier opinion on the likelihood of finding more bodies was wrong, brought a team of divers including Donovan to the wreck, and over the next two months eighty-six more bodies were recovered.[51] Winchell spent most of his time at Vanderbilt Reef, examining each body as it was brought to the surface. Each time he was disappointed, though for some unexplained reason his wife's handbag was discovered in the overcoat pocket of an Alaskan from Tolovana named James G. Nichols–another minor mystery that no doubt raised some eyebrows in the north. The divers told him that the bodies were found all over the *Princess Sophia*–'between decks and up on the boat deck, and in various places . . . most of them were taken out of the social hall.'[52] By the summer, the search was taking its toll:

> Winchell is an old man now. His friends say that he has grown old since the Sophia went down. He lives with but one thought and one end and that is expressed in the line of a letter he wrote a few days ago, which says: 'I hope there is a God in heaven who will favor me by giving me my poor Ilene. I am nearly all in.'[53]

Finally, at the end of July, Ilene Winchell's body was brought to the surface. Al took her back to California and buried her at San Francisco near her mother. Keeping his promise had cost him more than $1000 and five months of searching at Vanderbilt Reef.[54]

On 12 August the body of Edgar Seneff was recovered from the wreck, probably the last to be discovered by the salvage-company divers, who suspended operations that day for three weeks and apparently did not start up again. Seneff, the 18-year-old son of a Fairbanks couple, was working as a watchman on the river steamer *Reliance*, and had decided to go south to join the war effort. His parents had written Governor Riggs a month after the disaster, asking if their son's body had been found, and the exchange of letters, typical of dozens of others that Riggs answered that month, shows once again the human side of the tragedy:

> Fairbanks, Alaska, Nov. 25th, 1918.
> Dear Mr Riggs,
> Mrs Seneff and I wish to thank you for the part you took in the recent disaster of the Princess Sophia . . . We certainly appreciate the noble work done by you in searching for the lost ones, and shall always feel very kindly towards you for it. Edar [sic] was our only child and of course was very dear to us, he was eighteen years old last May–at the time of his fate he was on his way outside to attend a naval school–as he wished to get in that branch of the service.
>
> Up to this writing his body has not been found and we will thank you to inform us if the search is still in progress, also if the divers have gone through the ship–and what their findings were. We have been led to believe that most of the missing bodies still remaining unaccounted for are in the ship–if the bodies are not in the ship what is your opinion about finding them?
>
> Is it a fact that all the passengers could have been saved had the captain of the Sophia permitted it to be done?
>
> We understand that there is an investigation being held at this time,

> if this is a fact we would like to know the outcome of the investigation. Thanking you for any information you may be able to give us at this time and for your interest shown the bereaved ones of the Princess Sophia.

Governor Riggs replied on 13 December:

> It is not possible that very many of the bodies are still in the ship, as the wreck did not come as a surprise and all the bodies recovered showed that the passengers were aware of the danger just before she sank, having all been equipped with life preservers. It is entirely probable, however, that the fear of meeting death by drowning impelled some to remain in their staterooms until the end. How many might have done so, however, can only be conjectured . . .
>
> Your question as to whether the passengers could have been saved if the master had permitted them to take to small boats is one that it is very difficult to answer, in view of the many conflicting opinions. It must be borne in mind that most of them are personal opinions or else are influenced by sentimental or material interest. If you feel inclined to rely upon any opinion that may be expressed, it should come from an entirely disinterested source, and, of course, no one is qualified to give an opinion unless he were in the immediate vicinity from the time the Sophia struck until she sank. Some who were at the scene the morning after she grounded on the reef claim that it was entirely possible to have removed the passengers, while others express doubt. However, in view of the investigation which will be held in Victoria sometime in the near future, it is only proper that the decision of the Wreck Commissioner should be awaited before voicing one's sentiments.[55]

Sadly, the Seneffs were to wait nearly nine months before their son's body was found. The final disposition of the case was to take much longer.

8. AFTERMATH

> The Sophia is a jagged, white mound on the bottom. Virtually no part has escaped the attachment of the large sea anemone, Metridium senile. The effect is eerie–thousands of white anemones slowly and silently extending, then contracting their tentacles . . . Because of the dense covering of anemones and the broken and twisted condition of the hull, the lines of the ship are so indistinct that it was only after many trips to the reef that [the divers] . . . agreed on what they were seeing. The Sophia lies on her side, gradually settling into the bottom, with her bow in about 60 feet of water and her stern at about 100 feet. Hull plates lie twisted and broken, pieces of her masts and superstructure are strewn about, there are gaping holes in her sides–all testimony to her last violent moments and years of slow decay.[1]

By the end of the summer of 1919, all the mortal remains of the *Princess Sophia*'s passengers and crew that would ever be found had been recovered and buried. Yet the story was not over, for the public, and particularly the victims' relatives, demanded that a cause for the disaster be found and blame assigned. Some three hundred and fifty people had died under circumstances that cast grave doubts on the competence and integrity of Canada's most famous private corporation. Now it was the turn of the lawyers.

Within weeks of the disaster the federal government ordered the establishment of a commission of inquiry. At the same time proceedings were begun before the Workmen's Compensation Board to obtain a cash settlement for families of the ship's crew. The question of salvaging the vessel had to be dealt with. Finally, a civil case was launched in the American courts to seek damages for the relatives of the passengers. Extensive testimony was heard–particularly at the commission of inquiry and in the American courts–and the evidence produced eventually filled many volumes. The wheels of justice turned at their usual glacial pace, and almost fourteen years were to pass before the final judicial decisions were rendered.

The favourite targets were the Canadian Pacific Railway and its employees. To many in the general public, and certainly to the victims' families, the company was obviously guilty of gross negligence. The common perception of the disaster was very simple. The *Princess Sophia* had steamed in pitch dark at full speed down a narrow channel in the middle of a blizzard, had got off course, and had run aground. Rescue vessels had come to offer aid, but the company had refused these offers, preferring to wait for one of its own ships to take off the passengers in better weather. But the weather had worsened, and when it was too late for rescue, the *Princess Sophia* had called for help and then sunk. How could such a catastrophe not be someone's fault? Many Canadians believed as an article of faith that the CPR was a pinchpenny outfit, the scourge of prairie farmers; many were ready to believe that it had scrimped on safety measures and sacrificed passengers and crew to save a few thousand in rescue fees.

On one side was a generally unpopular corporation, then capitalized at well over a billion dollars–an immense sum for those days. On the other side were scores of widows and dependent children who had lost their breadwinners and found themselves in difficult circumstances. Surely, they believed, the rich, powerful

CPR would do the decent thing and pay compensation. They were dead wrong; far from paying compensation, the CPR fought the idea through the courts with a tenacity that only a large company, with plenty of money for lawyers' fees, could muster.

From the CPR's point of view, it was obvious that the claims for damage could not be admitted. To do so would have cost the company a great deal of money. Over two hundred claims were filed for the maximum allowable amount of $10,000 each, and $2 million was a large sum to pay for what the company considered to be an act of God. To admit liability would have also been a terrible blow to the company's pride and the professional character of its operations.

All sorts of rumours were circulating among the public and the press at the end of 1918. They were gathered, collected, and amplified by the lawyers acting on behalf of the victims' relatives. Captain Locke was drunk; he was carousing in his cabin with loose women; he was senile; he was subject to fits of wild rage; the *Sophia*'s crew was made up of untrained boys rather than seamen; the CPR had refused to accept the proffered aid because it was too stingy to pay for it; passengers had tried to get off the ship on their own but had been forced back and shut in their cabins at gunpoint; victims had been found riddled with gunshot wounds; the *Sophia* was not seaworthy; her compass did not work; there were not enough lifeboats; the pilot was a novice. All these stories and more provided rich fodder for the lawyers, and were the subject of many allegations raised in court. There are relatives of the victims still alive who firmly believe they are true. Any assessment of the blame for the disaster cannot ignore them.

The disaster also attracted the usual unbalanced publicity seekers. A Miss Vienne Field of Potter Valley, California, claimed in January 1919 to be the 'only Sophia survivor' and to have suffered 'no ill effects of the perilous experience other than a severe cold'. The Juneau *Empire* scornfully dismissed this fantasy with the comment that Miss Field had spoiled a future opportunity, both for herself and for anyone else–it was too soon after the disaster to get away with 'an only *Princess Sophia* survivor story, particularly if one is so near at hand as California'.[2]

While the rumours continued to circulate, the legal proceedings began. The first was the commission of inquiry set up by the Canadian Department of Marine and Fisheries to investigate the affair. There was some difficulty about this at first; the wreck had occurred in American waters, and American officials were expressing interest in conducting an investigation. The Alaska Territorial Senate did pass a resolution to do so,[3] but the idea was eventually dropped, and the investigation was carried out by Canadian officials. On 15 November 1918 a telegram from Ottawa arrived in Victoria, ordering Captain J.D. Macpherson, Wreck Commissioner for British Columbia, to organize a hearing into 'the loss of the steamer Sophia'. As the Victoria *Daily Colonist* observed, everyone knew what the cause of the loss was: the ship had run on a reef and sunk. What was in question was the responsibility for the disaster, and that would presumably be settled in a civil court.[4]

The suggestion that hundreds of people had died in a disaster that might well have been prevented had there been a light on Vanderbilt Reef was one with political overtones. Alaskans had been complaining for years about the lack of lighthouses and adequate lighted buoys in the coastal waters, and the *Sophia* disaster seemed to lend weight to these complaints. In fact, a buoy with a gas light and bell was placed on the reef within weeks of her sinking, and in 1921 it was replaced by a steel tower on a substantial concrete base. Raised 36 feet above the water, bearing a 230 candlepower light, it is still warning mariners away from the rocks today.[5]

The first session of the commission of inquiry was opened in Victoria on 6 January 1919, before Justice Aulay Morrison and Captain Macpherson, with E.H. Martin in an advisory position. Lawyers attended on behalf of the CPR, the government of the Yukon, and several relatives of the victims.[6] The *Dawson Daily News* employed G.C. Macleod, a reporter for the Vancouver *Sun*, to telegraph a report to Dawson each day the committee sat. Extensive testimony was given by Captain J.P. Davis of the *Estebeth* and Captain Miller of the *King and Winge*, and the inquiry then adjourned.

On 31 January the commission sat at Vancouver, and on 10 and 11 February a second session was held in Victoria. In the time between the first and second sessions it was decided to hold a special hearing in Juneau, since that was where most of the witnesses to the disaster lived, and on 26 and 27 February the inquiry met there. A final session was then held in Victoria on 10, 11, and 20 March, and the Commission's report was tabled in the House of Commons on 23 April 1919.

The transcript of the *Princess Sophia* inquiry is voluminous: 522 pages of typewritten testimony were taken at Victoria, and another 250 or so at Juneau. There were essentially two issues in question: how the ship came to hit Vanderbilt Reef, and whether the passengers could have been taken off in safety before she sank. The first question could not be answered; the *Sophia*'s log was never found, and since all the ship's officers had perished, it was simply a matter of conjecture as to how she had got off course. For the second question there were plenty of witnesses, particularly the captains of the rescue ships that had spent a day and a half circling the stricken vessel on Vanderbilt Reef. Some of them were of the opinion that the passengers could have been taken off the ship, but the majority believed they would have been in considerable danger, and that it was not unreasonable for Locke to assume that his ship was in no immediate peril. There was a photographic record of conditions at Vanderbilt Reef during the time the *Princess Sophia* was perched on it. E.P. Pond, the professional photographer from Juneau who had gone out on the *King and Winge* on its rescue mission to Vanderbilt Reef, submitted prints of his pictures.[7] Taken about 11.00 a.m. on 25 October, the day the *Sophia* sank, they show the waters of the Lynn Canal as extremely rough, and make Captain Locke's decision not to offload his passengers seem more reasonable.

Mr Justice Morrison's report was dry and concise, filling fewer than eight pages, several of them statistical. His conclusion too was brief:

> The evidence is that Captain Locke was under no restraint, dictation or interference in the navigating of his ship in any way by the owners, or their agents or servants. Owing to the conditions prevailing at the time, the cable and wireless services were very much impaired.
>
> From the evidence adduced, the conclusion arrived at by your Commission is that the ship was lost through the peril of the sea.
>
> As to why the passengers were not landed is a matter of conjecture,

> but your Commissioners beg to submit that from the evidence of all the surrounding circumstances, such as the ship being staunch, and well officered; other craft being in the vicinity and other ships approaching; the inhospitable shores and lack of shelter sufficiently near; the time of year and weather conditions; we are not prepared to find that it was unreasonable for Captain Locke not to land his passengers.[8]

And with that resounding triple negative–saying, in effect, that the decision not to take the passengers off was what sportswriters term a 'judgement call'–the report ended. The commission did not deal with the misery caused by the disaster, nor did it come to grips with the tremendous human loss involved. Much time was spent in discussion of technicalities and niggling points of procedure, such as how much per diem should be paid to the witnesses. Perhaps surprisingly, neither the British Columbia nor the northern newspapers castigated the inquiry for dealing with the disaster as a technical rather than a human matter, and there was no wave of public protest against the decision. The public seems to have accepted the belief of the majority of sea captains who witnessed the episode that it was an act of God.

In March 1919 a test case was brought by the CPR before the Supreme Court of British Columbia in Vancouver to determine whether the relatives of the *Princess Sophia*'s crew were eligible for benefits under the Workmen's Compensation Act. The matter was of more than academic interest to the CPR, since such benefits would have to be paid not by the government, but by the Workmen's Compensation Board out of a fund collected from 'certain groups of employers generally'. Since the relatives of about seventy-five crew members were involved, the sums to be paid were substantial,[9] and the CPR, as a large employer, would be responsible for a big share. More to the point, any imputation of blame to the CPR that might come out in the hearings would presumably have a damaging effect on the company in the civil suits, brought by relatives of the passengers, that were bound to follow in the courts. Lawyers for the CPR claimed that the Workmen's Compensation Act was *ultra vires* (beyond the authority) of the British Columbia legislature because the latter could not pass laws concerning accidents that might happen outside its own territory. The *Sophia* had sunk in United States waters, where the Workmen's Compensation Act had no force. The judgement, handed down on 13 March by Mr Justice Clement, upheld the company's position:

> Regretfully, his lordship states, he must hold that the Workmen's Compensation act, in so far as it applied to actual facts of this case, is beyond the power of the provincial legislature . . . there was by law of the [Alaska] territory very limited liability to pay damages, but there was no legislation akin to the Workmen's Compensation act of this province. This immunity enjoyed by the plaintiff company in respect of its navigation of Alaskan waters was clearly, in his opinion, a civil right existing beyond this province and that civil right would manifestly be rendered a delusion if the plaintiff company was forced to pay compensation in this province. Action might be brought in Alaskan courts, but, of course, without any possibility of success.[10]

It was 'Catch-22' in action: the Act of British Columbia was inoperative in Alaskan waters; the relatives of the crew might well be successful in bringing action under a Workmen's Act in Alaska; but there was no Workmen's Compensation Act in Alaska–therefore they were out of luck.

The decision was immediately taken to the Court of Appeal, which confirmed it, and then to the Judicial Committee of the Privy Council in Great Britain, a course of action that remained possible in Canadian civil cases until 1949.[11] In the Judicial Committee of the Privy Council Viscount Haldane delivered a judgement reversing the original decision. The Workmen's Compensation Act, he said, was 'not one for interfering with rights outside the Province. It is in substance a scheme for securing a civil right within the Province. . . . It makes no difference that the accident insured against might happen in foreign waters.'[12]

The compensation paid to the relatives of the crew was based on the relationship involved and the age of the claimant. Although the awards were as high as $3500, they were paid in instalments, as a monthly pension. Widows received $20 per month, and $5 for each child. If a widow remarried, she was given a lump sum of $480 and no further payments. Dependent parents got between $5 and $20 a month, according to their circumstances. The total value of the awards was about $83,000.[13] Having applied for and accepted compensation, the relatives of the crew members were prevented by the Workmen's Compensation Act from suing the company for further damages.

By August 1919, when this judgement was delivered, the law seemed to be favouring the victim's families. Compensation had been awarded to the estates of the crew members, and the relatives of the passengers had every reason to believe that they would be equally successful in the courts. But they would wait a long time to find out, for the final chapter of the legal proceedings associated with the *Princess Sophia* was also the most prolonged.

The initial legal skirmishing took place even before all the bodies had been found, when relatives of the passengers began hiring lawyers to sue the CPR for damages. The CPR's countermove was to initiate legal proceedings for limitation of liability in the American courts, and to that end the company hired the Seattle law firm of Bogle, Bogle, and Gates. As part of this action, the CPR had to surrender title to the *Princess Sophia* to the court in Seattle, which then permitted the company to continue work in the summer of 1919 searching for bodies and attempting salvage work.

The CPR arranged with the Deep Sea Salvage Company to raise the wreck, and efforts were made in the late summer and fall of 1919 to do so, but without success. In October 1919 rumours circulated in Juneau and Whitehorse that the *Sophia* had been raised by cables and towed to Bridget Cove, or had been raised and then slipped back into the water, but these were unsubstantiated.[14] During the winter of 1919-20 the salvage company raised over $40,000 from investors anxious to share in the treasure that was supposed to be on board. In the summer of 1920 work began again. The company reported that it had secured cables and chains around the ship, and was ready to winch it to the surface. A motion-picture photographer arrived in Juneau to film the event for the Gaumont newsreel company. But at the end of the summer the salvage company went bankrupt, and work stopped. Since the ship's Wells Fargo safe had already been found, there was more than a whiff of fraud about the whole affair:

> For two years the newspapers of the north have been filled with the doings of the Deep Sea Salvage Co., and, in the earlier stages of the proceedings, the company carried big display ads in the Juneau papers inviting the public to buy shares in an enterprise . . . that would return

> to the stockholders unheard of dividends . . . $50,000 in cash and gold dust in the vessel's safe . . .
>
> Many people were found gullible enough to accept the statements of the promoters as true . . . And now, after two years of worry and disappointment, in which time several unsuccessful attempts have been made to raise the wreck of the Princess Sophia, the disillusionment comes. The purser's safe on board that vessel was recovered a few days ago, . . . only about $10,000 in cash and gold dust.
>
> As the *Douglas Island News* remarked . . . 'It was a romance all right, but sordid romance, with a touch of bitterness in it at the end.'[15]

While the vultures were picking the carcass of the *Princess Sophia* clean, court proceedings were beginning in Seattle; because the accident took place in American waters, the case was heard in American courts. The lawyers for the CPR attempted a pre-emptive strike by obtaining a legal limitation of liability, which would defuse any effort on the part of the victims' relatives to obtain compensation. The legal grounds for such tactics were quite straightforward. Both Canadian and American law provided for a limitation of liability in cases such as that of the *Princess Sophia*. The Canadian law[16] held that ship owners should not be held answerable for losses of life or property for more than $38.92 for each ton of the ship's tonnage, if the loss was without knowlege or privity (fault) of the owner. The American law was the same, except that the liability was limited to the value of the ship, freight, and passenger ticket sales. Since the ship was valueless, the total sum of the liability amounted to the value of the ticket and freight sales–about $9,000–unless it could be proven that the disaster was due to the company's negligence and not to an act of God.

Some lawyers felt from the beginning that the relatives would not win. F.T. Congdon, a Vancouver lawyer who had practised for many years in Dawson and had once served as Territorial Commissioner, wrote a memo in 1919 saying that his 'advice to claimants would be to settle and get what they can and not incur the risk of expensive actions in which defeat seems almost inevitable'.[17] Others, however, felt that the relatives had a good case. Prominent in this group was William Martin, a Seattle attorney of the firm of Martin and Myers, who eventually was hired to represent the interests of the relatives of 225 passengers. Martin worked on a contingency basis, his clients agreeing to pay him 40 per cent of any damages recovered, plus court costs.[18] He seems to have represented his clients energetically and ably, participating in all the numerous hearings that took place on the case, and keeping his clients informed during the long years of proceedings.

Under American law, it did not matter if Captain Locke or his pilot had made a terrible mistake, as one of them evidently had, so long as he was a competent mariner, had a trained crew, and commanded a seaworthy ship. This was why much of Martin's case depended on being able to prove that Locke and his crew were not competent, and that the *Princess Sophia* was not seaworthy.

First, however, as Martin explained, he had to answer the CPR's petition before a United States Commissioner, stating his clients' claims. At the end of 1919 he did so, filing a claim for each client to the value of $10,000, the maximum permitted under the laws of Alaska. This meant that the total claim against the CPR came to $2.25 million. The company objected to the claim, which meant, said Martin, that it doubted its ability to win limitation of liability, since if it were to succeed in limiting liability, it would not matter how large the claim was.

On the main point, the limitation of liability, Martin set out for his clients the points of his case. First, he intended to prove that the officers of the *Princess Sophia* were neither qualified nor competent, that they were alcoholics and were drunk on the fatal voyage; that the crew was made up of boys and men rejected by the army for physical disability; that the *Sophia* did not have a full complement of crew as required by American law; and that the CPR knew these facts and was thus guilty of negligence.

Second, he intended to prove that the CPR had for years been in the habit of running its ships at full speed in bad weather, even when the 'points of departure', or places where changes were made in the ship's course, could not be seen, which was a violation of both US law and international rules of navigation; since the company knew that this was done, it was at fault: 'Where the officers of a vessel are in the habit of navigating the vessel in fog and thick weather at full speed and the company does not stop them, it . . . becomes a party to the negligence itself.'[19] Since there was little doubt that the *Princess Sophia* was going at full speed when it hit Vanderbilt Reef, said Martin, it remained only to prove that running at top speed in bad weather was common practice, and that the company knew it.

The third point was Martin's contention that the CPR could easily have removed the passengers in perfect safety, and that Captain Locke had originally wanted to do so, but that the company had instead ordered him to keep them on board until the *Princess Alice* could be sent to Vanderbilt Reef. The reason for this, said Martin, was that the CPR wished to save the expense of transferring passengers to the boats standing by. He was confident that, even though some crucial wireless messages had been destroyed, he could prove this point, which was vital to the case. By November 1920 he had visited Ketchikan, Juneau, and Skagway to take testimony before a commissioner, and planned to spend three more months taking further testimony on the matter.

The first point to be decided in the courts was the matter of limitation of liability. In January 1921 a trial lasting two weeks was held at Seattle before the Honorable Jeremiah Neterer. It produced thousands of pages of testimony, but since a good deal of the case turned upon what might have been done and was not, much of the 'evidence' was contradictory and speculative. One interesting point, for example, was the question of whether or not the *Atlas* could have taken off the *Sophia*'s passengers by means of a breeches buoy, a contrivance by which a kind of chair is rigged to a rope passing between the two vessels. Captain C.W. Call, master of the *Atlas*, testified under examination by William Martin that this could easily have been done (Mr Bogle was the counsel for the defence):

Q. [Martin] How long would it have taken you to transfer the passengers from the 'Sophia' to the 'Atlas' in the manner which you speak of?

A. [Call] That is hard to say, sir. You can only handle one man at a time with a breeches buoy,–one person at a time.

Q. How close would you have been able to go up to the 'Princess Sophia' with the 'Atlas'?

Mr Bogle–I shall object to this. The witness wasn't there, and doesn't know the conditions.

Q. You are familiar with the conditions of water about Vanderbilt Reef,–depth, etc?

A. Yes, sir.

Q. You may state how close the 'Atlas' could have come up on the lee side of Vanderbilt reef.

Mr Bogle–Objected to as pure speculation.

The Court–Let him answer.

A. We could have gotten close enough to have thrown a rock there. . . . Our plan, your Honor, was to go up under the lee of the vessel and use the line as I said, and if our ship was tailing off, to have a tail anchor to hold her in position while we were doing our work. . . .

Q. Would you have encountered any difficulties in transferring the passengers in that manner from the 'Sophia' to the 'Atlas'?

Mr Bogle–Objected to as pure speculation, the elements as to the weather conditions not being known to the witness.

The Court–Let him answer.

A. No difficulty. . . .

Q. [Bogle] Was the 'Atlas' fitted with a breeches buoy:

A. She had a Lyle gun, and that goes–

Q. She had what?

A. A Lyle gun. And a breeches buoy is a very easy thing made.

Q. Had you made one during those two hours?

A. Preparations were under way when we got the second wire.[20]

Q. Now, in operating a breeches buoy of that kind, isn't it pretty difficult when you are in a heavy sea?

A. It is.

Q. Every surge of the ship, there is a sag in the line?

A. More or less.

Q. There is great danger of loss of life in that method, where a ship is rolling in a sea, and not stationary?

A. There is some.

Q. There is a great deal of danger of it, isn't there; you can't keep that line stationary; it sags with each roll of the ship?

A. Yes. . . .

Q. Could you have done it at night?

A. It has been done many times.

Q. Have you often done it yourself?

A. Never.

Q. How often have you saved lives, or removed passengers from a vessel at sea?
A. At no time.
Q. Never. Is it practical to operate this breeches buoy unless your ship is at anchor? . . .
A. It depends on the stress of the weather and the seas running. . . .
Q. So that your proposed method of rescuing the passengers would depend upon the ability to anchor the 'Atlas' to the leeward of the 'Sophia'?
A. That was our whole method, sir. . . .[21]

Captain Call, who admitted that he had not been a witness to the events of 24 and 25 October, was not a strong witness. His testimony was further weakened by the fact that Captain Leadbetter of the *Cedar* had actually tried and failed to anchor his ship downwind of the *Princess Sophia* with a view to picking up the ship's passengers in lifeboats. A great deal of the testimony heard by the court was equally unhelpful.

On 30 September 1921 Judge Neterer filed his decision, denying the petition of the CPR, giving it limitation of liability only for the value of the cargo and holding it liable, if negligence were proven, for the payment of all damages sustained by passengers and crew – a payout of $2.5 million by the CPR and a fee of $1 million for Martin's firm. In his decision, Judge Neterer said that the circumstances of the accident were of paramount importance:

> Ordinary care on the part of the lookout and moderate speed would have prevented the catastrophe. Navigating through a storm of the character disclosed by the testimony, at a speed which would carry the vessel upon the reef 72 feet, inflicting the injury disclosed under the circumstances shown in the testimony, is contrary to the International Rules of Navigation . . . and a violation of the rule of ordinary prudence in navigation, and establishes a presumption of negligence, which, unless overcome, is conclusive.[22]

But this was just the first round. The CPR immediately filed a petition for rehearing before Judge Neterer, which was granted, and the case was re-argued on the same testimony he had already considered over the summer of 1921. Ten days after the re-argument, the judge filed a second decision reversing the first and granting the company the right to limit its liability to $9,000 (and Martin's fee, consequently, to a maximum of $3,600).

The next step was to appeal this decision, and at the same time take testimony to establish the actual damages sustained in order that a final decree might be entered as to the share of whatever sum might be assessed. When the CPR had objected to the size of the claim, it had set up another issue for the courts to decide: the value of each victim's life. Martin was correct in saying that if the company won its case on limitation of liability, it would not matter if each life was worth $100 or $1 million, but–either as a fall-back position, or perhaps simply on the principle that the best defence is a good offence–the CPR vigorously contested every claim. This meant that the relatives of the victims or the administrators of their estates had to provide testimony on the lives, careers, employment history, health, and spending habits of each victim, along with other personal information. They did not all have to attend court personally; a list of questions (interrogatories) was drawn up–and there was great legal wrangling over the form of the questions–and sent to the home towns of those relatives who did not live on the west coast; the questions were then answered under oath before a commissioner of oaths. Other family members did attend court to answer the questions. In either case, the questioning must have been painful for the relatives, but it provides some fascinating insights into the lives of hundreds of otherwise obscure people. Not surprisingly, for the most part their survivors testified that the deceased had been hard workers, good providers, great savers of money, and in perfect health. They testified to the latter even in instances where the victims had left the north precisely in order to seek medical treatment. It was a matter of speaking nothing but good of the dead–particularly advantageous where hopes of financial compensation were involved.

Judge Neterer's reversal of his decision was a serious but not fatal setback, for there were appeal courts before which the case could be re-heard. Martin now took it to the United States Circuit Court of Appeals at San Francisco, where three judges would try it *de novo*: all over again from the beginning. Despite the fact that the CPR seemed to be winning, it continued to fight on the question of

lus exhibits) was that the lawyer for
number of frivolous and unsubstan-
PR and its employees. In trying to
as incompetent, they made charges
re at best irrelevant and at worst
ngthy exchange between Martin and
ed to show that Locke was some sort
of, incredibly, rested on an advertis-
shown Locke dancing with a female
al to the CPR, was an unco-operative

Troup, if Captain Locke was not in the
with women on the boat, and you knew

im dancing around on the boat with

nowledge,–never even heard of it.

of him with women dancing around on the

at, if the Court please, as incompetent and

didn't know.
there; and I ask if that is the regular
out?
amphlets.
good many times, haven't you?
an official circular or publication of the

It is published by the passenger depart-

this in evidence, and ask that it be
espondents' Exhibit 20.

competent and immaterial.

by the passenger department.

of its transcript (8,500 pages
the victims' relatives made a
tiated allegations about the
prove that Captain Locke v
about his character that w
scurrilous and stupid. In a l
Captain Troup, the lawyer t
of carousing playboy. His pr
ing pamphlet that might hav
passenger. Troup, fiercely lc
witness:

Q. I will ask you, Captain
habit of dancing arounc
it.
A. No, sir.
Q. You never knew of
women?
A. Never to my personal k
Q. Never heard of it?
A. No.
Q. Never saw any pictures
boat?
Mr Bogle.–I object to t
immaterial.
The Court.–He said h
Q. Look at this pamphle
pamphlet that you got
A. I don't get out these p
Q. You have seen them a
Q. (By the Court.) Is tha
company?
A. Yes; undoubtedly it
ment.
Mr Martin.–We
marked as Clair
The Court.–A
Mr Bogle.–
The Cour
Mr Bogl

(Whereupon the court admitted in evidence as Claimants' and Respondents' Exhibit 20, the pamphlet referred to).

Q. I will ask you to look at the top photograph in this pamphlet which you have issued and circulated all over the country.
Mr Bogle.–I object to the statement, and ask to have it stricken.
Q. And ask you who the gentleman is there with the uniform on, dancing with the large lady?
Mr Bogle.–We object to that as incompetent and immaterial,–entirely immaterial.
Q. Doesn't it look like Captain Locke?
A. I wouldn't be sure of that.
Q. Wouldn't you?
A. No, sir.
Q. Wouldn't be sure whether that was Captain Locke or not?
A. But even though it was Captain Locke, I don't see that it would be any harm.
Q. Is it or not a picture of Captain Locke?
A. I couldn't tell you. It is nearer his figure than Captain Slater's.
Q. Decidedly nearer his figure than Captain Slater's. A very stocky man.
A. But it might not have been Captain Locke at all.
Q. You can see the picture.
A. I can see the picture. I don't know where it was gotten.
Q. In your best judgement, is that a picture of Captain Locke in that pamphlet, on the after deck of the 'Sophia'?
A. Well, I must say I wouldn't be sure that is Captain Locke.
Q. What is your best judgement about it?
Mr Bogle–He has answered it, if the Court please, and it is an immaterial matter. I ask to have the question stricken; the fact whether the man danced or not wouldn't affect his navigation.
Mr Martin.–No; nothing affected his navigation.[27]

It is hard to believe that either lawyer was unaware that captains of passenger ships not only regularly danced with female passengers but were expected to do so by the shipping companies. Not all the lines of questioning were this inane, but a considerable amount was almost equally silly, such as the testimony about Locke's opinion of Americans. A private letter was produced in court in which Locke wrote: 'There are some fine USers, but they are few and far between . . . I have sailed under their rotten flag and know it.'[28] How was this relevant? Was Martin suggesting that

Locke sank his ship out of hatred for the US, or refused aid because he would not let himself be helped by Americans? It seems unlikely. Other lines of questioning were patently offensive, as when Martin engaged in prolonged questioning of a young woman who was a friend of Locke's family. Martin strongly insinuated that Locke was the father of the woman's daughter, whom he had apparently adopted. Even if these allegations were true, they were not even remotely relevant to the events on Vanderbilt Reef.[29]

Judge Sawtelle's decision, commendably lucid, took issue with the haggling on both sides, pointing out that the work of the court had been made more difficult by the fact that 'counsel are in sharp disagreement as to the facts, and in their briefs accuse each other of bad faith and unprofessional conduct'. 'It is unfortunate,' he continued, 'that the court could not have had the temperate argument that the record requires and the importance of the case demands. When counsel accuse on another of bad faith, naturally the court is unable to accept the assertions in the briefs at face value, and can, of necessity, take nothing for granted.' The judge was also understandably annoyed at the ponderous weight of briefs, arguments, and counter-arguments, which amounted to 'repetition of matters contained in the original briefs, with very few really new points discussed'.[30]

On the main point, whether the passengers could have been taken off safely had Locke so wished, the court quoted the testimony of Captain C.E. Tibbits, a long-time mariner in the Juneau area and a founder of the Juneau Ferry and Navigation Company:

Q. The first thing to do is to consider the safety of the passengers, isn't it?
A. Yes, sir.
Q. And if it is safe,–if the passengers are safer on the vessel than they would be if an attempt were made to remove them, why the safe course would be to keep them on the vessel, wouldn't it?
A. Certainly.
Q. And that all depends upon the condition of the weather that exists at the time the vessel is stranded?
A. Yes, sir; certainly.
Q. And the condition of the sea, and the condition of the point where

the vessel strands. All those matters have to be taken into consideration in determining wherein the safety of the passengers lies?

A. Certainly.

Q. And those are matters which can be best determined by the master and officers in charge of the stranded vessel?

A. He is supposed to be the judge of those matters.

The court also quoted a report of W.J. Manahan, officer in charge of the US Naval radio station at Juneau:

> The second officer of the USS Cedar told me during our conversation that on Friday they perhaps could have taken off the passengers, if they were put into a boat alongside of the Sophia and let drift with the current, but by doing this in all probability many of them would have been lost. If this had been done and some were lost and later the ship held fast, and the remainder were taken off the Sophia direct, there would be a blame for the seemingly rash act of taking off the people in a small boat when they could have remained on board and been taken off in a better manner later on. It is the opinion that this was the Captain's idea in keeping his passengers on board. Both the Captain of the Cedar and the King and Wing[e] stated that they would have done exactly as Captain Locke did, keep the people on board.
>
> The general opinion is that Captain Locke cannot be blamed in any way for his actions, and he acted according to his best judgment and lost.[31]

In the court's opinion, the disaster was not caused by inadequate equipment. None of the rumours about Captain Locke's incompetence or drunkenness was substantiated. Nor did the wireless messages indicate that the CPR had ordered Locke not to take the passengers off the *Sophia* before the *Princess Alice* got to the scene. Nor were any of the other points raised by the lawyers for the victims' relatives found valid. Concluding that 'it is beyond cavil that the ultimate decision rests with the captain of the ship, and an error of judgment on his part cannot be imputed to the owner', the court upheld the CPR's petition for limitation of liability.

This meant that the CPR was liable to pay out only the amount of the value of the cargo and perhaps the ticket revenue. In 1919 this had amounted to $8,000 or $9,000, but by 1932 court costs had whittled the total amount available for payment of claims to about $600. This paltry sum–about $2.50 each–was the only money that the 225 clients of William Martin had a legal claim upon. As he said disgustedly to the Court of Appeals: 'That is it. It is all gone. It is not worth considering at all.'[32] That being the case, the court did not bother to deal with the relative merits of the 225 individual cases, as to whose life or earning potential was worth more or less than another's. There was no $2.5 million. After nearly fourteen years of litigation, hundreds of hours of testimony, thousands of pages of typed and printed pleas, the estates of the passengers on the *Princess Sophia* got precisely nothing.

Some people who are interested in the story–mostly relatives of the victims–believe that the outcome of the *Princess Sophia* story represented an outrageous miscarriage of justice. First of all, there is little question that the court's decision was correct in law. The law stated that the CPR was not liable for damages unless it could be proven that the company was knowingly negligent in equipping or manning the ship. As the Court of Appeals correctly stated, there was no real evidence–wild rumours and the lawyer's allegations notwithstanding–that the *Sophia* was badly manned or equipped with fewer lifesaving devices than the law required; nor was there any evidence at all that Locke was less than a competent captain. Despite the public hostility to the CPR, which was not without some justification, it strains credulity to believe that the company would have put more than three hundred and fifty lives at risk to save a few thousand dollars in rescue costs; at any rate, the aftermath of the disaster cost it many times more than that. The funeral expenses alone cost the company over $70,000 (see Appendix D) and the lawyers' fees must have been enormous. It is true that the ship was going at full speed, or nearly so, in bad weather, but had she been going at half or quarter speed, she would have fetched up on the reef all the same. The buoy that marked Vanderbilt Reef is invisible in bad weather, and the *Sophia* ran on the reef through an error in navigation, not because of her speed. This error could not have been foreseen by the CPR; thus the company was not liable. As to the question of taking off the passengers, again the court was correct in saying that this was entirely the decision of Captain Locke. The CPR had nothing to do with it; if he made a wrong decision, it was not the company's fault. Thus under the law the CPR was not liable, and the appeal court ruled correctly.

But if this decision was right in law, was it also right in fact–was it morally just? The crucial question is whether the passengers could have been taken off in safety on 24 or 25 October, while the *Princess Sophia* sat perched on Vanderbilt Reef. There is contrary evidence on this point. Some of the witnesses who were present during those two days said that it might have been done, although perhaps with some loss of life; others–the majority–said that it could have been done only at great risk, and that they would have acted just as Captain Locke did. E.P. Pond's photographs of the scene show that on the 24th the water was rough, though apparently not perilously so, and much rougher on the 25th. Perhaps Captain Locke was thinking of the 1904 *Clallam* disaster, when the passengers put into boats had died while those remaining on the ship survived. The *Princess Alice* was on the way; the weather was bound to moderate; the *Sophia* was firmly on the reef. Why should he risk his passengers in open boats on rough and cold waters? A fair summary of opinion on the question was given by Inspector Bell of the Mounted Police: 'There is a prevailing sentiment that many of them could have been taken off but that at no time could all of them have been transferred without loss of life.'[33] In the end, it was Locke's decision to make; it proved to be horribly wrong, but that does not mean it was unreasonable.

As to fairness: the relatives of the crew received $3,000 from the Workmen's Compensation Board and the relatives of the passengers got nothing, while the CPR collected a quarter of a million dollars in insurance money from Lloyd's of London.[34] This certainly seemed unfair, though a hard-hearted observer might say that this is what life insurance is for, and that there was nothing to prevent the passengers from insuring their lives as the CPR had insured the vessel; indeed, some of them had done so. But the law did not deal with such questions; it was designed to protect the shipowners in just such cases as that of the *Princess Sophia*, and it was the court's business not to weigh the misery and privation of the relatives, but to interpret the law. The question of fairness, as the bereaved relatives understood it, had no place in the courts that ruled on the case.

On 7 October 1919 the *Dawson Daily News* published an editorial entitled 'Remember the Sophia', which reminded readers that although Dawson had given 'heavily of her richest blood on the battlefields of Flanders, here at her threshold the toll she paid was by far heavier than she sustained in all the world war'. The *Dawson Daily News* called for all flags in town to be lowered on 25 October, the first anniversary of the disaster: 'The heroes and the heroines of Dawson and the rest of the broad Northland who went to their reward with the Sophia are enshrined forever in the hearts of Dawson.' But it was one of the saddest aspects of the whole episode that this pious statement proved to be untrue. The story of the sinking of the *Princess Sophia* quickly faded from popular consciousness, even in the north; within a surprisingly short time, northerners had all but forgotten about the disaster, and it was not until recently that interest in it has reawakened.[35]

During the seventy years that have passed since the *Princess Sophia* disaster there have been people who have kept the memory of the event alive: friends and relatives of the victims, and maritime buffs in particular. Over the past few decades, short articles have appeared from time to time in popular publications recounting the episode, often inaccurately. In 1958 Edison Marshall, an author of historical novels, wrote a book entitled *Princess Sophia*.[36] Whatever its merits as a piece of fiction, as an account of the *Sophia* story it has little to do with history. In the book, the ship is named after a southern belle called Sophia Hill, who comes from a South Carolina plantation. A far-fetched twist of the plot brings her to Alaska, where she dies in childbirth. Then Captain Locke, a secret admirer, names his new ship after her. In October 1918 Locke runs this vessel aground and says 'Good God, I've run up on Vanderbilt Reef!' In any case, the most interesting aspect of the book is the question of how Marshall happened on the subject. This particular mystery has been solved by R.N. DeArmond of Juneau, who reports that around 1956 Marshall spent a week or so in the town looking for material for a novel on the north. He spent a good deal of time in the Alaska Historical Library, and presumably came across the *Sophia* story there.

But in the Yukon River valley, the area most affected by the disaster, it was until very recently all but forgotten. There are two war memorials in the Yukon, but not a single physical monument to the victims of the *Princess Sophia* in the Yukon or Alaska. In the years after 1918 it was kept alive in the hearts of a shrinking minority, but in the public consciousness there was no trace of it. The disaster has even escaped professional historians. In their survey history of Alaska, Claus-M. Naske and H. Slotnik ignore the episode, as does Morris Zaslow in his study of the Canadian north after 1914.[37] The question that remains, obviously, is why.

At the beginning of this book some answers to this question were suggested, among them the absence of famous people aboard the ship and the peripheral importance of the north, particularly to Canada. But there are reasons that spring specifically from the nature of northern society itself. For one thing, the *Princess Sophia* disaster was not the only blow to hit the far northwest in 1918. The economies of both the Yukon and Alaska had been badly damaged by the war, particularly by the departure of hundreds of young men for military service. A depression affected the entire region–in sharp contrast to the energy and excitement of the gold-rush era. Particularly in the Yukon, a series of devastating government economy measures had undercut much of the region's confidence in the future; the federal government had slashed the budget, savaged the civil service, and removed a large amount of political power from the people.

In the natural course of events, a disaster such as the sinking of the *Princess Sophia* would dominate the North American press for months, as did the *Challenger* disaster of 1986, particularly as the public pondered its causes and significance. But the coincidence of the episode with the end of the First World War drew public attention away from it. In November 1918 the people of North America were in a mood to celebrate; they did not wish to mourn or engage in a long post-mortem. Even Dawson City–though the local newspaper was full of the *Sophia* for weeks–stood back from the event, and launched a series of parades and dances to mark the peace in Europe.

Another unusual feature of the *Sophia* story was the fact that, for the most part, the mourning took place far away from the region most affected. Because the families of the victims were scattered around the Pacific northwest and across North America, the grieving was fragmented; personal and collective memories of the event were not concentrated in one place, and thus were weakened. For people in the far north, the mourning was limited to symbolic memorial services. There were no mass funerals–indeed, no funerals at all–and hence no major community focus for grief. Without such a focus, the sense of loss was dissipated, and the fact that the victims were buried outside is the most likely reason that a memorial was never built to them in the north.

Because the victims' families were so widely scattered–in itself an indication of the tremendous mobility of people in the far northwest–the story did not become entrenched in the regional consciousness; it remained important only to individual friends and relations who had virtually no contact with each other. This isolation was confirmed by attempts made in the summer of 1988 to solicit reminiscences and other information on the sinking. Family members and old-timers in the Vancouver, Seattle, and Vancouver Island areas were very forthcoming with information and assistance, but almost no one from the far north came forward to share personal recollections.

Although the sinking of the *Princess Sophia* served to illustrate the interconnected nature of life in the Yukon and Alaska, that same interconnectedness meant that the story could not be captured by one political jurisdiction or even one nation. It was a story of passengers from the Yukon (some of whom were American) and from Alaska (some of them Canadian) heading for destinations in British Columbia, Washington, Oregon, California, and more than a dozen other states and provinces,[38] travelling on a Canadian ship through American waters; the subsequent court cases and inquiries too were held in both Canada and the United States. The fact that it was neither 'Canadian' nor 'American' made it difficult for any one region or group to claim the story as its own, let alone to identify in it elements that might be illustrative of national or regional characteristics.

Although the central themes of the *Princess Sophia* story–the transiency and mobility of the far northwest, the post-gold-rush gloom, the wartime collapse of the northern economy–are representative of the processes of change in the region, they are negative, unhappy themes, ones that the region would just as soon forget. Any country's memory of its past is inevitably imprecise and incomplete; many elements are ignored while others, typically those deemed to illuminate positive aspects of the national character, are highlighted and even mythologized.[39] The *Princess Sophia* disaster was not this kind of story, for it reminded Yukoners and Alaskans of the very elements in their society that they wished to ignore–the impermanence and transiency, the lack of commitment. Given a choice between the upbeat, exciting stories of the Klondike gold rush, with its tourist-attracting themes of greed, hardship, lust, and triumph over the frontier, popularizers have until very recently found little of interest in the sad story of the *Princess Sophia*.

The major explanation, however, must rest not with the event itself, but with the north. The mobile nature of northern society that was made so clear by the *Sophia* story was symptomatic of a much broader tendency in the far northwest. It was a society with shallow roots, constantly on the move. Few families remained there long; most northern residents were either single men or husbands and fathers who left their families in the south. There was consequently little persistence in the population. Of the 6,000 or 7,000 people who lived in Dawson City in 1907, only 7 per cent were still there in 1923.[40] Such impermanence, coupled with the steady loss of population in the territory–from over 27,000 in 1901 to 8,500 in 1911 and only 4,100 in 1921–reflected the remorseless decline of the north after the gold rush.

This transient quality was accentuated by the fact that there the people who generally pass on regional culture and consciousness in a community were themselves on the move. Missionaries, teachers, political leaders, journalists, lawyers–those who would usually be expected to keep the flame of regional memory alive–were among the most mobile northerners, most of them leaving after only a few years' confinement in the land of the midnight sun. Only a handful were left over the years to retain and pass on the memory, ensuring that as time passed, fewer and fewer people in the north would have any personal memories of the disaster or its victims.

Where the story has survived over the past seventy years is not in the Yukon River valley that was wounded so grievously by the episode, but in the Pacific coastal towns, where maritime buffs have kept it alive.[41] Here the long-ignored disaster epic is slowly re-entering the regional lexicon. Mary Lou Spartz of Juneau has written and staged a short play, targeted at the city's growing tourist trade, entitled *The Real Story of the Princess Sophia.* It takes great liberties with the facts, especially Captain Locke's character–he is in his cabin dancing with two ladies named Rose and Dolly when the ship grounds on the reef–and is in fact anything but the 'real' story. Moreover, Spartz's play, like Sheila Nickerson's evocative rendering of the disaster in her poem *On Why the Quilt-Maker Became a Dragon*, focusses only on the events on Vanderbilt Reef and after; there is no attempt to understand the origins of the disaster or to carry the story into the interior of the far northwest, where the losses were most deeply felt.[42] Steve Hites, Manager of Passenger Operations for the White Pass & Yukon Railway–reopened in 1988 to carry tourists once more over the White Pass, along the route followed in 1918 by the *Sophia*'s victims–has written a song called 'The Last Voyage of the *Princess Sophia*', a powerful piece in the tradition of maritime disaster epics. But it too describes only the salt-water part of the journey that carried some three hundred and fifty people to their deaths.

The *Princess Sophia* disaster marked the end of an era–a time of northern optimism, when, in the lingering twilight of the gold rush, people still believed that the Yukon River valley had a bright future. In this respect, the episode was like the *Titanic* disaster of 1912. Coming in the last days of the Edwardian era, at the end of a century of peace and prosperity (some minor colonial wars notwithstanding), the sinking of the *Titanic* struck a blow to the hitherto unshakeable confidence of the British Empire and western Europe generally, serving as a prelude to the holocaust of the First World War and the decline of European power that followed it. Just as the *Titanic* disaster illustrated many of the failings of British society in the first years of this century, so too the sinking of the *Sophia* revealed the structural weaknesses in the far northwest.

Consider, for example, the double meaning in the subtitle of this book: 'Taking the North Down with Her'. While it refers directly to the experience at Vanderbilt Reef, it also alludes to the essential pattern of northern life whereby each autumn the *Sophia* and other ships took a sizeable portion of the North's non-Native population down south with them. This yearly migration drained much of the vitality from the region, hampering economic growth and forestalling the kind of social and political development that might have been expected: people who were unhappy with conditions in the region simply left, never to return. Each year, therefore, the coastal steamers left behind a mere shell of the functioning, vibrant society that had operated briefly in the valley of the Yukon River.

And then one of these ships was lost. That the *Princess Sophia* came to grief in late October ensured the loss of dozens of the fall migrants–a cross-section of northern society on the move. The fact that the episode occurred in 1918, following years of economic decay and the upheaval of the First World War, guaranteed that the ship would be carrying a number of people leaving the north forever. Drained of any lingering optimism or confidence in the region, hundreds simply said good-bye and headed south for new opportunities and a warmer climate.

The loss of the *Princess Sophia*, then, can be seen as symbolic both of the seasonal migration and of the painful atrophy of a unique society. But there is more than symbolism in the disaster at Vanderbilt Reef. Even a cursory glance at the passenger list reveals the depth of the loss. One Yukon witness recalled: 'Our loved Northland never recovered from the blow. I doubt if there was one person in all the country who had not been bereft in some way. In the eyes of many there remained always the look of one wounded unto death.'[43] But the damage went far beyond the personal suffering and bereavement, important though that was in sapping much of the region's remaining spiritual strength. A number of leading businessmen were lost, and no one was left behind to take their places. The White Pass & Yukon Route lost parts of five separate riverboat crews–skilled workers whose disappearance stripped the company of much of its knowledge of Yukon River navigation.

It is impossible to quantity the economic and social devastation that followed the sinking of the *Sophia*, but it is clear that the direct loss was traumatic. The Alexanders' Engineer Mine, the great hope of the period, all but died with them; it was tied up in litigation for years after 1918 and never gave the region the economic shot in the arm that had been expected. And this story can be multiplied dozens of times: businessmen from Dawson City, Circle, Eagle, Ruby, and Iditarod perished. So did miners like William Scouse, one of the largest independent operators in the northwest, and John Hellwinkle, owner of dozens of properties in Dawson City.

Many of the North's 'best and brightest' went down with the *Princess Sophia*. William Harper carried with him the dreams of the missionaries in Alaska, particularly Hudson Stuck. William O'Brien might have been lost to the north in any case, but the people of Dawson City particularly mourned the loss of this political and community leader. And so the list continues: Edmund Ironside, Oscar Tackstrom, Dave Williams, George Mayhood, Thomas Turner, Ulysses Grant Myers. The *Princess Sophia* also took a number of working people to their deaths. Their obituaries seldom ran to more than a few lines, but Arnoux Pellison, Arthur Lewis, Peter Peterson, and the others were a vital element in northern society. Working on the riverboats and dredges, in the laundries, hotels, and stores, providing much of the energy for the north's many fraternal organizations, they were not easily replaced.

When the *Sophia* sank off Vanderbilt Reef, it struck a severe blow at a vulnerable society and accelerated a decline that was already underway. It would take another war to lift the far northwest out of the doldrums. Until 1942, when the first American troops arrived to begin construction of the Alaska Highway–a bonanza of a different kind–the region remained locked in decline, unable to escape the combined effects of economic collapse and southern indifference.

Ironically, the population movements that were so much a part of the *Sophia* story ensured that the disaster was largely forgotten in the region most affected. While memories of it remain relatively strong in coastal areas–Skagway, Haines, Juneau, Victoria, Vancouver, and Seattle–they have all but disappeared in the Yukon River basin. The impermanence and transiency of the region have until recently prevented it from producing or sustaining an image of itself; the permanent population has been too small to create or preserve a usable sense of its past. The vacuum has been filled by southern popularizers reflecting southern attitudes towards the north. The narrow stereotypes of cold, cabin fever, Mounties, painted ladies, huskies, and the men who moil for gold have found their chroniclers in writers like Robert Service, Jack London, and Pierre Berton. The images of the frontier that such popularizers have created are among the most powerful elements in the popular culture of both Canada and the United States. But it is time to assess more critically the degree to which these images have sprung from the frontier itself; having done so, one is likely to conclude that in fact they have their roots in the south, and have served as an effective means of cultural colonization. The virtual disappearance of the *Princess Sophia* story from the collective memory of the Yukon River valley is symptomatic of the cultural loss associated with this process. Until the far northwest begins to generate its own popular culture, and starts to explore its past for events that speak to the reality of life in the Yukon and Alaska, the region will continue to be defined by outsiders.

What we have attempted to do in this book is to revive interest in the full story of the *Princess Sophia*–not only the disaster itself, but the seasonal closing of the region, the ritual departures, the efforts to seek redress, and the disappearance of the story from the folk culture of the Yukon and the Alaskan interior. We hope too that this knowledge will raise questions about the state of northern life and culture, and encourage northerners and southerners alike to examine those forces have locked the northwest into a pattern of boom and bust, impermanence and transiency.

Our last wish is that the memory of the victims–of Billy O'Brien and his parents, of Lulu Mae Eads, of the Harpers, the Tackstroms, and the hundreds of others–will be revived and preserved. Each fall when the temperature plummets, when the snow begins to stick to the ground and ice takes over the Yukon River, we hope that people, especially northerners, will remember the fatal migration of 1918: the pain of those left behind, wondering if their friends would return, or if they too would join the exodus the following year; the false joviality of Ruby, Iditarod, Tanana, Dawson, Whitehorse, and Skagway as the citizens gathered to say goodbye; the brutal combination of boredom and fear that gripped the passengers aboard the *Princess Sophia* as she sat caught on Vanderbilt Reef, a bitter storm swirling around her; the brave men of Juneau who risked these dangerous waters in response to the call for help; Frank Lowle, tending the CPR office in Juneau, frantically putting together a rescue effort, then becoming morgue attendant to a catastrophe; the families and friends of the victims as they worried and waited for news, and then, their worst fears confirmed, waited days or months for the bodies of loved ones to be recovered and buried; the love and commitment of Al Winchell, driven by a promise to his wife; the sense of loss in the northwest as citizens gathered to honour their dead, denied the opportunity to mourn properly and bury their friends; and, finally, the many women left widows, the children growing up as orphans, the parents left to mourn their lost children.

In recalling the suffering of the *Princess Sophia*'s victims, and in seeking to understand the significance of the greatest disaster in the history of the Pacific northwest, we honour the memory of those who died and those who would have saved them, and we pay tribute to those who suffered personal loss. In remembering, we hope to help the region reclaim an important part of its past, and to assist the people of the Yukon River valley in coming to terms with elements in their history that have been too long ignored. In his song about the disaster, Steve Hites also asked if the message about the *Princess Sophia* has been heard:

And the summer tourists come by the thousands to see
  if the Inside Passage is all that it claims to be.
And I wonder if any of them pause to hear
  the crashing of the waves on the rocks so near.
And I wonder as I watch the lowering sky
  if we're going to have a storm
when you cast off
  tonight?

APPENDIX A:
Letters from Jack Maskell and Auris McQueen

Shipwrecked off
coast of Alaska.
S.S. Princess Sophia
24th Oct 1918.

My Own Dear Sweetheart,

I am writing this dear girl while the boat is in grave danger. We struck a rock last night which threw many from their berths, women rushed out in their night attire, some were crying, some too weak to move, but the life boats were soon swung out in all readiness, but owing to the storm would be madness to launch until there was no hope for the ship. Surrounding ships were notified by wireless and in three hours the first steamer came, but cannot get near owing to the storm raging and the reef which we are on. There are now seven ships near. When the tide went down two thirds of the boat was high and dry. We are expecting the lights to go out any minute, also the fires. The boat might go to pieces, for the force of the waves are [*sic*] terrible, making awful noises on the side of the boat, which has quite a list to port. No one is allowed to sleep, but believe me dear Dorrie it might have been much worse. Just hear[d?] there is another big steamer coming. We struck the reef in a terrible snowstorm. There is a big buoy near marking the danger but the captain was to port instead [of] to starboard of [the] buoy. I made my will this morning, leaving everything to you, my own true love and I want you to give £100 to my dear Mother, £100 to my dear Dad, £100 to dear wee Jack, and the balance of my estate (about £300) to you, Dorrie dear. The Eagle Lodge will take care of my remains.

In danger at Sea.
Princess Sophia
24th October 1918.

To whom it may concern:

Should anything happen [to] me, notify Eagle Lodge, Dawson.

My insurance, finances and property I leave to my wife (who was to be) Miss Dorothy Burgess, 37 Smart St., Longsight, Manchester, England.

J. Maskell

SOURCE: This letter was reprinted by many newpapers, each giving a different version. The original is in the Yukon Territorial Archives, Seddon Collection, 86/49 pt. 1. Punctuation has been added for the sake of clarity. The version of the will in the Archives is a typed copy of the original.

In the Lynn Canal off Skagway,
10-25-18

Dear Mama,

The man who wrote 'On a Slow Train Through Arkansas' could write a true story of a 'Slow Trip Through Alaska' if he had been with a party of a few soldiers. We were sure making a slow trip. We were on a government steamer from Fort Gibbon to Whitehorse and had no pilot who knew the river, so had to tie up nights, and at that got stuck on six sand bars. We were 19 days on that 11-day trip up the Yukon.

Then at Skagway the stampede of people out of the Interior had got ahead of us and we had to miss three boats and only got on this one by good luck. Now, this ship, the *Princess Sophia*, is on a rock and when we can get away is a question.

It's storming now, about a 50-mile wind, and we can only see a couple of hundred yards on account of the snow and spray. At 3 a.m. yesterday she struck a rock submerged at high tide, and for a while there was some excitement, but no panic. Two women fainted and one of them got herself into a black evening dress and didn't worry over who saw her putting it on. Some of the men, too, kept life preservers on for an hour or so and seemed to think there was no chance for us. But we passed through the first real danger point at high tide at 6 a.m. when it was thought she might pound her bottom out on the rocks, and everybody settled down to wait for help. We had three tugboats here in the afternoon, but the weather was too rough to transfer any passengers. The most critical time, nobody but the ship's officers, we soldiers and a few sailors amongst the crew and passengers were told of it, was at low tide at noon when the captain and chief officer figured she was caught on the starboard bow and would hang there while she settled on the port side and astern. They were afraid she would turn turtle, but the bow pounded around and slipped until she settled into a groove, well supported forward on both sides. The wind and the sea from behind pounded and pushed her until she is now, 30 hours after, on the rock clear back to the middle and we can't get off.

She is a double-bottom boat and her inner hull is not penetrated, so here we stick. She pounds some on a rising tide and it is slow writing, but our only inconvenience is, so far, lack of water. The main steam pipe got twisted off and we were without lights last night, and have run out of soft sugar. But the pipe is fixed so we are getting heat and lights now, and we still have lump sugar and water for drinking.

A lighthouse tender, big enough to hold all the 400 passengers, and one big launch are standing by. And as soon as this storm quits we will be taken off and make another lap to Juneau. I suppose after 3 or 4 days there, we can go to Seattle, after I reckon we will be quarantined, as there are six cases of influenza aboard. The decks are all dry, and this wreck has all the markings of a movie stage setting. All we lack is the hero and the vampire. I am going to quit, and see if I can rustle a bucket and a line to get some sea water to wash in. We are mighty lucky we were not all buried in the sea water.

Lovingly,
Auris

SOURCE: Reprinted in the *Alaska Daily Empire*, 30 Oct. 1918.

APPENDIX B:

Awards made under the Workmen's Compensation Act to Relatives of the *Princess Sophia*'s Crew

CREW MEMBER	DEPENDENT	PER MONTH	VALUE
John Mitchell Clark	Agnes Clark (M)	20	2678.48
William K. Liggett	Margaret Liggett (W)*	20	3514.86
	Patricia Liggett (D)*	5	557.43
	Robert A. Liggett (S)*	5	460.44
Jeremiah C. Shaw	Agnes Shaw (W)*	20	3364.27
Victor C. Whitecross	E. Whitecross (M)	20	3266.63
Charles G. Beadle	Irene Beadle (W)*	20	3080.68
Arthur G. Murphy	Nita E. Murphy (W)	20	2855.57
Frank Gosse	Mabel Gosse (W)*	20	3147.75
	Gordon V. Gosse (S)*	5	572.68
Alfred Cartwright	Fanny Cartwright (W)	20	2880.77
	John Cartwright (S)	5	97.02
	William Cartwright (S)	5	267.79
	Thomas Cartwright (S)	5	318.10
	Sidney Cartwright (S)	5	501.79
Frederick Harvey	Florence Harvey (W)	20	3514.86
	Marjorie Harvey (D)	5	573.64
	Norman Harvey (S)	5	441.85
	Harry Harvey (S)	5	248.87
	Edward Harvey (S)	5	168.55
George G. Booth	Nina Booth (W)	20	3147.75
	Dorothy Booth (D)	5	462.08
	Wilbur E. Booth (S)	5	569.91
Charles H.E. Waller	Elizabeth Waller (W)*	20	3364.27
	Dorothy Waller (D)*	5	441.76
	Vera Waller (D)*	5	548.25
	James Waller (S)*	5	584.31

O.M. Phillips	Valerie Phillips (D)*	10	969.32
	Margaret Phillips (D)	10	1115.88
Charles Newberg	John Newberg (F)	10	1222.73
	Sophia Newberg (M)	10	1750.86
James W. Massey	Pearl Massey (SS)	20	1064.43
William McLennan	Lucy McLennan (M)	20	3514.86
	Lloyd McLennan (B)	5	290.73
	Dunalda McLennan (SS)	5	551.80
William MacLachlan	E. MacLachlan (M)*	20	3334.55
	Mary MacLachlan (S)	10	1389.48
Duncan Ross	Ellen Ross (W)	20	2702.08
	Grace Ross (D)	5	589.85
Leonard Locke	Emily Locke (W)*	20	2249.49
	Leonard Locke (S)*	5	588.59
William C. Dibble	Cecelia Dibble (W) (Saskatoon)	20	3506.56
	Ivy L. Dibble (D)	5	236.39
	Edna W. Dibble (D)	5	347.30
	Frances L. Dibble (D)*	5	573.03
George A. Dallas	Ursula Dallas (M)*	10	1406.85
Michael Doris	Mary Anne Doris (W) (Greenock, Scotland)	20	3501.72
	Mary Doris (D)	5	316.45
	Bridget Doris (D)	5	427.74
Sit, L.	Sit Chin Shih (W) (China)	20	3439.67
	Sit Wen (S)	5	317.87
Lee Hong	Kam Yuk (D)*	10	412.34
	Kam Yit (D)*	10	619.68
Lionel A. Olson	Laura E. Olson (M)	20	3439.67
Edgar Doughty	Eleanor Doughty (M), (Surrey, England)	5	485.75
Gordon Templeman	S.C. Templeman (M), (Winnipeg)	10	1667.27

(B) brother; (D) daughter; (F) father; (M) mother; (S) son; (SS) sister; (W) widow

* living in Victoria. Those for whom a city is not indicated were living in Vancouver.

SOURCE: Case #6390, pp. 6498-513.

APPENDIX C:

Passengers and Crew on *Princess Sophia*
Sailing from Skagway, 23 Oct. 1918.

NOTE: There are many versions of the crew and passenger lists in the records, and no two of them agree. These are the lists published in the court records; they almost certainly miss some passengers and crew members. The notation WP indicates that the passenger was an employee of the White Pass & Yukon Route or an employee's dependent. These people were given a discount of $12.50 for the trip, a practice that would have been illegal under the Interstate Commerce Act had the ship been registered in the United States. Apparently the discount was extended to other favoured customers such as Edmund Ironside, who was a civil servant, his mother, and the O'Briens.

PASSENGER'S NAME	DESTINATION	TICKET
J. Allmark	Vancouver	37.50
W.S. Amalong	Seattle	37.50
Mrs W.S. Amalong	Seattle	37.50
J.P. Anderson	Seattle	37.50
Mrs J.P. Anderson	Seattle	37.50
F. Aitken	Seattle	25.00 WP
G.W. Allen	Vancouver	37.50
A.W. Anthony	Vancouver	25.00 WP
Joe Able	Seattle	25.00 WP
Capt. Alexander	Vancouver	37.50
Mrs Alexander	Vancouver	37.50
A.S. Bourne	Seattle	37.50
Mrs J. Beaton	Seattle	37.50
Beaton (child)	Seattle	18.75

Beaton (infant)	Seattle	2.50
S.J. Baggerley	Seattle	37.50
Mrs S.J. Baggerly	Seattle	37.50
C.M. Bell	Seattle	37.50
Mrs C.M. Bell	Seattle	37.50
Bell (infant)	Seattle	2.50
Bell (infant)	Seattle	2.50
O. Backman	Seattle	37.50
J.M. Beyer	Seattle	25.00 WP
H. Bennett	Seattle	25.00 WP
P. Bowker	Seattle	25.00 WP
C.W. Barlow	Seattle	37.50
N.G. Blyth[e?]	Victoria	25.00 WP
C.J. Bloomquist	Victoria	25.00 WP
H.M. Bridges	Vancouver	37.50
Mrs H.M. Bridges	Vancouver	37.50
Frank Brown	Vancouver	37.50
Allen Barnes	Vancouver	37.50
Walter Barnes	Vancouver	37.50
Geo. J. Baker	Vancouver	37.50
W. Barton	Vancouver	25.00 WP
Brown	Vancouver	25.00 WP
J.A. Clark	Prince Rupert	20.00
C. Castleman	Seattle	37.50
J.M Colver	Seattle	37.50
Marie Colombara	Seattle	37.50
J. Crone	Seattle	25.00 WP
Chas. Craven	Seattle	25.00 WP
Chas. Chantquist	Seattle	37.50
Sam. Chanquist	Seattle	37.50
C.E. Clark	Seattle	25.00 WP
Mrs Chas. Cousins	Victoria	25.00 WP
J.S. Chisholm	Vancouver	37.50
Mrs J.S. Chisholm	Vancouver	37.50
J. Christiansen	Vancouver	37.50
A. Campbell	Vancouver	25.00 WP
C.S. Chinery	Vancouver	25.00 WP
Mrs W.S. Carr	Vancouver	37.50

Thos. J. Collins	Prince Rupert	20.00
R.H. Davis	Seattle	25.00 WP
Mrs R.H. Davis	Seattle	25.00 WP
Jas. Dubois	Seattle	37.50
S.M. Dalby	Seattle	37.50
G.M. Dano	Seattle	25.00 WP
M. Davis	Seattle	37.50
H. Davis	Victoria	25.00 WP
Mrs H. Davis	Victoria	25.00 WP
Capt. J.P. Douglas	Vancouver	25.00 WP
F.W. Elliott	Seattle	37.50
M.S. Eads	Seattle	37.50
Mrs M.S. Eads	Seattle	37.50
John Eyre	Seattle	37.50
W.A. Foster	Vancouver	37.50
R. Findlay	Vancouver	25.00 WP
J.J. Flannagan	Prince Rupert	20.00
A. Fleming	Prince Rupert	20.00
W.H. Grover	Seattle	37.50
Peter Gurkovitch	Seattle	37.50
F.S. Gibbs	Seattle	37.50
Chas. Guy	Seattle	25.00 WP
A.L. Garner	Seattle	37.50
A.J. Grenny	Seattle	25.00 WP
J.C. Green	Seattle	25.00 WP
Mrs J.C. Green	Seattle	25.00 WP
Mrs Dan Gillis	Victoria	37.50
O.A. Gidlund	Prince Rupert	20.00
O. Garner	Seattle	37.50
Mrs O. Garner	Seattle	37.50
Thos. Hennessey	Seattle	37.50
H.E. Hardin	Seattle	37.50
R.M. Hall	Seattle	37.50
Sam Henry	Seattle	37.50
Mrs Sam Henry	Seattle	37.50
W. Harper	Seattle	37.50
Mrs W. Harper	Seattle	37.50
Hendrix	Seattle	37.50

J.W. Helwinkle	Seattle	37.50
L.A. Hanson	Seattle	37.50
Jack Haynes	Seattle	25.00 WP
Carl Headlund	Seattle	25.00 WP
Chas. Holmes	Seattle	25.00 WP
J. Howard	Seattle	25.00 WP
Mrs Jas. Hall	Vancouver	37.50
T.L. Hoering	Vancouver	25.00 WP
R.C. Haws	Vancouver	25.00 WP
Geo. Howey	Vancouver	25.00 WP
R. Hager	Prince Rupert	20.00
Wm. Haggerty	Vancouver	37.50
E.S. Ironside	Vancouver	25.00 WP
Mrs M. Ironside	Vancouver	25.00 WP
E.J. Johnston	Vancouver	25.00 WP
Mrs E.J. Johnston	Vancouver	25.00 WP
Arthur Johnston	Prince Rupert	20.00
J.F. Kelly	Seattle	37.50
C. Knutson	Seattle	37.50
Sam Kolonas	Seattle	25.00 WP
T. Kagawa	Vancouver	37.50
A.W. Kendall	Vancouver	25.00 WP
C.E. Kilway	Vancouver	25.00 WP
H.J. Kenyon	Vancouver	25.00 WP
D. Kink	Vancouver	37.50
J. King	Prince Rupert	13.35 WP
J. Kirk	Vancouver	37.50
I. Labrai	Seattle	37.50
J.A. Laird	Seattle	37.50
W.S. Liber	Seattle	37.50
G.S. Leavit	Seattle	25.00 WP
H. Lawless	Seattle	25.00 WP
L.M. Lee	Seattle	25.00 WP
G.H. Lisson	Seattle	37.50
W. Lidgett	Vancouver	25.00 WP
A.D. Lewis	Vancouver	25.00 WP
Mrs Lenez	Vancouver	25.00 WP
Mrs Geo. Markus	Seattle	37.50

Markus (infant)	Seattle	2.50
W. Murphy	Seattle	25.00 WP
U.G. Myers	Seattle	37.50
G.F. Mayhood	Seattle	37.50
Geo. Milton	Seattle	37.50
Joe Maskell	Vancouver	37.50
T. Mabins	Seattle	25.00 WP
Thos. Milne	Prince Rupert	20.00
W.T. McArthur	Seattle	37.50
D.A. McDonald	Seattle	37.50
A.W. McQueen	Seattle	37.50
Guy McCrait	Seattle	25.00 WP
J. McNeil	Victoria	37.50
Thos. McMahon	Victoria	37.50
R. McLachlan	Vancouver	37.50
Mrs. R. McLachlan	Vancouver	37.50
A.R. McLean	Vancouver	37.50
Wm. McWaters	Vancouver	25.00 WP
John McLeod	Vancouver	37.50
Alex. McLeod	Vancouver	25.00 WP
W.H. McDonald	Vancouver	37.50
Mrs W.H. McDonald	Vancouver	37.50
McDonald (child)	Vancouver	18.75
McDonald (infant)	Vancouver	2.50
McDonald (infant)	Vancouver	2.50
N. McLeod	Vancouver	37.50
Mrs N. McLeod	Vancouver	37.50
R. McTavish	Vancouver	25.00 WP
G.A. Niles	Seattle	37.50
J.G. Nichols	Seattle	37.50
S.A. Nelson	Seattle	37.50
Thos. Neilson	Victoria	25.00 WP
W.J. O'Brien	Vancouver	25.00
Mrs W.J. O'Brien	Vancouver	25.00
O'Brien (child)	Vancouver	25.00
O'Brien (child)	Vancouver	12.50
O'Brien (child)	Vancouver	12.50
O'Brien (infant)	Vancouver	2.50

O'Brien (infant)	Vancouver	free
J.F. Pugh		pass
A.D. Pinska	Seattle	37.50
Mrs A.D. Pinska	Seattle	37.50
Mrs C.J. Perkins	Seattle	25.00 WP
H.B. Parkin	Seattle	25.00 WP
O. Poppert	Seattle	37.50
A. Pellison	Seattle	25.00 WP
P.W. Peterson	Seattle	37.50
O.D. Pratt	Seattle	25.00 WP
Nick Peterson	Seattle	37.50
John Peterson	Vancouver	37.50
C.C. Queen	Vancouver	37.50
H. Russell	Seattle	25.00 WP
H. Rutherford	Seattle	25.00 WP
H.F. Robinson	Vancouver	25.00 WP
Leo Ryan	Prince Rupert	20.00
H.A. Robinson	Vancouver	37.50
G.C. Randolph	Vancouver	37.50
Mrs J.A. Segbers	Seattle	37.50
H.A. Somerset	Seattle	37.50
F.E. Soule	Seattle	37.50
William Scouse	Seattle	37.50
W.C. Sharon	Seattle	25.00 WP
Geo. L. Sholseth	Seattle	37.50
T.E. Sanford	Seattle	37.50
W.H. Smith	Seattle	37.50
H.M. Swartz	Seattle	37.50
John Schenck	Seattle	37.50
E. Seniff	Seattle	25.00 WP
W.F. Shaw	Seattle	25.00 WP
D. Satomyer	Seattle	25.00 WP
J. Santine	Seattle	25.00 WP
Fred Smith	Seattle	25.00 WP
W.W. Shillinglaw	Victoria	25.00 WP
W.P. Smith Jr.	Victoria	25.00 WP
R.H. Smith	Victoria	25.00 WP
M. Stange	Vancouver	37.50
Tom Sinich	Vancouver	37.50

Wm. Steinberger	Vancouver	37.50
Capt. A. Steward	Vancouver	37.50
N. Stewart	Vancouver	37.50
H. Strain	Vancouver	25.00 WP
Joe Shimada	Vancouver	25.00 WP
A.H. Southerland	Prince Rupert	20.00
Sam Sorensen	Prince Rupert	20.00
J.H. Smith	Prince Rupert	20.00
Mrs J.H. Smith	Prince Rupert	20.00
Smith (infant)	Prince Rupert	1.50
Smith (infant)	Prince Rupert	free
T.M. Turner	Seattle	37.50
T.E. Thorsen	Seattle	37.50
T.D. Tolbert	Seattle	37.50
E. Taggart	Seattle	25.00 WP
O.E. Tackstrom	Seattle	37.50
Mrs O.E. Tackstrom	Seattle	37.50
Tackstrom (infant)	Seattle	2.50
Tackstrom (infant)	Seattle	2.50
Geo. Tribe	Victoria	25.00 WP
R. Trucco	Prince Rupert	20.00
J. Trainer	Prince Rupert	20.00
W.A. Thomson	Seattle	37.50
W.P. Smith	Victoria	25.00 WP
B. Van Valkenberg	Seattle	25.00 WP
H.D. Vandecarr	Victoria	25.00 WP
P. Vant	Vancouver	25.00 WP
Miss N. Very	Prince Rupert	20.00
Miss E. Very	Prince Rupert	20.00
C.S. Verrill	Vancouver	37.50
Mrs Vifquain	Vancouver	37.50
Vifquain (child)	Vancouver	2.50
Mrs Al Winchell	Seattle	37.50
A.W. Walker	Seattle	25.00 WP
Frank White	Seattle	25.00 WP
B. Wilkinson	Victoria	25.00 WP
A.S. Winkler	Vancouver	37.50
C.H. Wilkinson	Vancouver	37.50
C.D. Williams	Vancouver	37.50

W. Wright	Vancouver	25.00 WP
C.E. Watson	Vancouver	37.50
E.G. Wheeldon	Vancouver	25.00 WP
R. Young	Seattle	37.50
J.D. Young	Vancouver	25.00 WP
John Zaccarelli	Seattle	37.50
C.W. Zylstra	Seattle	25.00 WP

SECOND-CLASS PASSENGERS

Dube Narcisus	Prince Rupert	11.00
C.A. Paddock	Prince Rupert	11.00
C.W. Shiarlin	Prince Rupert	11.00
K. Tzuzi	Vancouver	22.00
L. Heinzer	Seattle	22.00
Elmer Stitzel	Seattle	22.00
Nino Clemintino	Seattle	22.00
H. Wurgler	Seattle	22.00
R. Meston	Seattle	22.00
Chas. Nelson	Seattle	22.00
Jim George	Seattle	22.00
Wm Staples	Seattle	22.00
Sam Brown	Seattle	22.00
P. Kontes	Seattle	22.00
E.M. Nelson	Seattle	22.00
Joe Vito	Seattle	22.00
O.C. Salt	Seattle	22.00
J.L. Clay	Seattle	22.00
Thos. Wishart	Seattle	22.00
M. Moyer	Seattle	22.00
P. McCaskey	Seattle	22.00
O.H Strupp	Seattle	22.00
C.C. Faires	Seattle	22.00
C.W. Porter	Seattle	22.00
G.W. Wares	Seattle	22.00
E.A. Wendt	Seattle	22.00
A.J. Smyth	Seattle	22.00

TOTAL PASSENGERS 278

CREW MEMBERS, 23 OCT. 1918

NAME	AGE	OCCUPATION
DECK OFFICERS		
L.P. Locke	66	Master
Jerry Shaw	36	1st Officer
F. Gosse	28	2nd Officer
A. Murphy	46	3rd Officer
PETTY OFFICERS		
W. Evans	33	Quartermaster
W.K. Liggett	25	Quartermaster
F. Hyndman	18	Watchman
G. Glortue	38	Quarter Deck
L. Smith	18	Lookout
A. Walker	19	Stevedore
P. Burnham	43	Stevedore
H. Darling	38	Winchman
H. Walsh	53	Quarter Deck
ENGINEERS		
H. Solloway	–	2nd Engineer
D. Ross	–	3rd Engineer
J.W. Massey	–	4th Engineer
M. Doris	55	Fireman
E. Doughty	22	Fireman
L. Lapierre	19	Fireman
J. Dobbie	39	Oiler
M. McCormack	53	Oiler
T.M. Evans	32	Oiler
DECK HANDS		
F. Frau	–	
S.W. Macey	16	
P. Gaynor	37	
T. Park	20	
A.D. Park	18	
A. Munro	29	
G.A. Dallas	19	

W. McLaughlin	–	
J.M. Clark	–	
F. Burke	17	
L.A. Olson	16	

STEWARDS AND PURSERS

C.G. Beadle	33	Purser
C.J. Black	29	Freight Clerk
D.M. Robinson	20	Wireless
J. King	46	Chief Steward
A. Cartwright	47	2nd Steward
H. Browning	35	Stewardess
L. Wood	58	Barber
T.J. Galuth	44	Waiter
G.G. Booth	36	Waiter
J. Mossman	21	Waiter
G. Templeman	23	Waiter
J.H. Klein	16	Waiter
V. Whitecross	29	Waiter
McLennan	22	Waiter
F. Harvey	44	Waiter
H. Short	17	Waiter
T. Deans	55	Waiter
A. Coles	28	Waiter
H. Dolphius	32	Waiter
O.M. Phillips	26	Waiter

NOTE: There were also what the official list called '12 Chinamen in steward's department', whose names were not given. From other sources, they were

T. Jimms	Chief Cook
Hong Lee	2nd Cook
Hoy Lee	3rd Cook
Chee Fit	Pantryman
Man Set	2nd Pantryman
Joe Fee	Porter
Jim Get	Baker
Lee Sing	Porter

Set Leon	Porter
Young Lee	Porter
Yip Set	Porter
Chin Yuen	Porter

SOURCE: Case #6390, I.M. Brace et al. vs. CPR, Appellants' Supplemental Brief, Appendix II, and other documents.

TOTAL CREW	65
TOTAL PASSENGERS	278
TOTAL PASSENGERS AND CREW	343

NOTE: In addition, the inquiry was given a list of ten 'workaways' who boarded the ship in Skagway but were not mentioned in the printed lists of crew or passengers. They are Frank Hagan, Jack Hatcher, Alex Kline, Thomas Lepage, R. Matheson, Charles Neuberg, H. Plumb, G. Sangster, Alfred Smith, and Emil Tschierschkey. If these men were on the *Princess Sophia*, the number of victims would have been 353. The list of crew presented to the inquiry contains only 61 names, including several with marginal notations 'not on board,' Moreover, three awards were made under the Workmen's Compensation Act to relatives of men whose names do not appear on the crew list presented to the court. These men–Charles Waller, Charles Newberg (or Neuberg? one of the workaways?), and William C. Dibble–were presumably lost on the ship (the Compensation Board did not give money away lightly). This would raise the total to 356, assuming no errors were made in the other direction. It seems incredible that by 1929, when these lists were offered as evidence in court, they could still have been so inaccurate. In any case, it is evident that no precise figure can be given for the number of *Princess Sophia*'s victims; it is almost certainly more than 343, which has been the accepted figure for the past seventy years.

APPENDIX D:

'Statement of Expenses incurred up to January 31st 1919 in connection with the recovery, shipment and internment [sic] of bodies from the SS "Princess Sophia".'

1. Transportation and care of bodies per Dominion Express Co.		3,107.29
2. Undertakers:		
C.W. Young Co.	Juneau	47,411.00
Butterworth & Sons	Seattle	917.00
C.O. Lynn Ltd.	Tacoma	94.00
Collins Bros.	Seattle	51.50
T.J. Kearney & Co.	Vancouver	241.15
Grote Mortuary Co.	Vancouver	123.50
D.F. Jenkins	Nanaimo	103.50
Pearsons	Portland	-
C.L. Johnson	Lacey	100.00
Armstrong & Hotson	Vancouver	376.50
Bonny Watson	Seattle	842.27
Columbia Mortuary	Seattle	193.50
Sands Furnishing	Victoria	689.50
D. Belleghems	Peterboro	63.01
Brody & Harris	Ottawa	75.00
Murchie & Sons	New Westminster	56.00
B.C. Funeral Co.	Victoria	1,088.50
Center & Hanna	Vancouver	2,153.00
Munn Thompson & Clegg	Vancouver	302.50
S. Bowell & Co.	New Westminster	67.00
Funeral expenses at Saskatoon		35.50
	TOTAL	54,973.58

3. Boat Hire, etc.			
(a) Wages of boatmen at Rescue & Search			6,219.32
(b) Supplies to boats at Rescue & Search			4,871.81
(c) Hire of boats:			
'Excursion'	400.00		
'King & Winge'	1,845.50		
'Estebeth'	1,250.00		
'Woodrow'	80.00		
'Elsinore'	226.00		3,801.50
		TOTAL	14,892.63
4. Care of recovered baggage		TOTAL	148.20
5. Constructing Morgues & Medical Attendance etc.			
Vancouver	382.40		
Victoria	127.05		
Attendance, nurse, constable, etc	246.65		
		TOTAL	756.10
6. Free tickets issued relatives and vouchered			
At Vancouver	1,456.90		
At Seattle	727.66		
Travelling expenses refunded relatives	345.22		
		TOTAL	2,529.78
7. Photographing unidentified bodies		TOTAL	54.60
8. Telegrams		TOTAL	1,336.64
9. General Expenses:			
(a) Flowers	130.00		
(b) Gratuities to destitute widows	100.00		
(c) Advertising	12.00		
(d) Sundries	33.40		
		TOTAL	275.40
		FINAL TOTAL	$78,074.22

SOURCE: Inquiry, Exhibit 'G'

NOTES

The citation 'Case #4553' refers to United States National Archives, Seattle Branch, Record Group 21, US District Courts, Western District of Washington, Northern Division, Seattle, Admiralty on Appeal, #4553. The citation 'Case #6390' refers to United States National Archives, San Francisco Branch, Record Group 276, 9th Circuit, US Court of Appeals, Case #6390. The citation 'Inquiry' refers to the Sophia Inquiry, National Archives of Canada, Sessional Papers 21-24, vol. LVI, no. 7, 1920, Sophia file no. 110620, 1918-1919.

Introduction

[1] For example, Robert Turner's *The Pacific Princesses* (Victoria, BC: Sono Nis Press, 1977).

[2] Recently, Steve Hites, Manager of Passenger Operations for the White Pass & Yukon Route, Skagway, has written a song called 'The Last Voyage of the Princess Sophia', a copy of which was kindly provided to the authors by Patricia Buckway of the Canadian Broadcasting Corporation, Whitehorse. See Chapter 8.

Chapter Head A

[3] Davie, *The Titanic: The Full Story of a Tragedy* (London: Bodley Head, 1986), p. 215, disputes the assertion that the ship's builders had claimed she was unsinkable.

[4] Ibid., p. 44. A 'Titanic Historical Society' was founded in the United States in 1963. Since the recent discovery of the location of the ship, its membership has grown to 2,700. The society has established a permanent exhibit of relics and memorabilia of the ship at the Philadelphia Maritime Museum.

1. The North in Decline

[1] The story of Lindeberg, Brynteson, and Lindblom is well known in Alaska. See Claus-M. Naske and H. Slotnik, *Alaska: A History of the*

49th State, 2nd ed. (Norman: University of Oklahoma Press, 1987) p. 80.

[2] Judge Wickersham was an admirer of Senator Fairbanks, a leading figure in the Republican party who became Teddy Roosevelt's vice-president in 1904. Barnette agreed to name the town Fairbanks, and in return the judge promised to use his political influence to help the new settlement. 'Barnette later explained that both he and the judge thought the name Fairbanks for his trading post was a good idea, because should they ever need assistance in the nation's capital, they were assured of the friendship of someone who could help' (Naske and Slotnik, *Alaska*, p. 82).

[3] Iditarod was on the east bank of the Iditarod River, 7 miles northwest of Flat and 52 miles south of Holikachuk. By 1940 the town had only a single resident (D.J. Orth, *Dictionary of Alaska Place Names* [Washington: Government Printing Office, 1967]).

[4] Ibid.

[5] Case #6390, vol. 12, pp. 6115-17.

[6] Ibid., pp. 6083-92.

[7] Depositions made at the civil case that followed the sinking of the *Princess Sophia* provide three different ages for him; his father and his brother disagreed on it by two years.

[8] Case #6390, vol. 13, pp. 6737-44, Deposition of J.W. Castleman.

[9] *Victoria Daily Colonist*, 19 Nov. 1918.

[10] *Dawson Daily News* (henceforth *DDN*), 7 Nov. 1918.

[11] Laura Berton, *I Married the Klondike* (Toronto: McClelland and Stewart, 1954), p. 149.

[12] *DDN*, 7 Nov. 1918.

[13] Ibid., 14 Feb. 1919.

[14] Martha Black, *My Ninety Years* (Anchorage: Alaska Northwest Publishing, 1976), p. 111.

[15] *DDN*, 7 and 9 Nov. 1918.

[16] Case #6390, vol. 13, pp. 6940-1; *DDN*, 7 Nov. 1918.

[17] *DDN*, 7 Nov. 1918.

[18] Melody Webb, *The Last Frontier: A History of the Yukon Basin of Canada and Alaska* (Albuquerque: University of New Mexico Press, 1985), p. 283.

[19] *DDN*, 13 Dec. 1918.

[20] We are obliged for this suggestion to R.N. DeArmond of Juneau, who has helped us a great deal on points of Alaskan history.

[21] Berton, *I Married the Klondike*.

[22] *Victoria Daily Colonist*, 29 Oct. and 3, 7, and 14 Nov. 1918.

[23] *Vancouver Daily Province*, 28 Oct. 1918; *Whitehorse Star*, 1 Nov. 1918.

[24] Berton, *I Married the Klondike*, p. 148; *Nanaimo Free Press*, 30 Oct. 1918; Case #6390, vol. 13, p. 6992.

[25] Case #6390, vol. 13, p. 6997.

[26] National Archives of Canada, Yukon Territorial Records, RG 91, vol. 74, file 78.

[27] Berton, *I Married the Klondike*, p. 40.

[28] *DDN*, 3 Feb. 1919. See also David M. Dean, *Breaking Trail: Hudson Stuck of Texas and Alaska* (Athens: University of Ohio Press, 1988).

[29] Webb, *The Last Frontier*, p. 283.

2. Escaping Freeze-up

[1] Berton, *I Married the Klondike*, pp. 65, 136.

[2] 2 Oct. 1902.

[3] Yukon Territorial Archives, RG 1, Series 2, vol. 13, file 12333, Macaulay, Hon. C.D., Appointment, 1904-1944, letter from Commissioner Henderson to E.L. Newcombe, Deputy Minister of Justice, Ottawa, 3 June 1909.

[4] Berton, *I Married the Klondike*, pp. 96-7.

[5] Or at least who lived there; on occasion, the *Washburn* could not get to Iditarod. The *DDN* states that she did, but the Fairbanks *News-Miner* posted her only from Holy Cross to Dikeman (information kindly supplied by R.N. DeArmond, Juneau).

[6] The *Yukon* and *Alaska* were specially built, designed to work well in swift waters, to carry heavy loads on the downstream trips, and to run light on the upstream pull against the current.

[7] Yukon Territorial Archives, RG 1, White Pass & Yukon Route River Division, II-4-B, Sternwheeler Logs, vol. 36.

[8] *DDN*, 28 Oct. 1918, p. 1-2; 7 Nov. and 3 Dec. 1918; Yukon Territorial Archives, White Pass & Yukon Route Records, WP&YR River Division, II-8, Box 1, Personnel Records, 1903-1948, A-4, file 'G'.

[9] *DDN*, 7 and 15 Nov. 1918; Case #4553, file 16, Estate of Florence Beaton, Loretta Beaton and Neil Beaton, deceased. The 7 Nov. 1918 issue of the Dawson paper was a special memorial issue, and has extensive information about the victims of the *Princess Sophia*.

[10] *DDN*, 6 Aug. 1919; Case #4553, file 16, Estate of Ilene G. Winchell.

[11] Case #6390, vol. 12, pp. 6126-7; *DDN*, 28 Oct. 1918 (which gives her first name as 'Anna').

[12] *DDN*, 9 Oct. and 9 Nov. 1918.

[13] Case #4553, file 12, Charles Castleman testimony; file 16, Estate of Charles M. Castleman.

[14] *DDN*, 15 Oct., 28 Oct., and 7 Nov. 1918, 2 Jan. and 14 Feb. 1919; Case #4553, file 16, Estate of Oscar Tackstrom.

[15] *DDN*, 2 Jan. 1919.

[16] Case #6390, vol. 12, p. 6102.

[17] *DDN*, 31 Oct. and 7 Nov. 1918.

[18] Case #6390, vol. 12, pp. 6022-4; *Victoria Daily Colonist*, 3 Nov. 1918.

[19] *DDN*, 9 Oct. and 7 Nov. 1918.

[20] His name is incorrectly spelled 'Hagar' in many of the records. His grandson Robert Hager is chief of the Na-cho Nyak Dun Band, and numerous descendants, including great-great grandchildren, still live in the community (Case #6390, vol. 12, pp. 6006-7; letter to authors from Linda MacDonald, Secretary, Mayo Historical Society, 29 Nov. 1988).

[21] This was meagre only by northern standards. It would have been a good wage in the south: five years earlier Henry Ford had caused a sensation by offering his workers $5 a day without board. But living expenses were much higher in the north, and wages generally reflected this fact. When Laura Berton moved from Toronto to Dawson, her salary as a kindergarten teacher rose from $480 to $2100 per year.

[22] *Whitehorse Weekly Star*, 1 Nov. 1918; *DDN*, 28 Oct. and 7 Nov. 1918; Case #4553, file 16, Estate of Richard Harding Davis, Estate of Louise Davis.

[23] *DDN*, 7 Nov. 1918; Case #4553, file 16, Estate of James Dubois.

[24] *Vancouver Daily Province*, 30 Oct. 1918.

[25] Alaska State Archives, United States District Court for Alaska, First Division, US Commissioner's Probate Records, RG 506, Series 58, Box 4636.

[26] Berton, *I Married the Klondike*, pp. 39-40; *DDN*, 28 Oct., 7 Nov., and 20 Nov. 1918; *Vancouver Daily Province*, 30 Oct. 1918.

[27] *DDN*, 7 Nov. 1918.

[28] See Hal Guest, 'A History of Dawson City, Yukon Territory, 1897-1920', PhD dissertation, University of Manitoba, 1983.

[29] *DDN*, 9 Oct. 1918.

[30] William Morrison, 'The Unsinkable Martha Black', *Horizon Canada* 79; Martha Black, *My Seventy Years* (London: Thomas Nelson, 1938).

[31] *DDN*, 7 Nov. 1918.

[32] Ibid., 28 Oct. and 7 Nov. 1918.

[33] Berton, *I Married the Klondike*, p. 148; *DDN*, 28 Oct. and 7 Nov. 1918; Case #4553, file 13, Testimony of Zidania Scouse.

[34] *DDN*, 7 Nov. 1918.

[35] Case #6390, vol. 12, pp. 6248-9.

[36] *DDN*, 7 Nov. 1918.

[37] Ibid.

[38] Berton, *I Married the Klondike*, p. 147.

[39] *DDN*, 7 Nov. 1918.

[40] Berton, *I Married the Klondike*, p. 147; the story of the furniture is also recounted in the *DDN*, 7 Nov. 1918.

[41] Case #6390, vol. 12, pp. 6222-3.

[42] *DDN*, 7 Nov. 1918. There were a number of Japanese living in the Yukon. Jujiro Wada was a well-known miner who had been active in the country north of Dawson, and a key figure in the founding of Fairbanks. S. Kawakami was the proprietor of a Dawson store named 'The Japanese Bazaar', which sold the kind of goods Japan made for export in those days: 'silk goods, toys, matting, glass, china, porcelain, bamboo and lacquered ware' (National Archives of Canada, Yukon Territorial Records, RG 91, vol. 50, file 31126). Laura Berton gives an interesting description of Kawakami in *I Married the Klondike*.

[43] 8 Oct. and 7 Nov. 1918.

[44] 8 Oct. 1918.

[45] The probate documents gave his age as 45 in 1918; his obituary in the newspaper gave it as 41. Discrepancies such as this are quite common in the accounts of the *Sophia* victims. The Dawson newspaper often has the ages and even the names of the victims wrong. In most cases the court documents have been considered more reliable.

[46] *DDN*, 7 Nov. 1918.

[47] Ibid., 16 Oct. 1918.

[48] McQueen was not a member of the party of draftees, and while he went south on the *Princess Sophia*, they travelled on a different ship. See Chapter 3.

[49] *Alaska Daily Empire*, 30 Oct. 1918.

[50] *Skagway Daily Alaskan*, 21 Oct. 1918.

[51] *DDN*, 16 Oct. 1918.

[52] Ibid.

[53] Ibid.

[54] Ibid.

[55] Berton, *I Married the Klondike*, p. 97.

[56] Ibid., p. 131.

[57] *Victoria Daily Colonist*, 20 Oct. 1918.

[58] *Skagway Daily Alaskan*, 22 Oct. 1918.

[59] Gordon Bennett, *Yukon Transportation: A History*, Canadian Historic Sites Occasional Papers in Archaeology and History, no. 19 (Ottawa: National Historic Parks, 1978) p. 73.

[60] The White Pass & Yukon Route is the name used in the north for a 'family of companies', which includes the railway and riverboat companies (Roy Minter, *The White Pass: Gateway to the Klondike* [Toronto: McClelland and Stewart, 1987], p. 14).

[61] See Minter, *The White Pass.*

[62] *Atlin Claim*, special visitors edition, summer 1988.

[63] Reginald Brook, 'Story of Engineer Mine' (unpublished manuscript, cited with permission); *Vancouver Daily Province*, 28 Oct. 1918; *Whitehorse Weekly Star*, 20 Dec. 1918; *DDN*, 15 Nov., and 13 Dec. 1918.

[64] *DDN*, 10 Dec. 1918.

[65] *Skagway Daily Alaskan*, 22 Oct. 1918. Seventy-seven of the passengers were US soldiers from Fort Gibbon on their way south. They left early on 22 October on the Grand Trunk steamer *Prince Rupert.*

[66] *Skagway Daily Alaskan*, 21 Oct. 1918.

[67] Ibid.

[68] Ibid., 22 Oct. 1918.

[69] *Vancouver Daily Province*, 31 Oct. 1918.

[70] *DDN*, 9 Nov., and 15 Nov. 1918.

[71] Ibid., 26 Nov. 1918.

3. The *Princess Sophia*

[1] Pierre Berton, *The National Dream* (Toronto: McClelland and Stewart, 1970).

[2] This account of the company's history is based on George Musk, *Canadian Pacific: the Story of the Famous Shipping Line* (Toronto: Holt, Rinehart and Winston, 1981), and on Turner, *Pacific Princesses.* See also Norman Hacking and W. Kaye Lamb, *The Princess Story* (Vancouver: Mitchell Press, 1975).

[3] In a letter to Sir John A. Macdonald (Musk, *Canadian Pacific*, p. 11).

[4] Turner, *Pacific Princesses*, p. 41.

[5] Interview with Philip A. Hole, Victoria, August 1988.

[6] Interview with Mr J. Lenfesty, Vancouver, August 1988.

[7] Quoted in Musk, *Canadian Pacific*, p. 78.

[8] There may have been fog on the water, and the ship may have hit rocks rather than ice; testimony of witness conflicted (information kindly supplied by R.N. DeArmond, Juneau).

[9] Turner, *Pacific Princesses*, p. 45.

[10] Ibid. Musk (*Canadian Pacific*, p. 252) gives a total figure of 42 dead. In 1934 the *Islander* was raised and beached on Admiralty Island to recover the $275,000 in gold that was reputedly aboard; about $40,000 was found. She was scrapped in 1952.

[11] Turner, *Pacific Princesses*, p. 46.

[12] On 13 October 1918, the *Adelaide* went ashore at Georgina Point on Mayne Island in a blinding fog. All 360 passengers were transferred safely to the *Princess Alice*, and after five days' effort, the ship was pulled off the rocks. One of the passengers was a local mystic, 'Alexander, the man who knows'. It was reported that 'no one was more surprised when the vessel went ashore than the said Alexander, and he was the butt of a good many remarks, all to the general effect that either his faculties had failed him at the wrong moment or that he was not on the best of terms with the CPR' (*Victoria Daily Colonist*, 15, 16, 17, 19 Oct. 1918).

[13] Neither the *Irene* nor the *Margaret* went into service on the BC coast. Both were requisitioned by the Royal Navy for use as mine layers during the First World War.

[14] Vancouver City Archives, Captain Henry Mowatt Papers, Add. Mss. #136, vol. 3, file 6, *Princess Sophia*, J.W. Troup to A. Piers, Manager of Steamship Lines, CPR, Liverpool, 9 Jan. 1911.

[15] Accommodation plans for the *Princess Sophia*, 3 June 1912, Royal British Columbia Museum (information kindly supplied by Robert Turner). See also Vancouver City Archives, Specifications of the *Princess Sophia*.

[16] 21 May 1912.

[17] Interview with Philip A. Hole, Victoria, August 1988.

[18] Case #6390, vol. 4, pp. 1780-99, testimony of James McGown, Superintendent Engineer for the CPR. It was later alleged that she was hard to steer in a following sea.

[19] Information kindly supplied by R.N DeArmond, Juneau.

[20] In the late summer and fall of 1918 the *Princess Sophia* was scheduled to leave Skagway for the south on 21 and 31 Aug., 11 and 21 Sept., 2, 12, and 23 Oct., and 2 Nov.

[21] The 2 November voyage would take passengers from the Whitehorse and Atlin region, as well as some who had not been able to get on the ship on 23 October.

[22] *Vancouver Daily Province*, 17 Oct. 1918.

[23] Case #6390, Brief of Appellants, p. 12. 'It has been suggested that the Union Steamship Company or the GTP [Grand Trunk Pacific] send a ship there to help relieve the situation, but these companies state that it is impossible' (*Vancouver Daily Province*, 17 Oct. 1918).

[24] Inquiry, Testimony of James McGown, pp. 298-300.

[25] Letter of W.C. Dibble, 21 Oct. 1918, reprinted in 'Sophia, Princess of Death', in Ruth Greene, *Personality Ships of British Columbia* (West Vancouver, BC: Marine Tapestry Publications, 1969), pp. 194-211. In theory the ship could have carried as many as 500 passengers, but it was

likely not possible, given the time limitations, to increase the ship's accommodations that much.

[26] *Victoria Daily Colonist*, 29 Oct. 1918; *Vancouver Daily Province*, 28 Oct. 1918.

[27] Case #6390, vol. 8, p. 4120, Testimony of Cyril D. Neroutsos.

[28] Ibid., p. 4121.

[29] Interview with Philip A. Hole, Victoria, August 1988.

[30] *Victoria Daily Times*, 28 Oct. 1918.

[31] *DDN*, 3 Dec. 1918.

[32] 'Captain' was a courtesy title given to men who had earned their captain's papers, even though they might not actually be in command of a vessel.

[33] *Victoria Daily Colonist*, 5, 6, 7 April 1918.

[34] Ibid., 29 Oct. 1918.

[35] *Vancouver Daily Province*, 28 Oct. 1918; *Victoria Daily Colonist*, 29 Oct. 1918.

[36] 'Francis Burke, 1901-1918', recollections of Gerry Burke, kindly loaned by Eileen Burke, Vancouver. Lionel Olson was a year or so younger than Frank Burke.

[37] On this episode see R.J. Diubaldo, *Stefansson and the Canadian Arctic* (Montreal: McGill-Queen's University Press, 1978).

[38] *Victoria Daily Colonist*, 29 Oct. 1918.

[39] Interviews with Mrs K.E. Pearsall (Frank Gosse's sister-in-law), Victoria, October 1988, and Alan F. Gosse (Frank Gosse's nephew), Victoria, August 1988.

[40] Case #6390, vol. 8, p. 4058, Testimony of James McGown, Superintendent Engineer for the CPR; interview with Mrs M. McCall (the daughter who was not expected to live), Victoria, September 1988.

[41] Case #6390, Testimony of James McGown, Superintendent Engineer for the CPR, p. 43.

[42] Inquiry, part II, Testimony of L. Johnston, p. 208. There is no indication of what the *Sophia* carried on the trip north–likely general supplies for the communities along the coast, and bulk supplies for Skagway for trans-shipment to the interior.

[43] *Vancouver Daily Province*, 28 Oct. 1918, p. 13. The information on Robinson's additional responsibilities comes from Inquiry, p. 451, exhibit B.

[44] Case #6390, vol. 13, pp. 7140-58. In the original claimants' submission to the court, his age is given as fifty years and his name as Sit Yep (Case #4533, file 16, Estate of Sit Yep). While the Sophia Inquiry refers to him as Set Yip, newspapers too called him Sit Yep. The various records–

newspaper accounts, court documents, and inquiry exhibits–are very unreliable where the Chinese aboard the *Princess Sophia* are concerned.

[45] Case #6390, vol. 13, pp. 6064-70.

[46] Case #6390, vol. 8, p. 4051, Testimony of James McGown, Superintendent Engineer for the CPR.

[47] Case #6390, Appellants' Supplemental Argument, p. 11.

[48] Ibid., pp. 11-12.

[49] Dibble's letter of 21 Oct. 1918 was reprinted in Greene, *Personality Ships of British Columbia.*

[50] On the early role of the Collector of Customs, see T. Hinckley, *The Americanization of Alaska, 1867-1897* (Palo Alto: Pacific Books, 1972), p. 129.

[51] Case #6390, Brief of Appellees, p. 9; *DDN*, 25 Nov. 1918.

[52] Information kindly supplied by R.N. DeArmond, Juneau.

[53] Inquiry, Part II, Testimony of L.H. Johnston, p. 208; ibid., Testimony of B. Summers, p. 223.

[54] But not in the Yukon, whose isolation had made it immune. For a history of the influenza pandemic that followed the First World War, see Eileen Pettigrew, *The Silent Enemy: Canada and the Deadly Flu of 1918* (Saskatoon: Western Producer Prairie Books, 1983).

[55] Inquiry, Exhibit A; Case #4553, file 8, Exceptions to Findings. The CPR later claimed that these additional men had signed on as able-bodied seamen. From available biographical information on the 'workaways' (those who signed on in Skagway), it seems that they were waiters, not trained seamen.

[56] Inquiry, Part II, Testimony of L.H. Johnston, p. 208.

[57] *Vancouver Daily Province*, 5 Nov. 1918.

[58] *DDN*, 29 Oct. 1918.

[59] Ibid., 7 Nov. 1918.

[60] Ibid.

[61] Ibid., 10 Oct. 1918.

[62] Ibid., and 7 Nov. 1918.

[63] Ibid., 7 Nov. 1918.

[64] Ibid.

[65] Ibid.; and Berton, *I Married the Klondike*, p. 148.

[66] *DDN*, 24 Dec. 1918. If this is true, their names were not recorded, and did not appear on the official list of the dead.

[67] Inquiry, Part II, Testimony of L.H. Johnston, p. 208.

[68] Case #6390, Appellants' Supplemental Argument, Petitioner's Exhibit A-77, pp. 171-80. Other evidence suggests that the ship had a licence to carry 350 passengers. Why it did not carry that many (since some

would-be travellers were left behind at Skagway) was not explained–perhaps the company did not have time to crowd sufficient extra bunks into the ship on its last trip north. See Appendix C.

[69] Ibid.

4. Vanderbilt Reef

[1] Turner, *Pacific Princesses*, pp. 42, 46, 109-11.

[2] Orth, *Dictionary of Alaska Place Names*, p. 1017. The exact location of the reef is 'at the junction of Favorite Channel and Lynn Canal, 3.6 mi. NE of Little I. and 30 mi. NW of Juneau, Coast Mts.; 58° 35′30″ N, 135° 01′00″ W'. The *U.S. Coast Pilot*, on the other hand, ends Favorite Channel not at Vanderbilt Reef but at the north end of Shelter Island, 6 miles south of the reef.

[3] *U.S. Coast Pilot*, 8, 16th ed. (1984), p. 202. According to the Department of Commerce, US Coast and Geodetic Survey, the 'approximate mean range of all tides' in Lynn Canal was 13 feet, and the 'approximate mean great diurnal range of tide' was 15.5 feet. The great diurnal range of tide is the 'range between the higher high and the lower low water of each day' (Case #6390, p. 4675).

[4] *DDN*, 6 Nov. 1918.

[5] Perhaps the government should not be too harshly judged for not lighting Vanderbilt Reef. According to R.N. DeArmond (letter to authors), there were hundreds of requests for lights on rocks, reefs, and islands all over the northwest. And the light on Sentinel Island did not keep the *Princess Sophia* from running into it in 1913.

[6] US National Archives, Microfilm Publication #939, Roll 546, General Correspondence of the Alaska Territorial Governor, '*Princess Sophia*' file (henceforth MP #939), W. Redfield to Governor Riggs, 29 Oct. 1918; Riggs to Redfield, 9 Nov. 1918.

[7] 16th edition (1984), p. 200.

[8] The light on Vanderbilt Reef was put up after the disaster. See Chapter 8.

[9] Interview with Philip A. Hole, Victoria, August 1988.

[10] To avoid confusion, all times in the next three chapters have been converted to Alaska time–one hour earlier than Yukon and British Columbia time. The *Princess Sophia* ran on BC time.

[11] Various explanations have been advanced; see *DDN*, 20 Nov. 1918; Greene, *Personality Ships of British Columbia*, p. 202; Part I, Testimony of John W. Harrison, p. 335; ibid., Part II, Testimony of F.F.W. Lowle, p. 25.

[12] According to testimony (Sophia Inquiry, part I, p. 5, the ship should have passed to the west of the reef. But information supplied by

R.N. DeArmond indicates that the normal course for vessels bound south for Juneau was 'from a position close off Point Sherman, then 128 [degrees] true to pass east of Vanderbilt Reef and between Sentinel Island and Poundstone Rock . . . the course used today by the Alaska State Ferries'. This is confirmed by a report of 2 Nov. 1918 to the Commissioner of Lighthouses in Washington that 'the usual course lies about one mile to the eastward of the reef'. (US National Archives, RG 26, Selected Records from Lighthouse Service Correspondence, file 1028, Series of 1917). The Sophia Inquiry record is wrong, because of faulty testimony or an error in transcription; directions and distances are often confused in the printed records.

[13] Despite much legal wrangling, it was never established how fast the ship was going when it hit the reef. Given the time that elapsed between leaving Skagway and striking the reef, 11 knots is a reasonable guess.

[14] Inquiry, Part I, p. 5.

[15] *Vancouver Daily Province*, 31 Oct. 1918. The woman was likely Lulu Mae Eads.

[16] Inquiry, Part I, Testimony of J.W. Troup, pp. 211 ff.

[17] The *Peterson* was named for Major Matt Peterson, who died during the Spanish-American war.

[18] Inquiry, Part II, Testimony of J.P. Davis, pp. 98 ff.

[19] Ibid., Testimony of E. McDougall, pp. 136-7.

[20] Ibid., Testimony of C.W. Stidham, pp. 33-4.

[21] *DDN*, 15 Nov. 1918.

[22] Inquiry, Exhibit J.

[23] Inquiry, Part I, Testimony of J. Miller, p. 42.

[24] *DDN*, 14 Nov. 1918.

[25] Inquiry, Part II, Testimony of J. Clark Readman, p. 182.

[26] Ibid., Testimony of F.F.W. Lowle, p. 8.

[27] Ibid., pp. 5-6.

[28] Ibid., Testimony of J. Miller, pp. 122-3. How many boats were being lowered is not clear. A photograph taken of the starboard side of the ship on the morning of 24 October shows one lifeboat partially lowered. Perhaps Locke had one boat lowered on each side of the ship.

[29] Ibid., Testimony of J.P. Davis, p. 102.

[30] Ibid., p. 104.

[31] Ibid.

[32] Ibid., Testimony of Charles Duffy, pp. 178-180.

[33] Ibid., Testimony of A. Lucy, pp. 71-73.

[34] Correspondence with Edward P. Madsen, September 1988.

[35] Inquiry, Part I, Testimony of Alfred Baxter, pp. 419-20.

[36] Ibid., Part II, Testimony of E. McDougall, p. 138.

[37] *Alaska Daily Empire*, 30 Oct. 1918.

[38] Inquiry, Part II, p. 5, Maskell to Dorothy Burgess, 24 Oct. 1918.

[39] Notation on a copy of the will in Yukon Territorial Archives, Seddon Collection, 86/49 part 1.

[40] Inquiry, Part I, Testimony of J. Troup, p. 218.

[41] Ibid., pp. 220-1.

[42] Ibid., S.H. Brown to District Communication Superintendent, Puget Sound District, 26 Nov. 1918, pp. 503-4.

[43] Ibid., E.J. Haughton to Ben Wolf, 25 Oct. 1918, p. 494.

[44] Ibid., Testimony of J.W. Leadbetter, p. 52.

[45] Ibid., pp. 53-4; with 350 people, they would have had to stand shoulder to shoulder on the boat's deck.

[46] Ibid., Part II, Testimony of J.P. Davis, pp. 105, 132.

[47] Ibid., Testimony of C. Stidham, p. 42.

[48] Ibid.

[49] Ibid., Testimony of E. McDougall, p. 155.

[50] Ibid., Testimony of J.P. Davis, p. 141.

[51] Ibid., p. 111.

[52] Ibid., Testimony of E. McDougall, p. 136.

[53] Ibid., Testimony of F.F.W. Lowle, pp. 10-11; Exhibit J, Lowle to Captain James Troup, n.d.

[54] Ibid., Part I, Testimony of James Miller, pp. 3-5; *DDN*, 14 Nov. 1918.

[55] Ibid., Part II, Testimony of Abe Abrams, pp. 192-8.

[56] Ibid., Testimony of C. Stidham, p. 37.

[57] On 24 October the sun sets at Juneau at 4.30 p.m. Alaska time, and it is pitch dark by 5.12. Information obtained from the US national Weather Service Office, Juneau.

[58] Inquiry, Part I, p. 119, Leadbetter to Lighthouse Superintendent, 16th District, 30 Oct. 1918; Part I, Testimony of Captain Leadbetter, pp. 57-8.

[59] *DDN*, 24 Dec. 1918.

[60] Inquiry, Part II, Testimony of F.F.W. Lowle, p. 11.

[61] *DDN*, 14 Nov. 1918.

[62] Inquiry, Part I, Testimony of J.W. Leadbetter, p. 101.

[63] Ibid., Testimony of J.J. Miller, p. 22.

[64] Ibid., Testimony of J. Troup, pp. 224, 235-6; Testimony of William Logan, pp. 357-60.

[65] *Vancouver Daily Province*, 25 Oct. 1918.

[66] Inquiry, Part I, Testimony of J. Troup, p. 225.

[67] Ibid., Part I, Exhibit J.

5. The Sinking of the *Princess Sophia*

[1] *DDN*, 14 Nov. 1918.

[2] Ibid.

[3] Inquiry, Part I, Testimony of Captain Leadbetter, pp. 59-60.

[4] Ibid., Testimony of J. Miller, p. 26.

[5] Ibid., Exhibit J, Lowle to Troup.

[6] Ibid., Testimony of J. Troup, p. 220; Testimony of E.M. Miller, p. 137.

[7] Ibid., Testimony of Captain Leadbetter, p. 60.

[8] *Alaska Daily Empire*, 30 Oct. 1918; reprinted in a slightly amended form in the *Vancouver Daily Province*, 31 Oct. 1918; *DDN*, 15 Nov. 1918.

[9] Inquiry, Part I, Testimony of Captain Leadbetter, p. 63.

[10] Ibid., Testimony of C. Stidham, p. 43.

[11] Ibid., Testimony of J. Miller, pp. 1-49.

[12] Ibid., Testimony of J.P. Davis, p. 111.

[13] Ibid., Captain Leadbetter to Lighthouse Superintendent, 30 Oct. 1918, p. 119.

[14] Ibid., Part II, Leadbetter to Juneau radio, 25 Oct. 1918.

[15] *DDN*, 20 Nov. 1918.

[16] Pond aquired some blurry photographs taken the day before by Captain Davis of the *Estebeth*. He had the pictures made into postcards, and sold hundreds of them. Many of them are still in private collections.

[17] Inquiry, Part I, Exhibit J.

[18] Ibid., Testimony of Troup, p. 222.

[19] Ibid., Part II, Testimony of E. McDougall, pp. 136-59.

[20] Case #6390, vol. 12, p. 6616; Inquiry, Part II, Testimony of Lowle, p. 14.

[21] Yukon Territorial Archives, RG1, Series 1A, vol. 50, file 31126, Bell to Knight, 28 Nov. 1918.

[22] Inquiry, Part I, Testimony of Troup, p. 227.

[23] Ibid., p. 224.

[24] Ibid., p. 225; Part II, Testimony of Lowle, p. 7.

[25] *Vancouver Daily Province*, 25 Oct. 1918, p. 1.

[26] The report from the *Skagway Alaskan*, 25 Oct. 1918, is summarized in the *DDN*, 8 Nov. 1918.

[27] Inquiry, Part I, Testimony of E.M. Miller, p. 139.

[28] Ibid., p. 140; Part I, Exhibit J.

[29] *DDN*, 24 Dec. 1918.

[30] Miller testified that he said Benjamin Island.

[31] Inquiry, Part I, Testimony of E.M. Miller, pp. 149-50.

[32] Ibid., Testimony of J.J. Miller, p. 7-10; Testimony of Leadbetter, p. 64.

[33] Ibid., Testimony of J.J. Miller, pp. 44 and 25; Testimony of Leadbetter, p. 64; *DDN*, 14 Nov. 1918.

[34] Ibid., Testimony of Leadbetter, pp. 64, 106.

[35] Ibid., Part II, Testimony of F.F.W. Lowle, p. 15.

[36] Ibid., Part I, Testimony of E.M. Miller, p. 150; Testimony of Leadbetter, p. 65.

[37] Ibid., p. 151.

[38] Ibid., Testimony of J.J. Miller, pp. 11-2.

[39] Case #6390, p. 6615.

[40] On 25 October at Juneau the sun rises at 6.56 a.m. and sets at 4.28 p.m. Alaska time (information obtained from National Weather Service, Juneau).

[41] Inquiry, Part I, Testimony of J.J. Miller, p. 12; Testimony of Leadbetter, p. 66.

[42] Case #6390, p. 27.

[43] Ibid., p. 6615.

[44] *DDN*, 1 Nov. 1918; Inquiry, Part II, Testimony of J.P. Davis, pp. 132-3.

[45] Although there were no survivors of the disaster, the last hours of the *Princess Sophia* can be reconstructed from letters and diary entries found on the victims, as well as from the physical evidence.

[46] *Alaska Daily Empire*, 29 Oct. 1918.

[47] *DDN*, 18 Nov. 1918, 21 Dec. 1918; Yukon Territorial Archives, RG1 Series 1A, vol. 50, file 31126, Bell to Knight, 28 Nov. 1918.

[48] Inquiry, Part I, Testimony of John Donaldson, p. 387.

[49] *DDN*, 22 July 1919; *Whitehorse Star*, 14, 24 Feb. 1919.

[50] *DDN*, 30 June, 18 March 1919.

[51] Ibid., 2, 22 July 1919.

[52] Ibid., 18 Nov. 1918. The ship operated on Vancouver time, which was the same as Yukon time, and presumably the watches were set to that time.

[53] Yukon Territorial Archives, RG1, Series 1A, vol. 50, file 31126, Bell to Knight, 12 Nov. 1918.

[54] *DDN*, 20 Nov. 1918.

[55] Inquiry, Part I, Testimony of Selmer Jackson, p. 87.

[56] Jack London, 'The Sea-Wolf', in L. Teacher and R.E. Nichols, eds, *The Unabridged Jack London* (Philadelphia: Running Press, 1981), p. 842.

[57] *Vancouver Sun*, 28 Oct. 1918. There is a photograph, taken aboard the *Princess Adelaide*, of one of these flotation devices (Case #6390, Answer

to Appellee's Supplemental Brief, p. 35). It consists of two narrow wooden coffin-like boxes, about 2 × 2 × 8 feet each, fastened parallel to each other about 3 feet apart by boards nailed across each end. Ropes are looped around the outside, and it was obviously not designed to keep people out of the water.

[58] *DDN*, 21 Dec. 1918.

[59] CPR agent C. Garfield disputed that the footprints belonged to Gosse. (*DDN*, 13, 21 Dec. 1918).

[60] Five dogs were checked on the ship at Skagway (*DDN*, 15 March, 1 April 1919).

[61] Inquiry, Part II, Testimony of F.F.W. Lowle, p. 16.

[62] Ibid., Part I, Testimony of J. Troup, pp. 226, 255.

6. Finding the Victims

[1] Case #6390, vol. 12, p. 6616.

[2] Ibid.

[3] Inquiry, Part I, Testimony of Captain Leadbetter, p. 68.

[4] Ibid., Part II, Testimony of Captain J.P. Davis, p. 133; *DDN*, 14 Nov. 1918.

[5] *DDN*, 14 Nov. 1918.

[6] Ibid.; Inquiry, Part I, Testimony of Captain Leadbetter, p. 68.

[7] *DDN*, 14 Nov. 1918.

[8] Inquiry, Part II, Testimony of C. Stidham, p. 44.

[9] Ibid., Part I, Testimony of Captain Leadbetter, pp. 69-70.

[10] Ibid., Testimony of E. Miller, p. 160.

[11] Ibid., Part II, Testimony of E. Stidham, p. 44.

[12] Ibid., Part I, Testimony of Captain Leadbetter, p. 71; Log of *Cedar*, p. 132.

[13] *DDN*, 1 Nov. 1918.

[14] Inquiry, Part I, Testimony of J. Miller, p. 15.

[15] E.M. Miller, wireless operator on the *Cedar*, gave the earlier time. Thomas Riggs, Governor of Alaska, indicated that the first word reached Juneau at 9.00 a.m.

[16] Letter from Thelma Reid Lower, Vancouver, to authors, 9 Sept. 1988.

[17] Bruce Hutchison, *The Far Side of the Street* (Toronto: Macmillan, 1976), p. 55; telephone interview with Bruce Hutchison, Victoria, August 1988.

[18] Interview with Mrs M. McCall, Victoria, September 1988.

[19] *DDN*, 3 Dec. 1918.

[20] Ibid., and *Juneau Alaska Daily Empire*, 4 Nov. 1918. White was one of the few who got messages out from the *Princess Sophia* on 24-5 October.

[21] Case #6390, pp. 6014-15.

[22] Inquiry, Part II, Testimony of F.F.W. Lowle, pp. 18-19.

[23] Ibid., Exhibit J, Report of Lowle to CPR.

[24] Ibid., Part I, Testimony of Captain Troup, p. 228. The figures given for the number of passengers and crew were incorrect.

[25] Ibid., Part II, Testimony of Captain Stidham, p.247.

[26] The reply to his request read 'No boat available here for taking party [I]t is imperative that Peterson pick up hunting parties [on] account of them not having enough rations for prolonged stay' (MP #939, Kinney to Riggs, 26 Oct. 1918).

[27] *DDN*, 26 Oct. 1918.

[28] A Democrat in politics, he was named Governor of Alaska by President Wilson in April 1918. He served for three years, until he was replaced in June 1921 by Scott C. Bone, an appointee of President Warren Harding (C. Hulley, *Alaska: Past and Present* [Portland, Binfords and Mort, 1970], p. 317).

[29] MP #939, *Daily Alaskan* to Riggs, 26 Oct. 1918; Riggs to Editor, *Daily Alaskan*, 26 Oct. 1918 (plus passenger list).

[30] MP #939, Riggs to Lane, 26 Oct. 1918.

[31] The Gold Commissioner was the chief official in the Yukon after the office of Territorial Commissioner was abolished.

[32] MP #939, Riggs to Mackenzie, 26 Oct. 1918.

[33] A copy of the proclamation was printed in the *DDN*, 12 Nov. 1918.

[34] *DDN*, 31 Jan. 1919.

[35] Inquiry, Part I, Wireless Messages sent through the *Cedar*, p. 161.

[36] Ibid., Lowle to Captain Troup, CPR, p. 75.

[37] Ibid.

[38] *DDN* 20 Nov. 1918; MP #939, 'For the Press', memo by Thomas Riggs, c. 28 Oct. 1918.

[39] Inquiry, Part I, Testimony of Captain Leadbetter, pp.71-2; MP #939, 'For the Press'.

[40] Inquiry, Part I, Testimony of Captain Leadbetter, pp. 71-2.

[41] *Monaghan, King and Winge, Adolphus, Excursion, Estebeth, May, Sitka, Lone Fisherman, Wilson* (MP #939, Garfield to Riggs, 27 Oct. 1918).

[42] Inquiry, Part I, Testimony of Captain Leadbetter, p. 73.

[43] Ibid., Log of the *Cedar*, p. 134.

[44] Ibid., Testimony of Captain Leadbetter, p 74.

[45] *DDN*, 20 Nov. 1918.

[46] Inquiry, Part I, Log of the *Cedar*, p. 134.

[47] MP #939, Garfield to Riggs, 28 Oct. 1918.

[48] Since the Gold Commissioner was wintering in southern Canada, Knight was in charge of the civil administration of the Yukon.

[49] Brook, 'Story of Engineer Mine', p. 28.

[50] MP #939, Garfield to Riggs, 28 Oct. 1918.

[51] *DDN*, 20 Nov. 1918.

[52] In September 1971 a public building in Juneau again served as a temporary morgue for the victims of a disaster. In this case it was the National Guard Armoury, which served to hold the bodies of the 111 people killed when an Alaskan Airlines plane flew into a mountain. Again the townspeople pitched in to help identify, label, and prepare the bodies (*Vancouver Sun*, 7 and 8 Sept. 1971; *Portland Oregonian*, 7 Sept. 1971).

[53] *Vancouver Daily Province*, 2 Nov. 1918.

[54] *DDN*, 24 Dec. 1918. Presumably it was of comfort to the relatives of the deceased to know that the victims were being handled by men of business rather than just ordinary workers.

[55] This account comes from the *DDN*, 27 Nov. 1918. It stated that the victims' clothes and shoes were set aside 'to be utilized for Red Cross work'. This cannot be true; the bodies had to be clothed for their trip south. Either the report refers to clothes that were found in floating baggage, or it is simply a mistake.

[56] *DDN*, 24 Dec. 1918–an eyewitness account, probably written by Inspector Bell of the Mounted Police.

[57] Yukon Territorial Archives, RG1, series 1A, vol. 50, file 31126, A.L. Bell to Officer Commanding, RNWMP, Dawson, 6 Nov. 1918.

[58] *DDN*, 21 Dec. 1918.

[59] Ibid., 5 Dec. 1918.

[60] Ibid., 25 Nov. 1918.

[61] *Alaska Daily Empire* (Juneau), 30 Oct. 1918.

[62] Ibid.

[63] Ibid.

[64] Thomas Riggs, 'For the Press', Alaska State Archives, Territorial Records, Princess Sophia file.

[65] It disappeared after a few weeks–it may have blown down in a storm, though a rumour circulated that someone had chopped it down because the sight of it was too depressing.

[66] *Alaska Daily Empire*, 5 Nov. 1918.

[67] Case #6390, vol. 13, pp. 6951-5; *DDN*, 7 Nov. 1918; *Alaska Daily Empire*, 5 Nov. 1918.

[68] MP #939, Riggs to Wolf Templeman, Vancouver, 20 Nov. 1918.

7. In Memoriam

[1] *Vancouver Daily Province*, 11 Nov. 1918.

[2] Ibid.

[3] *Vancouver Sun*, 12 Nov. 1918.

[4] Ibid.

[5] 'Francis Burke, 1901-1918', recollections of Gerry Burke, kindly loaned by Eileen Burke, Vancouver.

[6] *Victoria Daily Colonist*, 13 Nov. 1918.

[7] Ibid., 14 Nov. 1918.

[8] *DDN*, 14 Feb. 1919.

[9] *Victoria Daily Colonist*, 14 and 15 Nov. 1918.

[10] *DDN*, 16 Nov. 1918; *Whitehorse Weekly Star*, 29 Nov. 1918. Santine's body was not found for nearly a year; in October 1919 his remains were found in Mud Bay. He was identified by some faded papers and an Elks pin attached to a scrap of clothing (*DDN*, 28 Oct. 1919).

[11] *DDN*, 16 Nov. 1918.

[12] *Whitehorse Weekly Star*, 29 Nov. 1918.

[13] *DDN*, 28 Oct. 1918.

[14] Ibid., 7 Nov. 1918.

[15] Ibid. The *Birkenhead* was a British troop ship that sank in February 1852 in Algoa Bay off the coast of South Africa, drowning most of the men on board, who stood at attention on deck while the women and children were loaded into the boats, establishing the convention of 'women and children first'.

[16] Ibid.

[17] Ibid., 4 Nov. 1918.

[18] Toronto *Globe*, 29 Oct. 1918.

[19] *DDN*, 2 Nov. 1918.

[20] Ibid., 4 Nov. 1918.

[21] Ibid. The men were Fred T. Congdon, a long-time Yukon politician; Walter Hamilton, a member of the Vancouver City Council; Charles Reed, secretary to the mayor of Vancouver; Captain Turnbull of the steamer *Whitehorse*; Bert Lamb; Harry Hosking; James Falconer; W. Drury.

[22] Ibid., 9 Nov. 1918.

[23] Yukon Territorial Archives, Corporate Record Group 1, series II-1, file 191B, White Pass & Yukon Route, Superintendent's Annual Report, 31 Dec. 1918.

[24] *DDN*, 4 Nov. 1918.

[25] Ibid., 2 Jan. 1919.

[26] Ibid.

[27] Ibid., 25 Nov. 1918. Gratitude was expressed to the Juneau Igloo of the Alaska Pioneers for their work in looking after the bodies.

[28] Ibid., 7 Nov. 1918.

[29] *Whitehorse Weekly Star*, 3 Jan. 1919.

[30] *DDN*, 24 Dec. 1918.

[31] The *Alaska Daily Empire* (Juneau) of 30 Oct. 1918 reported that 'Walter [sic] J. O'Brien's Body and That of His Child' had been found, the child 'Closely Clasped in Father's Arms'. Both identifications later proved incorrect.

[32] Toronto *Globe*, 4 Nov. 1918.

[33] *DDN*, 21 Dec. 1918.

[34] In 1923 her husband gave a deposition that his wife's health 'was of the best. She did not have a serious illness during the whole time of our acquaintanceship' (case #6390, vol. 13, p. 6883). This was one of several instances in which the best case was put on the condition or the prospects of the deceased in the course of legal action for damages. His testimony could be described as perjury; he might have said that her disease was incapacitating but not life-threatening. In any event, her health was hardly 'of the best'.

[35] *DDN*, 7 Nov. 1918.

[36] Yukon Territorial Archives, RG1, series 1A, vol. 50, file 31126, and series 2 1/3, vol. 14, file 17777; Case #6390, vol. 13, pp. 6712-29. Vancouver *Sun*, 13 and 15 Nov. 1918. His father gave the family birthplace as Hammer; the Dawson newspaper called it Homer. Neither place appears in the London *Times* world atlas; presumably it now has a Czech name. How his father learned of his death is not known.

[37] *DDN*, 7 and 15 Nov., 19 Dec. 1918. The newspapers did not follow this story through, so it cannot be determined who the little girl was, or whether Beaton's children were ever found.

[38] *Fairbanks News-Miner*, date obliterated.

[39] Case #6390, vol. 6, pp. 3063-4.

[40] *Vancouver Sun*, 13 Nov. 1918.

[41] *Vancouver Daily Province*, 31 Oct. 1918.

[42] *DDN*, 27 Feb. 1919.

[43] Congdon apparently maintained offices in both Dawson City and Vancouver. Like so many Dawsonites, he was only a seasonal resident.

[44] Case #6390, vol. 12, p. 6054.

[45] *DDN*, 12 Feb. 1919; *Victoria Colonist*, 29 Oct. 1918; National Archives of Canada, RG 42, vol. 290, file 47799.

[46] Information kindly supplied by Joan E. Harding, Vancouver.

[47] *DDN*, 3 Dec. 1918.

[48] *Whitehorse Weekly Star*, 22 Aug. 1919. The following account is based on the *DDN*, 22 July and 6 Aug. 1919, and the *Whitehorse Weekly Star*, 14 Feb., 14 March, 11 July, and 22 Aug. 1919.

[49] *DDN*, 6 Aug. 1919.

[50] In his testimony before the Canadian Royal Commission investigating the disaster, Jacobson stated that he was 'sent out from Juneau by the steamship company to see what bodies I could recover', which suggests that Winchell's story may have been exaggerated–perhaps he initiated the search, but once the first body was found, the CPR stepped in to continue it (Testimony of Selmer Jacobson, quoted in Case #6390, vol. 9, pp. 2913-25).

[51] The figure of 86 was given by John Donovan, who made a number of dives to the ship in July 1919 (Case #6390, vol. 9, pp. 2980-3). There is also some suggestion in the press accounts that the CPR waited until summer simply because it felt that diving was too dangerous in the winter.

[52] Case #6390, vol. 11, pp. 5482-4.

[53] *DDN*, 6 Aug. 1919.

[54] Case #6390, vol. 11, pp. 5482-4. In testimony given in 1923, Al Winchell described Ilene's health previous to her death as 'excellent'. Either his memory had failed, which seems hardly likely, or this was another case of perjured testimony designed to put as high a value as possible on the victim's life.

[55] Letter in authors' possession.

8. Aftermath

[1] Nancy Barr, 'The Princess Sophia Revisited', *Alaska Magazine*, July 1976.

[2] Juneau *Daily Empire*, 17 Jan. 1919.

[3] *DDN*, 18 March 1919.

[4] *Victoria Daily Colonist*, 16 Nov. 1918.

[5] Information provided by Department of Transportation, United States Coast Guard, Seventeenth Coast Guard District, Juneau, September 1985.

[6] The victims' relatives hired several different lawyers to represent them. Several people from Dawson retained F.T. Congdon, a Vancouver lawyer who had practised in Dawson and had once been Territorial Commissioner. Eventually all the cases were taken over by William Martin of Seattle.

[7] Two weeks after the disaster, Pond was advertising in the Juneau paper 'POST CARDS of Sophia wreck now ready' (*Alaska Daily Empire*, 7 Nov. 1918).

[8] National Archives of Canada, RG 42, vol. 290, file 47799.

[9] The act set out classes of industry, and provided that the accident fund for each class should be maintained by an assessment levied on employers according to the size of their payrolls, which in the case of the CPR would have been of considerable size.

[10] *Whitehorse Weekly Star*, 7 March 1919; *DDN*, 14 March 1919.

[11] Although the Supreme Court of Canada was established in the 1870s, appeals from it could be made to the Judicial Committee of the Privy Council in criminal cases until 1931 and civil cases until 1949.

[12] Great Britain, *House of Lords and Privy Council* (1920), pp. 184-93. As the *DDN* commented (7 Aug. 1919), the case launched in BC in March and decided by the Privy Council in August marked a 'record in the speeding up of the wheels of justice'–previous cases had taken as much as five years.

[13] See Appendix B.

[14] *Whitehorse Weekly Star*, 31 Oct. 1919. The second rumour may have been true. The ship may have been raised off the sea bed by cables, either partly or wholly to the surface. However, this may have been merely a rumour planted by the salvage company to raise working capital; the wreck certainly was not towed anywhere.

[15] *Whitehorse Weekly Star*, n.d. [September 1920]. See also 31 Oct. 1919; 5 March, 21 May, 25 June, 3 Sept. 1920.

[16] *Revised Statutes of Canada*, chap. 113, sec. 921.

[17] F.T. Congdon, 'Memo-Re-Princess Sophia Losses', 14 April 1919 (letter in authors' collection).

[18] Agreement between William Martin and H.A.P. Myers, attorneys-at-law and Yvonne Maxwell, administratrix of the estate of Maria Very, February 1920 (copy kindly provided by Robert W. Very, Vancouver).

[19] Martin to Yvonne Maxwell, 23 Nov. 1920.

[20] The message from the *Cedar*, saying the weather was too bad to attempt a rescue, after which the *Atlas* abandoned the plan of going to Vanderbilt Reef and returned to Juneau.

[21] Case #6390, vol. 9, pp. 4536-57.

[22] Judge Neterer's two decisions were printed in *The Federal Reporter*, vol. 278 (St Paul, Minn., 1922), pp. 180-207.

[23] Martin to Yvonne Maxwell, 18 Aug. 1922 (copy kindly provided by Robert W. Very, Vancouver).

[24] Case #4552, file 19. Mr and Mrs G.H. Hendrix, Terre Haute, Indiana, to Clerk of the U.S. District Court, Western District of Washington, 14 Oct. 1929.

[25] Case #6390, Brace, Administratrix, etc. vs. Canadian Pacific Railway Company, filed 3 Oct. 1932.

[26] Ibid.

[27] Case #6390, pp. 4750-2. Troup was under a tremendous strain. According to one source, 'the fact that one of his Princesses had occasioned the worst disaster in the history of coastal shipping affected Captain Troup deeply, and he suffered a breakdown in health from which it took him some time to recover' (Hacking and Lamb, *The Princess Story*, p. 251).

[28] Case #6390, vol. 6, pp. 3019-20.

[29] Ibid., pp. 3006-49.

[30] Ibid., Brace, Administratrix, etc. vs. Canadian Pacific Railway Company, filed 3 Oct. 1932, pp. 5-6.

[31] Ibid., p. 20

[32] Ibid., p. 32.

[33] Yukon Territorial Archives, RG1, Series 1A, vol. 50, file 37126, Bell to Officer Commanding B Division, RNWMP, Dawson, 28 Nov. 1918, Yukon Archives.

[34] A figure of $247,860 is given by the U.S. Coast Guard 'Report of Casualty', 3 Feb. 1919 (US National Archives, Seattle Branch, RG 26, US Coast Guard, Juneau, FRC 63309-Wreck Reports). The Wreck Register of the British Board of Trade gives the same figure, plus $5,992 insurance on the cargo. The total loss was stated to be $295,000 (National Archives of Canada, RG42, vol. 669, file 1918, West Coast ['Claimants' Brief on Petitioner's Objections to Commissioners Assessment of Damages' gives a figure of $270,860]). No information was available from the CPR.

[35] K. Coates and W.R. Morrison, 'The Sinking of the *Princess Sophia*: A Missing Element in the Cultural History of the Far Northwest', *Northwest Folklore*, 7, no. 2 (Spring 1989).

[36] New York: Doubleday, 1958.

[37] Naske and Slotnik, *Alaska*; Morris Zaslow, *The Northward Expansion of Canada, 1914-1967* (Toronto, McClelland and Stewart, 1988).

[38] The destinations of 101 of the passengers has been determined: 27 were bound for British Columbia, 18 for California, 17 for Washington, 11 for Oregon, 3 for New York, 2 for Ontario, and the rest for Wisconsin, Texas, Florida, Panama, Great Britain, and a variety of other places. The destinations of 49 of the White Pass & Yukon riverboat crew are

known: 31 were heading for British Columbia, 6 for Washington, 2 for California, and the rest for other places.

[39] Michael H. Frisch, 'The Memory of History', in Susan Benson et al., eds, *Presenting the Past: Essays on History and the Public* (Pittsburgh: Temple University Press, 1986). This issue is confronted on a grand scale in David Lowenthal, *The Past is a Foreign Country* (New York: Cambridge University Press, 1985).

[40] Information collected from Yukon Territorial Archives, Benjamin Craig Collection, 'Lists of Old-Timers, Dawson City'. See also K.S. Coates and W.R. Morrison, 'Transiency in the Far Northwest After the Gold Rush: The Case of the *Princess Sophia*,' in Coates and Morrison, *Interpreting Canada's North* (Toronto: Copp Clark, Pitman, 1989).

[41] Articles on the story have appeared regularly in the west coast and maritime press. See 'S.S. Princess Sophia', *The Skipper*, August 1959; Ruth Greene Bailey, 'Marine Notebook', *Harbour and Shipping*, March 1963; A.H. Wells, 'The Ship of Sorrow', *Victoria Daily Colonist*, 7 March 1971; T.W. Paterson, 'Sophia Disaster', *Victoria Daily Colonist*, 27 Oct. 1963; T.W. Paterson, 'B.C.'s Greatest Marine Tragedy', *Victoria Daily Colonist*, 28 Nov. 1976; N. Hacking, 'Divers Probe Old Wreck', *Vancouver Province*, 26 Nov. 1976; A. Cottrell, 'But Listen', *Vancouver Province*, 2 Nov. 1951; B. Bowman, 'All Lost When 'Sofia' [sic] Sank', *Nanaimo Daily Free Press*, 22 Oct. 1966; S. Levi, 'Blue Sea', *Sea Classics*, May 1988; Jim Nesbitt, 'The West Coast's Worst Disaster', *Maclean's*, 15 Oct. 1951; Nancy Barr, 'The Princess Sophia Revisited', *Alaska Magazine*, July 1976.

[42] Fairbanks: Vanessapress, 1985. Both of these items were kindly provided by the authors.

[43] Hugh D. Maclean, *Yukon Lady: A Tale of Loyalty and Courage* (Surrey, BC: Hancock House, 1985), p. 170.

BIBLIOGRAPHY

A: Primary Sources

There are three essential primary sources for a study of the *Princess Sophia* disaster. First is the record of the court case, which went on for thirteen years in Seattle and San Francisco. The records of the Seattle case can be found in manuscript form at the United States National Archives, Seattle Branch, Record Group 21, US District Courts, Western District of Washington, Northern Division, Seattle, Admiralty on Appeal, #4553. The records of the appeal in San Francisco (including copies of much of the material relating to the Seattle case) were printed together with supporting documentation, and can be found in the United States National Archives, San Francisco Branch, Record Group 276, 9th Circuit, US Court of Appeals, Case #6390.

The second source, also of great value, is the transcript of the Inquiry held before Mr Justice Morrison in the early months of 1919; it is available in the National Archives of Canada, Sessional Papers 21-24, vol. LVI, no. 7, 1920, Sophia file no. 110620, 1918-1919.

The third primary source consists of the contemporary newspapers, particularly the *Dawson Daily News*, which ran a lengthy (though frequently inaccurate) series of obituaries of the victims, the Victoria *Daily Colonist*, *Whitehorse Star*, Fairbanks *News-Miner*, Vancouver *Daily Province*, Vancouver *Sun*, Skagway *Daily Alaskan*, the Portland *Oregonian*, the Toronto *Globe*, and the Juneau *Alaska Daily Empire*. Other articles in newspapers and periodicals dealing with the ship are listed in the footnotes. The CPR archivist informed the authors that the company archives had no material on the *Princess Sophia*.

Other archival sources

Alaska State Archives: Record Group 506, US District Court for Alaska, First Division, US Commissioner's Probate Records; Record Group 101, Territorial Governor's Office, General Correspondence.

Anglican Church of Canada, General Synod Archives, Toronto: M 74-3, Stringer Papers.

British Columbia Provincial Archives: B2151, GR1323, BC Attorney General, Correspondence 1902-1937.

National Archives of Canada: Record Group 12, Department of Transport; Record Group 18, Royal Canadian Mounted Police; Record Group 42, Marine Branch; Record Group 91, Yukon Territorial Records.

Royal British Columbia Museum: Accommodation Plans for the *Princess Sophia*.

US National Archives, Washington: Microfilm Publication #939, General Correspondence of the Alaska Territorial Governor.

US National Archives, Washington: Record Group 26, Lighthouse Service.

Vancouver City Archives: Captain Henry Mowatt Papers; Add. Mss 782, Cadieux Collection, vol. 201, Specifications of the *Princess Sophia*.

Yukon Territorial Archives: Record Group 1, Territorial Government Records; White Pass & Yukon Route Records; Anglican Church Records; Yukon Order of Pioneers Papers, AC #02/454; Dorothy (Burgess) Seddon Papers, 86/49 part 1; Watt Papers, AC #82/196.

B: *Secondary sources: books*

Aitken, H.G.H. *Syntony and Spark–the Origins of Radio*. New York: John Wiley, 1976.

Bennett, Gordon. *Yukon Transportation: A History*. Canadian Historic Sites Occasional Papers in Archaeology and History, no. 19. Ottawa: National Historic Parks, 1978.

Benson, Susan, et al. *Preserving the Past: Essays on History and the Public*. Philadelphia: Temple University Press, 1986.

Berton, Laura. *I Married the Klondike*. Toronto: McClelland and Stewart, 1954.

Berton, Pierre. *The Last Spike*. Toronto: McClelland and Stewart, 1971.

———. *The National Dream*. Toronto: McClelland and Stewart, 1970.

Black, Martha. *My Ninety Years*. Anchorage: Alaska Northwest Publishing, 1976.

Black, Mrs George. *My Seventy Years*. London: Thomas Nelson, 1938.

Brook, Reginald Sr. *Story of the Engineer Mine*. Unpublished manuscript, Yukon Archives, n.d.

Coates, K.S. *Canada's Colonies: A History of the Yukon and NWT*. Toronto: James Lorimer, 1985.

Coates, K.S., and W.R. Morrison. *Land of the Midnight Sun: A History of the Yukon*. Edmonton: Hurtig, 1988.

————. *Interpreting Canada's North: Selected Readings*. Toronto: Copp Clark Pitman, 1989.

Coutts, R. *Yukon Places and Names*. Sidney, BC: Gray's Publishing, 1980.

Davie, Michael. *The Titanic: The Full Story of a Tragedy*. London: Bodley Head, 1986.

Dean, David M. *Breaking Trail: Hudson Stuck of Texas and Alaska*. Athens: University of Ohio Press, 1988.

Diubaldo, R. *Stefansson and the Canadian Arctic*. Montreal: McGill-Queen's University Press, 1978.

The Federal Reporter, vol. 278. St Paul, Minn.: West Publishing, 1922.

Fitch, Edwin M. *The Alaska Railroad*. New York: Frederick A. Praeger, 1967.

Green, Lewis. *The Gold Hustlers*. Vancouver: J.J. Douglas, 1972.

Greene, Ruth. *Personality Ships of British Columbia*. West Vancouver: Marine Tapestry Publications, 1969.

Hacking, N.R., and W.K. Lamb. *The Princess Story: A Century and a Half of West Coast Shipping*. Vancouver: Mitchell Press, 1974.

Hall, David. *Clifford Sifton: The Young Napoleon*. Vancouver: University of British Columbia Press, 1981.

Hinckley, T. *The Americanization of Alaska, 1867-1907*. Palo Alto: Pacific Books, 1972.

Howeth, L.S. *History of Communications-Electronics in the United States Navy*. Washington: US Government Printing Office, 1963.

Hulley, Clarence. *Alaska: Past and Present*. Portland, Oregon: Binfords and Mort, 1970.

Hunt, William R. *Distant Justice: Policing the Alaskan Frontier*. Norman: University of Oklahoma Press, 1987.

Hutchinson, Bruce. *The Far Side of the Street*. Toronto: Macmillan, 1976.

Lowenthal, David. *The Past Is a Foreign Country*. New York: Cambridge University Press, 1985.

Maclean, Hugh D. *Yukon Lady: A Tale of Loyalty and Courage*. Surrey, BC: Hancock House, 1985.

Marshall, Edison. *Princess Sophia*. New York: Doubleday, 1958.

Minter, Roy. *The White Pass: Gateway to the Klondike*. Toronto: McClelland and Stewart, 1987.

Morrison, David R. *The Politics of the Yukon Territory, 1898-1909*. Toronto: University of Toronto Press, 1968.

Morrison, William R. *Showing the Flag: The Mounted Police and Canadian Sovereignty in the North, 1894-1925.* Vancouver: University of British Columbia Press, 1985.

Musk, George. *Canadian Pacific: The Story of the Famous Shipping Line.* Toronto: Holt Rinehart and Winston, 1981.

Naske, Claus-M., and Herman E. Slotnik. *Alaska: A History of the 49th State.* 2nd ed. Norman: University of Oklahoma Press, 1987.

Nickerson, Sheila. *On Why the Quilt-Maker Became a Dragon.* Fairbanks: Vanessapress, 1985.

Orth, Donald J. *Dictionary of Alaska Place Names.* Washington: Government Printing Office, 1967.

Pettigrew, Eileen. *The Silent Enemy: Canada and the Deadly Flu of 1918.* Saskatoon: Western Producer Prairie Books, 1983.

Rea, Kenneth J. *The Political Economy of the Canadian North.* Toronto: University of Toronto Press, 1968.

Teacher, L., and R.E. Nichols, eds, *The Unabridged Jack London.* Philadelphia: Running Press, 1981.

Turner, Robert. *The Pacific Princesses.* Victoria: Sono Nis Press, 1977.

United States Coast Pilot, 8. 16th edition. Washington: Government Printing Office, 1984.

Webb, Melody. *The Last Frontier: A History of the Yukon Basin of Canada and Alaska.* Albuquerque: University of New Mexico Press, 1985.

Wedlake, G.E.C. *SOS: The Story of Radio-Communication.* Newton Abbott, UK: David & Charles, 1973.

Zaslow, Morris. *The Northward Expansion of Canada, 1914-1967.* Toronto: McClelland and Stewart, 1988.

C: *Secondary sources: articles and dissertations*

Bailey, Ruth Greene. 'Marine Notebook'. *Harbour and Shipping,* March 1963.

Barr, Nancy. 'The Princess Sophia Revisited'. *Alaska Magazine,* July 1976.

Bowman, B. 'All Lost When "Sofia" [*sic*] Sank'. Nanaimo *Daily Free Press,* 22 Oct. 1966.

Burke, Gerry. 'Francis Burke, 1901-1918'. Unpublished manuscript.

Coates, K.S. 'Best Left as Indians: The Federal Government and the Indians of the Yukon Territory, 1840-1950'. *Canadian Journal of Native Studies* 4, no. 2 (Fall 1984).

Coates, K.S., and W.R. Morrison. 'The Sinking of the SS Princess Sophia: A Missing Element in the Cultural History of the Far Northwest'. *Northwest Folklore* 7, no. 2 (Spring 1989).

Cooper, Richard W. '293 Prayed as the Gale Raged'. Victoria *Times-Colonist*, 22 Oct. 1989.

Cottrell, A. 'But Listen'. Vancouver *Province*, 2 Nov. 1951.

Guest, Hal. 'A History of Dawson City, Yukon Territory, 1897-1920'. PhD dissertation, University of Manitoba, 1983.

Franks, C.E.S. 'How the Sabbath Came to the Yukon'. *Canadian Public Administration* 10 (March 1967).

Hacking, N. 'Divers Probe Old Wreck'. Vancouver *Province*, 26 Nov. 1976.

Levi, S. 'Blue Sea'. *Sea Classics*, May 1988.

Nesbitt, Jim. 'The West Coast's Worst Disaster'. *Maclean's*, 15 Oct. 1951.

Paterson, T.W. 'Sophia Disaster'. *Victoria Daily Colonist*, 27 Oct. 1963.

————. 'BC's Greatest Marine Tragedy'. *Victoria Daily Colonist*, 28 Nov. 1976.

'SS Princess Sophia'. *The Skipper*, August 1959.

Spartz, M.-L. *The Real Story of the Princess Sophia*. Unpublished script.

Wells, A.H. 'The Ship of Sorrow'. *Victoria Daily Colonist*, 7 March 1971.

INDEX

INDEX